OF DREAMS DEFERRED, DEAD OR ALIVE

African Perspectives on African-American Writers

Edited by
FEMI OJO-ADE

Contributions in Afro-American and African Studies, Number 180

GREENWOOD PRESS
Westport, Connecticut • London

Library of Congress Cataloging-in-Publication Data

Of dreams deferred, dead or alive : African perspectives on African-
   American writers / edited by Femi Ojo-Ade.
      p.   cm. — (Contributions in Afro-American and African
   studies, ISSN 0069-9624 ;   no. 180)
   Includes bibliographical references and index.
   ISBN 0-313-26475-9 (alk. paper)
   1. American literature—Afro-American authors—History and
criticism.   2. American literature—Afro-American authors—
Appreciation—Africa.   3. Africa—In literature.   4. Afro-Americans
in literature.   I. Ojo-Ade, Femi.   II. Series: Contributions in
Afro-American and African studies ; no. 180.
PS153.N503   1996
810.9'896—dc20   95-45960

British Library Cataloguing in Publication Data is available.

Library of Congress Catalog Card Number: 95-45960
ISBN: 0-313-26475-9
ISSN: 0069-9624

First published in 1996

Greenwood Press, 88 Post Road West, Westport, CT 06881
An imprint of Greenwood Publishing Group, Inc.

Printed in the United States of America

The paper used in this book complies with the
Permanent Paper Standard issued by the National
Information Standards Organization (Z39.48–1984).

10 9 8 7 6 5 4 3 2

for Africa
our source of strength
our place of pride
forever
for the children of Africa
dispersed despised but undefeated
determined in our desire to be free
e fara yin mora, omo Africa!*
Come together, come together, you children of Africa!

*Lyrics of Yoruba song still heard today in the diaspora, particularly in Brazil's *candomblé* ceremonies.

Contents

Acknowledgments

As usual, I thank my family for unalloyed love and support.

St. Mary's College of Maryland has made me feel welcome and has encouraged my research.

All the contributors to this project deserve to be praised for finding time in spite of myriad constraints and circumstances that often make writing essays a privilege of the fat chosen few.

Last, but not least, I once again express my gratitude to my mentor and brother, Fred Case, while remembering my friend Dayo, who passed away too soon.

Introduction

FEMI OJO-ADE

This collection of essays is meant to present African perspectives on African-American writings on Africa; more precisely, the idea is to examine, through the written text, connections between the African American and Africa. While outsiders have had ample opportunity to assess that complex relationship, Africans, the insiders, have largely been silent. Hopefully, this work will contribute meaningfully to the ongoing debate on Africanity and the linkage between the ancestral continent and the diaspora.

The dream motif is very much part of the American phenomenon, and this is most appropriate for a people whose lives have been marked by slavery, spite, deracination, and dehumanization. As part of the whole process of constructing cleavage from Africa, the master tried to transform dreams into nightmares; hence, for the African American (a terminology that Africans find most interesting), Africa became the quintessential nightmare best left dead in the past. Nevertheless, the master forgot that lies could not triumph forever, especially given the lived and living nightmares of slavery and racism within the proclaimed paradise. Langston Hughes's poetry gave the editor of this volume an idea for the collection's title: Perhaps more than any other African-American writer, Hughes describes with poignancy the nightmarish side of the Dream while insisting on the Blacks' determination to fulfill it.

The lead essay attempts to make a critical and historical analysis of the totality of African-American writings as they concern Africa, from the slave period till the present. The analysis deals with a vast number of writers and issues, including those not addressed in other contributions to the collection.

In the essays following, critics discuss individual writers and thinkers. A decidedly African outlook is visible in the essays; for, the imposition of Euro-American tradition has made for many of the misconceptions about Africa. In reading the literature in question, these African critics recognize, as Vincent Odamtten succinctly states in his essay, "the historical conditioned continuities and apparent dislocation of over three hundred years of slavery, colonialism, and neocolonialism as they are manifest in the texts under discussion.'' In essence, complementarities and influences are found between African-American and African writers: for example, Gloria Naylor, Ama Ata Aidoo, Sembene Ousmane, and Ayi Kwei Armah; Harlem Renaissance and Negritude writers; W.E.B. Du Bois and Pan-Africanism; Marcus Garvey and Africanity. The significance of Oral Tradition (derived from Africa) in African-American writing is discussed, with attention to the notion of hearing giving new meanings and voices to written texts and thus continuing the interaction between artist and audience.

The theme of women and their conditions in society is given in-depth interpretations; and critics analyze the works of two major women writers, the Nobel laureate Toni Morrison (rightly dealt with by two different critics) and Alice Walker. As others have stated concerning other aspects of African culture and experience, these critics affirm that, in regard to the much debated issue of feminism, "concepts of patriarchy, masculinity, and femininity should be problematized rather than assumed" (Kieti). Unfortunately, writers such as Alice Walker fail to problematize concepts when they contemplate the African woman.

Contributors to this collection also use the insights of eminent African writers, such as Chinua Achebe, Ngugi wa Thiong'o, and Es'kia Mphahlele, as bases for viewing the literature written by those taken overseas. The idea of writing as an act of atonement with the past is posited. Finally, two strands of attitudinal positions are easily delineated in regards to Africa: while some African Americans consciously attach themselves to Africa, others forcefully reject such Africanness. The critics in this collection have tried to explain those positions.

What these essays prove beyond doubt is the importance of Africa to the African American, even in cases where a deliberate attempt is made at repudiation. The fact is the American Dream has by and large remained a mirage. Africa as symbol survives "because it holds the hope of legitimating the black self in a discursive formation which has often denied its very existence" (Gikandi).

Finally, it is appropriate to explain some stylistic aspects of the collection, particularly with regard to the use of upper- and lowercase in words such as "dream," "civilization," and "black." The American Dream is very well known all over the world; just ask the millions abroad praying to obtain a visa at the much-dreaded U.S. consulate. One notes the potency (not to forget the potential) of the Dream, and the urgency, which would explain a certain desperation to succeed on the part of many and, overall, the feeling that it is such a tall order that only the extraordinarily strong and the exceedingly fortunate will achieve the goal. To begin to participate in the Dream is, first, to cross the ocean from hell into heaven. Thus, America becomes the center of civilization, the Civilization, the one and only place worthy of anyone's interest. And the myth dates back to centuries when the slaves were brought from Africa. In using the capital letter, one is emphasizing the particularity of Civilization, implying at once its opposite, another absolute: Savagery. If America is Civilization, Africa, naturally, is Savagery—the condition, the society of Black people. As for the latter word, Black, some confusion might arise regarding its use as qualifier or as substantive. One might say that the descriptive (adjective) should be written in lowercase (yet one does not question "Western" culture . . .). Now, given the fact of self-affirmation and a kind of revolutionary stance in the face of centuries of racism, many Blacks have decided to capitalize even the descriptive, to affirm their humanity. That, indeed, is interesting; one does not have to think of how to appropriately write the word "white." White, being the norm, the "normal," the accepted standard, the reference point, is spared the agony of defining and determining how and why.

In reading these essays, therefore, some attention has to be paid to such details that might be considered unimportant in other circumstances. Maybe when the world arrives at a point of color blindness; when the rainbow replaces the several qualifying colorations determining human quality, beginning with black at the bottom and moving upwards to white at the top; when, finally, the human is the only factor governing our existence, then we will not have to give thought to these details and others addressed in the Afterword.

Africa and America: A Question of Continuities, Cleavage, and Dreams Deferred

FEMI OJO-ADE

I am a Negro:
Black as the night is black,
Black like the depths of my Africa.[1]

You are an African. You must accomplish things, for yourself, for your race,
for mankind, for literature.[2]

While we are an African people, we are not Africans.[3]

I must insist that, for me, this journey [spiritual, to Africa] is not just a dream.
I know that I am a product of Western civilization, but nevertheless, I need
my African references.[4]

Over the years, Blacks from Africa and those in the United States have enjoyed
what may be called a love-hate relationship, a fact that only the hypocritical on
both sides would attempt to deny. Those of us from the motherland who have
been students and workers in the "New World" have noticed, sad to say, a
general deterioration in the relationship. The era of Kwame Nkrumah, Ghana's
first president, and Nnamdi Azikiwe, Nigeria's prominent nationalist—both students at Lincoln University in Pennsylvania—as well as Hezekiah Oluwasanmi,
architect of the glory enjoyed by the University of Ife, Nigeria, and former
student at Morehouse College in Atlanta, coincided with the Harlem Renaissance
and no doubt constituted the happy days of harmony, commitment, and complementarity. The joys of brotherhood and sisterhood would be matched later
in this critic's generation of the activist 1960s when, as students whose thoughts
were honed by the heady dreams of rights and self-determination of destiny all
suffused in the ecstasy of African independence, we envisioned not only a Pan-
African republic but also a universal black community stretching from Atlanta
to Abidjan, from New York to Nairobi, from Salvador-Bahia through Washing-

ton to Ouagadougou, without forgetting Lagos, London, and Los Angeles, and Cuba and Canada—indeed, anywhere in which our people have been compelled to settle. Black aesthetics, an amalgam of artistic, cultural, and political commitment, was our model. We were following in the footsteps of our ancestors, singing songs of freedom, declaring pride in our blackness, building bridges of love.

Unfortunately, in our euphoria, we forgot to concretize ideas thrown out in moments of mirthful madness, just as we in Africa failed to see through the mirage of independence. Regarding the latter, needless to say, we are now paying the heavy price for our naivete, as we are being trampled upon by monsters hiding behind masks of messiahs; highway robbers posing as revolutionaries; sellers of the nation back to Civilization preaching sermons of saviors actually sent to us from hell. As for the former relationship culminating in Pan-Africanism, we are reluctantly coming to terms with the consequences of our overzealous expressions of love: if you chase the shadow without catching and holding onto the substance, you risk losing love and living hate. For commitment to last, you must base it upon concrete, dynamic substance to which you must continue to add positive elements. For Blackness to be meaningful, we must go beyond negative notions of suffering and misery, which, although these have been our shared experiences, must be transformed into acts of survival and growth in order for us to march forward to the beat of our own music. The maelstrom of militancy swept us along towards what we saw as the ultimate world of our dreams, supposedly back to our heritage, but, in actuality, we were being led to the precipice where dreams were liable to die as the fires ebbed in the soul of folks finally forced to attend once again to basic aspects of self-survival.

Those of us from Africa did not know our American brothers and sisters. They were ignorant of us. In Africa, foreigners included Blacks from the diaspora. The Yoruba word *oyinbo* means not only "white" but "foreigner." And we recall that colonial officers, especially in francophone Africa, were quite often black. Besides, continental Africans, due to the ignorance of racism used to dehumanize those taken abroad and due to our good fortune in remaining as majority on our land, could not understand why Blacks from America would be so desperately in need of an explicit emphasis on blackness. For their part, the latter could not understand our ignorance; and in addition, there arose from time to time the whispered question: "Why the hell did you all sell us into bondage, you savages from the jungle?"

Today, that question remains unanswered or, indeed, transformed into an accusation of criminality, even as our brothers and sisters appear to have chosen for themselves a name that includes the word *African*. Many Africans are wondering what happened to the solidarity expressed in joyful greetings and shared activities. This critic believes that an examination of the ideas of those involved in the American Dream would lead us to an understanding of the essence of that vaunted solidarity and Africanity, as well as an adequate assessment of their psyche and position vis-à-vis African heritage.

Slavery milked the myth of White superiority and Black savagery. Even as the slaves were struggling to regain their freedom, White America was repressing the fight with bogus reasoning marked by "fear to let black men even try to rise lest they become the equals of the white" (declaration of the Niagara Movement meeting in 1906 to commemorate John Brown's one hundredth birthday; see Du Bois' *A.B.C. of Color*, 32). The slaves' struggle did not dent the enslavers' propaganda. The dichotomy was absolute: brilliant, progressive America was an overwhelming winner over barbaric, retrogressive Africa. Yet, in spite of that propaganda, there were those slaves that reversed the equation and preferred until death to return to Africa. Guinea became a symbol of the lost heritage, most especially in Caribbean literature. An excellent example is the poetry of Haitian Jacques Roumain.[5] The belief was that the soul of the dead slave went back home.

The end point of the slaves' complex reactions was ambivalence towards Africa. Through a combination of positive and negative emotions consequent to the presence of the conquering alien culture and the absence of the conquered one (the Other over the Self), one could list a series of aspects of that double consciousness making for the dilemma that has lasted until today: acceptance-denial; resignation-rejection; love-hate; assimilation-alienation. Everything depends largely on the instant, the state of mind, the mentality, the modalities of manipulation. As human beings, the slaves could be expected to undergo different stages of reacting to the bombarding forces of Civilization (that is, Western civilization, which supposedly enjoyed absolute superiority over any other, specifically and especially the African, marked out as the quintessence of Savagery!).

A former missionary to Liberia, Hon. J. H. Smyth, makes one common early observation of the dilemma about Africa: "[Negroes] are averse to the discussion of Africa, when their relationship with that ancient and mysterious land and its races is made the subject of discourse or reflection." This worthy man of God also believes that Negroes should go to Africa as missionaries, as enlightened, civilized people; it is this belief that has been part of the problem in the relationship between Africans and African Americans. According to Smyth, the Negro should go to Africa "seeking a home because he has none . . . , goes from a sense of duty imposed by his Christian enlightenment, and not unprovided with ability and previous experience to organize and control labor" (Smyth, 69). In essence, the Negro would return to the ancestral continent as a modern master fashioned by Western (that is, American) civilization.

However ambiguous their feelings on Africa might be, Africa remained a constant presence in the minds of African Americans. Africa, either envisioned or vilified, always beckoned to its departed children. Yet, one cannot forget that the outward journey of those children was final.

Similar to the African situation, the Black condition in America imposes a social role on the writer, who, while of course interested in writing well, cannot but deal with real matters of his and his people's survival. Art for art's sake would hardly be adequate in such circumstances: "We must begin by dispelling the false notion that an artist is an artist, no matter what his color, and that being black imposes no special responsibility on him."[6]

Another factor in assessing the relationship of Blacks in America to Africa is religion, a factor that most critics have not considered to date. Christianity has been made out to be the only true religion, as if Africa did not have any religion of its own. In reviewing African-American literature, one is struck by the very deep acceptance of Christianity, whereas in other parts of the African diaspora, African religions are much propagated by writers either as a chosen alternative to Christianity or as an essential component of syncretism. The critic Martha Cobb notes the closeness of African ethos and religion in the works of the Haitian Jacques Roumain and the Cuban Nicolás Guillén, as opposed to that of the American Langston Hughes: "One reason is that syncretism between Catholicism and Yoruba religions expressed in the Vaudou of Haiti and Santería and Ñañiguismo of Cuba offered materials to Guillén and Roumain not available to Hughes" (Cobb, 40–41).

In a nutshell, Hughes and almost every other American writer of African descent were fed with the myth of African paganism. They generally have heeded the advice of missionaries such as the already quoted Smyth.[7]

Olaudah Equiano's *The Interesting Narrative of the Life of Olaudah Equiano, or Gustavus Vassa, the African* is an excellent example of a slave exhibiting unusual pride in his race. One notes in the title of the text the epithet "the African," which immediately sets Equiano apart from others as a nonassimilated person. Indeed, the African as depicted in the literature of the slave era connotes either a first-generation slave from the ancestral continent or one that was especially proud of his or her linkage to the motherland. In both cases, there would appear to be a tacit understanding that such a person was not considered American, that he was therefore inferior to other Blacks. Equiano remains an almost unknown entity in the literature of the slavery period.

Phyllis Wheatley, like Equiano abducted from Africa, was glaringly anti-Africa and supportive of the racist establishment. Wheatley was actually elated with Thomas Jefferson, who had stated his belief in Black inferiority to Whites in both body and soul. She regularly expressed her gratitude for having been saved from African savagery by civilized America:

> Twas mercy brought me from my Pagan land,
> Taught my benighted soul to understand
> That there's a God, that there's a Savior too.
> Once I redemption neither sought not knew.

To Wheatley's mind, the curse of Cain was an accepted part of Black heritage. She was overwhelmed with ecstasy to have been saved. Refined, she gladly joined the angelic train (and, of course, we remember that the devil is black, the angels, white).[8] Wheatley's overtly anti-African viewpoint would harmonize perfectly with that of Booker T. Washington, whose autobiography, *Up from Slavery*, is described by Ngugi wa Thiong'o as "a song in praise of social and mental subjugation, fawning, self-humiliation and self-abjection" (Ngugi, 133).

Two slave narratives help us understand the process of Americanization of the Negro and the attendant degradation of Africa and the color black. In *Incidents in the Life of a Slave Girl* (originally written in 1861), Linda Brent describes the horrors of slavery, how she escaped to the North, traveled to Europe as a servant, returned to America, and gained real freedom within the law. She notes in reference to her work as a nurse: "I was the only nurse tinged with the blood of Africa" (181), which at once makes her inferior to the others. Besides, she herself does not have anything to do with Africa: "Who *are* Africans? Who can measure the amount of Anglo-Saxon blood coursing in the veins of American slaves?" (45).

Brent implies a concurrence with the belief that Africans are savages; the only point of disagreement is that savages reside in Africa, not in America. Secondly, the fact of racial mixture (Brent was a mulatto) is underlined: mulatto is superior to black and is very close to heavenly white. Brent is ignorant of Africa. As she continues to condemn slave-holders for their horrible behavior, including the refusal to allow slaves to learn to read and write, she establishes her missionary motif, maintaining that their savagery is only comparable to that of barbaric Africans and that both groups need to be saved and civilized: "They send the Bible to heathen abroad, and neglect the heathen at home . . . .Talk to American slave-holders as you talk to savages in Africa" (75).

The analogy is an eye-opener: slaves aspiring to "the light of knowledge" become the equals of whites. Slave-holders would, through the lessons of the Bible, maintain or reassume their original superiority. Brent maintains the qualitative hierarchy imposed by color distinctions. Looking back on her life, she claims to find solace from tender memories of her grandmother, "like light, fleecy clouds floating over a dark and troubled sea" (208). White, as usual, triumphs over black.

Our Nig (originally written in 1859) is an autobiographical novel by Harriet Wilson. The descriptions of the horror of slavery are very poignant and compelling. We are especially struck by those episodes concerning African heritage. First, Frado, the poor mulatto protagonist, is a girl abandoned by her White mother, Mag Smith, at the home of a White family, the Bellmonts. Frado's nickname (which she has humbly allowed to stick), "Our Nig," is a stigma stamped on her by her new owners, like a brand on a horse.

The most interesting episode concerns the marriage of Frado's parents, Mag and Jim. Jim is "a kind-hearted African" (9), who supplies fuel to the neighborhood where Mag is withering away in a hovel. Orphaned early and convinced of her inferiority, Mag falls in love with a white man whom she considers an angel, "alluring her upward and onward" (6). Pregnant, she is abandoned by the vicious lover. The child dies. Mag moves away out of shame, then returns and decides to hide in a hovel, totally removed from "those innocent years when the coronet of virtue was hers" (9). That is the woman (an avowed trash abandoned by society) that the "kind-hearted African," Jim, decides to marry. Mag is convinced that the union is part of her punishment. Jim is also much aware of his inferiority to Mag: "He thought of *the pleasing contrast between her fair face and his own dark skin; the smooth, straight hair, which he had once, in expression of pity, kindly stroked on her now wrinkled but once fair brow*" (11).

Not only is she good enough for him. Jim believes that the marriage will lead to his own superioration and help confirm the humanity denied to date: "I's black outside, I know, but I's got a white heart inside" (12).

The only reason Mag accepts Jim's offer is that it is the sole alternative to begging; there's never a question of love. That notwithstanding, the narrator sees no reason to criticize Mag. The union with the African is viewed as such a major degradation that Mag is ever so eager to rid herself of the offspring, called "black devils" (16). Throughout the story, no more reference is made to Frado's African father. She is to all intents and purposes American; and what we witness, as she battles racism, learns to read the bible, and generally struggles to survive, is the process of civilization and initiation into the American dream.

From the slave narratives and other artistic productions of that period, one realizes that the dream stood deferred and, sometimes, there were signs of desperation and disillusionment on the Negro's part. After two revolutions, the independence war and the civil war and reconstruction, Blacks still remained outsiders. In most cases, that did not lead to the other dream, of Africa, because Africa remained a nightmare. One remarkable exception arrests our attention: Marcus Garvey.

Garvey founded the United Negro Improvement Association (UNIA) in 1919 under the slogan "Africa for Africans." He called out to Whites to clear out of Africa. His position was that if Whites lynched a Negro in America, Negroes would lynch a White in retaliation. Garvey was imprisoned in 1926 and died a death of disgrace and despair—and, some would say, a well-deserved one—in 1940.

Garvey's back-to-Africa movement was not an escape but a serious desire to return home. On the African continent, people welcomed his movement with zeal, calling him "Moses Garvey." Some critics have called Garvey a narcissistic chauvinist, a "demagogue [who] exploited the disillusionment of American Negroes" (Logan, 219).

For his part, Richard Wright berated the Garveyists for their simplemindedness which, he believed, led them into the error of seeing America as a place impossible to live in.[9] Garveyphobia was one more pretext to pounce upon a Black that dared dream of Africa not as an agent of colonialism (witness the work of missionaries) but as a son of the soil sharing the culture of his kin on the ancestral continent. The obituary written for Garvey dwells at length on his having "attracted a larger following than any Negro" and on his extraordinary achievement without owing his prominence, as many usually do, mainly to White men "who considered such spokesmen as those persons through whom they could work to keep the Negro in his place."[10]

The American origin of Pan-Africanism remains undeniable. The Nigerian scholar Abiola Irele remarks that the Negro's African heritage made for his supposed inferiority, not the mere fact of being Black.[11] Anthropologists like Charles Silberman and Harold Isaacs actually try to eradicate the Negro past and limit Negro experience to slavery. They also limit the Negro's horizon, claiming that only America can shape his or her personality and that any effort at African linkage can only be futile.

White civilization did create the myth of savage Africa. Pan-Africanism was a concerted movement to set the record straight. However, from the outset, complete rehabilitation was impossible; for, the Negro's desire to superiorate the African image for his own sake was most significant. Garveyism as a mass movement was unacceptable: it was too extremist for the moderate Pan-Africanists, who were bourgeoisie. To a large extent, Africa could still be considered savage once the Negro succeeded in saving himself by creating his own Africa.

The evolution of the Negro mind is well illustrated by the greatest symbol of Pan-Africanism, W.E.B. Du Bois. In his *The Souls of Black Folk*, Du Bois describes the state of Blacks shut out from the White world by "a vast veil" and states that the end of the Negro's striving is "the kingdom of culture" (46). That, of course, would mean America, and the Negro's desire would be acceptance side by side with Whites. That American dream does not directly include Africa; indirectly, it does, in the sense that Negroes would bring to the negotiating table a heritage affirming their humanity. White America has been intransigent. Reconciliation of "the two warring ideals" of White and Black America has proved impossible; hence, the African consciousness and alienation from America are fortified.

In *Dusk of Dawn*, Du Bois declares: "I was not an American. I was by long education and continual compulsion and daily reminder, a colored man in a white world" (136). Dreams of contributing as "a co-worker in the kingdom of culture" have been forgotten. Du Bois, in Pan-Africanism, emphasizes the Afrocentric ideal.

Now, it should be stated that Pan-Africanism insisted upon linkage with Africa, specifically and especially on the Negro's terms. Africa, colonized, was to be saved from the colonizers. The saviors, Negroes from America, wanted to run the show. No wonder when, in the 1950s, Africans decided to take hold of their destiny and thereby pushed the diasporan mentors to the background, the latter were dismayed and disappointed. The consolation is, that individuals such as Du Bois chose the African side. Du Bois left America to live in Ghana, where he died in 1963.

The Harlem Renaissance is another manifestation of the complex, controversial Africanity of the Negro. Alain Locke, philosopher-scholar-critic, coined the neologism, "the New Negro," as symbol of the rebirth of the Black race. It was during the horror-filled 1920s in the South where Blacks were summarily sentenced to lynching for committing the great sin of looking at White women, fine flowers in the White man's rose garden. Blacks, alienated, were bristling at social conditions that were burying Blacks deeper in the hell-hole meant "for coloreds only." The exodus to the liberal North, therefore, began in earnest. Harlem was the center of attention in that magic moment of freedom. Locke's *The New Negro* (1925) enthusiastically defines Harlem as the laboratory of a great race-welding where the "New Negro" has a new consciousness of opportunity and socioeconomic emancipation and a unique drive to improve his or her condition despite the greatest odds. Reading Locke carefully, one finds that the *American* component in the Negro's search is extremely strong; indeed, it appears to dominate everything else. According to Locke, the Negro is "a typical American." Locke also states that one of the most important roles of the American Negro is the future development of Africa.

The sense of mission of the New Negro, the subtly expressed superiority, the racial solidarity with Africa as springboard, such are the ideas emanating from Locke's beautifully crafted work. Also noteworthy is the fact of diversity in that solidarity: New Negroes had no slogan; individualism was the vogue. Langston Hughes's 1926 statement has been used by some people as a manifesto of the movement:

We young Negro artists who create now intend to express our individual dark-skinned selves without fear or shame. If white people are pleased we are glad. If they are not, it doesn't matter. We know we are beautiful. And ugly, too. The tom-tom cries and the tom-tom laughs. If colored people are pleased we are glad. If they are not, their pleasure doesn't matter.[12]

A manifesto of freedom of expression, of individualism without any strings attached, without any desire to please either Whites or Blacks. A strange solidarity, indeed.

Depending on which critic one is reading, opinions on Harlem go from the positive (for example, see Francis and Val Ward, 25) to the negative (see Emanuel, 53). Reactionary critics (for example, Harold Isaacs), unimpressed by any attempt by Negroes to move beyond the slave status and psyche, make an insensitive portrayal of Harlemites, stressing the shallow exoticism of those that Wallace Thurman, in *The Blacker the Berry*, calls "nigeratti," and Hughes, "the Harlemites of the balling and brawling 'Roaring Twenties' of midnight cabarets and bootleg gin."[13]

It is easy to find in all this something deeper than the image of brawlers and bar-hoppers. The matter of exoticism must be understood within the explanation given by Alain Locke. Harlem brought together Blacks and Whites, the former as players, the latter as mentors. White interest was essential to the Black players. Primitivists, such as the novelist Carl Van Vechten (*Nigger Heaven*) and the playwright Eugene O'Neill (*Emperor Jones* and *All God's Chillun Got Wings*) were at the forefront of the Black vogue as they gleefully exploited Black "basic savagery." The New Negroes "projected the feeling that in Harlem good writing might be done and that in downtown New York it might be published."[14]

The truth was not unknown to the New Negroes that, even though Harlem was not the South, it was still in the United States (which a character in Claude McKay's novel *Banjo* terms "the United Snakes"). The themes of solitude, despair, lack of love, all marked by a certain violence—a desire to destroy the oppressive-impressive Other—permeate the works of that period.

Primitive is a word that is repeated endlessly whenever Africa is mentioned, and it immediately connotes a series of images: noble savage in the jungle; elemental *joie de vivre* of the innocent (that is, backward people fit to be treated like children) untouched by civilization; intuitive reaction to things. What set apart the Negroes from others was their determination to see something "positive" in the overall dark image of Africa, whereas the "civilized" denigrators saw only the barbarity of cannibals, the irrationality of inferior beings closer to monkey than man. The New Negroes never said that Africa was civilized. Rather, they often sought refuge in an idyllic, innocent Africa. An African observer would admit that there is a tenuous Africanness in it all, but its authenticity and depth are debatable.

Another word that recurs over and over again in the literature of Harlem is *jungle*. One image is constant: Black savages happy in the simple existence of their *jungle*, dancing passionately to the rhythm of the *drums* and praying to their *pagan* gods.

Women writers of the Harlem Renaissance were as involved as the men in making exotic descriptions of Africa even if their numbers were not as great. Helene Johnson, in "Poem," dreams of drums while admitting her ignorance of their meaning. For her, Africa is a mystery. She closes her ears. Someone is singing a song but she actually hears "tom-toms" beating out loudly in her ears. She is most fascinated, not by the rhythm, not by the thud of the tom-toms, but by the very word, which, according to her, "belongs to us" (see Bontemps, *American Negro Poetry*, 101). The irony of closing one's ears and hearing tom-toms suggests the gap existing between the persona of this poem and Africa; for, when one closes one's ears, one normally hears nothing. The sounds heard would therefore come from within. The tragedy is that within lie the sounds of "civilization"; without, the sounds of confusion.

Gwendolyn Bennett, in "Heritage," also uses the tympanic motif. She expresses a desire to hear songs around a "heathen fire" and describes the race from which the song originates as "black" and "strange" (see Honey, *Shadowed Dreams*, 103). The word "heathen" fits perfectly well with the notion of a strange Black race and Africa is, of course, their home! Bennett deftly links the ancestral race to the victimized transplanted descendants now forced to smile and play the fool in order to survive. The title, "Heritage," is significant: present is thus linked to past, but only in memory, only in the mind desperately seeking solace of happiness while being overwhelmed by racist attacks in the poet's present abode. Songs are constantly being sung (the first meaning of poetry).

Mae Cowdery (see Honey, 119) underscores the dilemma of the race constrained to smile in sorrow. Her belief in such "blessed heritage" is fraught with irony and makes one think of the slave's experience in America. In another poem, Cowdery dreams of transforming Black men. Playing the role of prophet and magician, she declares her intention to dig deep into the hearts of Black men and change their unuttered "coarse" prayers into something beautiful, but still particular to the jungle of their origins (Chapman, *Black Voices*, 537). The poet is thus interested in eradicating Black men's fear, in making their dreams come true. The point of reference, the jungle, is Africa. Alain Locke considers the poet's words as "advance statement" on the transposition of the substance of primitivity to modern ways and means of insight. That analysis is quite strange because the beauty of the jungle can never be "modern" and one is not sure of the content of the prayers of Black men. Would it be a desire to be accepted into civilized society? A desire to valuate African heritage in its elemental form as posited by Blacks (or by civilization?) in order to be able to live it? If the objective is modernization, as Locke claims, then one can see that there is a move away from, and not towards, Africa. The only certain aspect of Cowdery's poem would be her vision of beauty in Africa. As a rule, however, that beauty, *exotic* to the Western observer, is hardly well defined. An ambivalence is noticeable in women's poetry, similar to what we have witnessed among the men. Indeed, the theme of blackness poses a dilemma.

In women's prose of the Harlem period, Nella Larsen stands out for distancing herself from everything African. That is hardly surprising, given the fact that, as a mulatto, she was obsessed with the question of "passing" (the title of her second novel): that is, passing for White, trying desperately to be assimilated into White America.[15] The heroine of Larsen's first novel, *Quicksand* (1928), Helga Crane, moves full circle from southern United States to the North, including Harlem, then to Europe and back to the South, all in search of an identity. It is interesting that in the introduction to the 1971 edition of the novel, Adelaide Hill states that Larsen "was a product of three cultures and that [she] lived in two societies" (14). The third culture is African, but its glaring absence in the novelist's contemplation of reality does not seem to bother critics.

Axel Olsen, Helga's White lover, tells her: "You have the warm impulsive nature of the women of Africa, but, my lovely, you have, I fear, the soul of a prostitute. You sell yourself to the highest buyer" (Larsen, *Quicksand*, 149). The combination, the contrast, may be seen as ingratiating to Africa, but only on the surface. For one thing, Axel knows nothing about African women. For another, there has never been any other reference to Africa in their conversations. Larsen is probably working on the stereotype of Black women's wild, sexy ways. The only other times when memories of Africa well up are in descriptions of *wild* dance in Harlem cabarets.

Helga becomes lost in the rhythm of the drum; she is transported to the jungle only to be brought back, ashamed, to civilization. Larsen's heroine equates blackness to being an African and she is therefore obsessed with never getting close to the horrible status of the savage African. When, at the end of her tragic life, Helga tries to find peace of mind in Christianity, Larsen informs us of its inadequacy: "Especially [Christianity] had its uses for the poor—the blacks. For the blacks. The Negroes. And this, Helga declared, was what ailed the whole Negro race in America, this fatuous belief in the white man's God" (219).

Unlike Nella Larsen, Zora Neale Hurston, novelist, folklorist, and Alaine Locke's student at Howard University, paints a somewhat positive picture of African culture. A professional, she was concerned with aesthetics and gave a deep dimension—much beyond propaganda—to "New Negroism" (see Hemenway, *Zora Neale Hurston*, 38). Hurston left the city and went into the rural areas, some still close to genuine Afrocentric ethos. Besides her collections on folklore, she wrote fiction in which one finds Blacks living their culture. In the novel *Jonah's Gourd Vine*, the drum and African dance come into play in John's sermon and the congregation's reaction.

John, the Christian, is mysteriously taken back into his African tradition through symbols of the drums, *Kata-Kumba* and *O-go-doe*, which critics have indicated as an example of Black people's ability to particularize Christianity through a pre-Christian (African) culture (see Larry Neal's introduction to the 1971 edition of *Jonah's Gourd Vine*). Robert Hemenway does a convincing reading of the Africanity of Hurston's novel. His only objection is that the African past still is made to connote barbarity, a state into which Blacks are prone to descend from time to time. Hurston's preacher, John, meets his death at the hands of White, mechanized civilization. Hemenway mentions the novelist's failure to "fictionally resolve either the bicultural trade-offs inherent in being black in America or the relationship between the individual artist and the community" (Hemenway, 201). Our own concern would be to know why trade-offs should be at all necessary. It is undeniable that the Christianization of Blacks in America is a force of de-Africanization. Her alienation notwithstanding, Larsen's Helga is lucid enough to realize that the Christian god, White, cannot accede to the prayers of the enslaved. It might also be mentioned that Zora Hurston traveled to Haiti to study the African religion there, and, in her *Tell My Horse* (1938), she gave the religion the respect that many a western critic would not accord it.

Of all those who sang of Africa in the 1920s, Langston Hughes was one of the very few who had been there. (We are talking specifically of Black Africa, not Arab Africa.) This may be why he sometimes sang of Africa in a key different from the rest (see Isaacs, 247–48). Isaacs's ahistorical and rather racist analysis of Black heritage in America has already been mentioned; it is therefore not surprising that he paid Hughes an underhanded compliment. Others before and after Hughes have traveled to Africa (one of them, Richard Wright, is praised to high heavens by Isaacs) without writing in a key even close to Hughes's. While it is true that first-hand knowledge attained by visiting a place helps authenticate one's opinion, such lucidity is achieved only by an open-minded, understanding visitor. Hughes would appear to have had that quality. He associated himself with Africa out of love and humility, out of pride in his race and heritage. Hughes was a mulatto. He could have tried to pass, but he chose to be Black. "My main material," he declared, "is the race problem" (quoted in Ward, 26). When Du Bois said, in 1903, that "the problem of the twentieth century is the problem of the color-line" (*The Souls of Black Folk*, 1969 ed., 54), he was anticipating the life-long work of individuals such as Hughes and, of course, the long struggle against racism that lay ahead for Blacks the world over. Hughes's autobiography, *The Big Sea* (1945), describes a hurting experience on his first African trip: "The Africans looked at me and would not believe I was a Negro. You see, unfortunately, I am not black" (10–11). Africans call him a White man. He meets a mulatto boy with a similar dilemma. Here is Isaacs's cynical comment on the problem: "Langston Hughes never did write a poem about Africans calling him 'a white man.' Instead he wrote lots of poems about being black, black, black" (Isaacs, 252). What irks Isaacs is Hughes's insistence upon solidarity with Africans.

Hughes's position is that the White man is guilty of creating the color problem, not Blacks. "Mulatto" (*Selected Poems*, 160) cries out that the Black is the White man's "Bastard boy," while Whites, including his racist father, shove him back into the night of oblivion and disgrace. Hughes perceives the supposedly superior civilization as the real jungle. The poet works at, and succeeds in, bridging the gap with Africa. In one of Hughes's earliest poems on Africa, "Afro-American Fragment" (Chapman, *Black Voices*, 425), he laments the seemingly too long distance and the insurmountable barrier between him, the departed son, and the motherland. He hears a song but, unfortunately, it is unintelligible because its creators are foreign to the culture. Nonetheless, the poet asserts that it is a matter of blood relations—deep, indelible, everlasting. The song heard may be unintelligible, but it is there; subdued, it refuses to go away. Little by little, the exile, as a result of his determination, will make the connection and concretize the continuity.

For Hughes, the dilemma of exile and de-Africanization is only temporary, as he is determined to wake up—and Africa with him. In "Africa" (*Selected Poems*, 284), the great continent is viewed as a giant in repose, with lightning and thunder visible in his smile. The metaphor brings forth images of power and rage, under control but ready to burst out at any moment. And the idea comes from Africa's geographical and natural realities: rain brings with it a storm that can destroy everything in its way. So also will Africa raze to the ground the enemy menacing to enslave it. Hughes sees the giant's "waking eyes," which makes one think of a people finally awakening from their slumber of oppression and deprivation into a dawn of consciousness about their rights, their power, and their potential in a world where much that belonged to them has been stolen and used to further dominate them.

Hughes insists on his blackness and his and his people's estate as victims. While others are bent upon sharing in the American dream at all costs (the trade-offs), Hughes sees such assimilation as a nightmare. Witness the verse of "Nightmare Boogie" (*Selected Poems*, 258): the poet relates a dream he had, not an ordinary one but "a nightmare dream" in which he saw a million Black faces which, suddenly, in a flash, turned "dead white."[16]

Hughes uses the dream motif more than any other poet of his or any other generation. The unique characteristic of the Hughesean symbol is its realism and its grounding in Black ethos and experience. The American Dream is well known for its inaccessibility to Blacks on their own terms.

"Lenox Avenue Mural" (in Bontemps, 67–70) contains Hughes's most striking lines on the theme. The poet addresses "the Great Migration" of Blacks to Harlem, all with eyes aglow with dreams of attaining and affirming the human status denied them in the South. The tragedy is that Harlem constitutes another cul-de-sac from the very first, and the perspicacious ones are quickly disabused. The nagging question is, "What happens to a dream deferred?" Mired in nothingness, impotence, and confusion, kicked around, the dream risks a death of ignominy, particularly when those struggling to give meaning to this harried existence realize that "they don't kick dreams around downtown." The poet, not one to be absolutist without reason, gives some room for doubt. He says that they may, indeed, kick dreams around over there, but quickly reminds us that his focus is Harlem, a hell in contrast to the heaven downtown. This emphatic statement places Hughes's interest squarely in the center of the suffering Black race. The dream continues to be deferred in spite of every effort to make it real. Yet Hughes never relents in his struggle. Africa is no longer too far away for Hughes, and that connection remains the closest he comes to resolving the dilemma of the dream deferred, but not dead.

The three acclaimed fathers of the movement of African cultural consciousness and liberation, Negritude, Aimé Césaire, Léon-Gontran Damas, and Léopold-Sédar Senghor, have all expressed their debt to the Harlem Renaissance. Hughes himself declared: "Had the word *negritude* been in use in Harlem in the twenties, Cullen, as well as McKay, Johnson, Toomer, and I might have been called poets of negritude" ("The Twenties," 16).

Africans and African Americans have mutually benefited from the cultural complementarity. What Pan-Africanism (in politics) and the Renaissance (in culture and literature) did for the Africans was to arouse their consciousness, their political commitment to the cause of independence, as well as a sense of brotherhood and sisterhood with their kin in the diaspora. On the other hand, Africans gave African Americans an opportunity to retrieve their lost heritage, a sense of pride and place, as well as their humanity.

Alain Locke's comparison of Hughes and Countee Cullen is revealing:

If Cullen has given us the exotic, emotional look on the race past, Hughes has given us what is racially more significant,—a franker, more spiritual loyalty, without sense of painful choice or contribution, a retrospective recall that is intimate and natural. (in Chapman, 537)

Countee Cullen is one of those poets who would feel very uncomfortable if called a "racial poet." In a 1926 article, he takes Hughes to task for falling "into the gaping pit that lies before all Negro writers, in the confines of which they become racial artists rather than artists pure and simple."[17] Cullen is, however, compelled by circumstances to face the fact of race, to "marvel at this curious thing that makes a poet black, and makes him sing!" (see *Color*, 1969 edition, 3). The Black poet cannot—and Cullen is never able to rid himself of that black cross—live in an artistic paradise where he is free to sing as he wishes. Cullen's struggle to resolve the problem shows his basic abhorrence for what he calls "paganism of blood," a state of savagery irreconcilable with his Christian, civilized upbringing. His exacerbated ambiguity carries over to his relationship with Africa.

One is astounded by the widespread praise showered on the poem, "Heritage" (Cullen, *Color*, 36–41), specifically in regard to the poet's relationship with Africa. The very first line asks the question, "What is Africa to me?" The beginning of a search, one might say. But it is far from being a normal search arising from a conscious or voluntary desire for knowledge. Cullen is bothered by his blackness and Africanity. His search is, to put it mildly, involuntary. A primitivist full of exotic ideas about the ancestral land, he imagines idyllic jungles inhabited by bronzed men and women and forest lovers; barbaric birds; great, thumping drums. He is an outcast in the midst of this uncultured life. As the questioning on Africa continues, we find that Cullen moves further and further away from the jungle and its barbarity symbolized in his mind by people's nakedness and nature's wildness. Cullen contrasts "here" with "there" where young bodies dripping wet in the tropical rain make love. "Here" is America, devoid of elements of nature (animals, trees, rivers) and savages.

Because America rejects him, Cullen becomes obsessed with images of Africa: no peace; a lot of pain; heathen gods. To solve the religious problem, he wishes for a Black Christ, but in vain. He shows remorse for daring to express such a sacrilegious desire and ends with a prayer of penitence, a blueprint of what he must do. The final lines are printed in italics, to accentuate the absolute urgency. He has to act with firmness and tenacity, all day and all night long, he has to do but one thing: "quench" his pride and "cool" his blood, that is, break every link with his ancestry and free himself from the "hot" blood for which his race is known. The fear of retrogressing, of returning to savage ways, is overwhelming here, but so also is the resolve not to do so: a single-minded decision, no doubt, this search, not for Africa, but for civilization. "They," the unflappable "other," are White. Africa and its savagery—the "boiling blood" making Cullen express anger, "my heart is pagan mad," he intones in "Pagan

Prayer'' (*Color*, 20–21)—belong to the past, and he would do whatever is necessary not to bring them back to life. As he tells it, the repercussion, the punishment for failure in his quest for Civilization is truly tragic: he would ''perish in the flood.'' Cullen finally converts to Christianity, the ultimate symbol of Civilization. He sees that as the only road to salvation.

On the theme of love, critics have affirmed Cullen's preference for a brown maiden as opposed to a White (see Nicholas Canaday, Jr., in Bontemps, *The Harlem Renaissance Remembered*, 100–10). Interestingly enough, however, no critical comment has been made on the character of the maiden. Canaday quotes from ''A Song of Praise'':

> Her walk is like the replica
> of some barbaric dance
> Wherein the soul of Africa
> Is winged with arrogance.

Similar to some of the most striking lines of the Negritude poet Senghor (see ''Femme noire'' in *Anthologie de la nouvelle poésie nègre et malgache*, 151), Cullen's poem, which Canaday describes as being of ''haunting and sensuous beauty,'' goes a long way toward depicting African woman's barbarity. She is all beauty and hardly any brain. Although one might claim that her warmth is to be preferred to the White woman's coldness, one must note that Cullen's emphasis on physical qualities is easily transformable to a stereotypical posturing, which, indeed, an African critic would see in his poetry. In his essay, Canaday makes the valid point that Cullen opposes brown/sensuality/paganism to white/spirituality/Christianity/cold sterility. Yet that would be only cold comfort when one considers the insidiousness of age-long Afrophobia stemming from the insistence on one group's hypersensuality. In matters of life, love, reason, and religion, Cullen's biases are much in tune with those of mainstream America, even while he keeps calling up images of Africa. In addition, the image of a brown maiden makes one think of a mulatto, a mixture of Africa and America, a big step removed from savagery and towards civilization!

Richard Wright belongs to the immediate post-Harlem Renaissance generation. His first novel, *Lawd Today* (1937), denigrates Garveyism. *Black Boy* and *Native Son*, arguably Wright's best-known novels, address his harrowing dilemma. His self-hate, resulting from White racism and Black rootlessness, pushes him to become the *Outsider* (the title of another of his works). The pity of it all is that the proclaimed outsider, deep down, hungers for America. He has never, indeed, left America, to which he remains attached psychologically and ideologically after he has dabbled into communism and after his self-exile in Paris. Wright moves from a moderate Black nationalism to Marxism, to a life of exile, settling down in Paris, ''City of Lights,'' center of civilization, epitome of Enlightenment—that enlightenment which, according to Wright, Africa lacks and must have.[18]

The critic Berghahn (164) mentions Wright's ambivalence towards Africa. One would rather call it abhorrence stemming from an intellectualist superiority complex that hides a deep feeling of lack of self-fulfillment within the Western world. The accident of color, the unwanted ancestry, those are the problems bothering Wright. He must have died wondering: "What does being *African* mean?" (Wright, *Black Power*, 4). Berghahn exaggerates when he likens Wright's relationship with the African continent to the attraction-repulsion between Wright and America. The fact is, Wright cast Africa out of his psyche; not the other way round. He demanded everything, but gave nothing. And it is strange when a man, alone, says that he does not care being alone.

Présence Africaine eulogized Wright thus, with a promise: "They [Africans] will see to it that even in the text-books of the humblest schools in the New Africa, the name of Richard Wright will be a familiar one . . . a vibrant symbol of strenuous dedication to the spirit of fraternity between all men."[19] This was, no doubt, a bourgeois exaggeration; but, at least, that class of privileged Africans did welcome back the lonely, departed son.

James Baldwin, an icon in his own right, would fall into the Zora Neale Hurston school of fighters against the sobbing school of Negrohood. Baldwin has written at length about Richard Wright's bleak landscape in an effort to understand the man. As he continues to examine Wright, Baldwin begins to modify his position because he, too, stands at a dangerous distance from the African:

[Wright] cut himself off from his roots. . . . I defended Richard when an African told me, with a small, mocking laugh, *I believe he thinks he's white.* . . . I did not think I was white, either, or I did not *think* I thought so. . . . I could not help wondering if he [Wright], when facing an African, felt the same awful tension between envy and despair, attraction and revulsion. I had always considered myself very dark, both Negroes and whites had despised me for it, and I had despised myself. But the Africans were much darker than I; I was a paleface among them, and so was Richard. (*The Price of the Ticket*, 280–81)

The difference between Wright and Baldwin is that the latter exteriorates more, he grapples more consciously and more openly with the dilemma. He owns up to his American complex and personal confusion built upon the myth of Africa that has been inculcated into his psyche. Berghahn mentions the difficulty in making clear-cut statements on Baldwin's relationship with Africa due to the diversity of Baldwinian positions. That is correct to a large extent; but there is a constant: Africa, in Baldwin's opinion, is inferior. America is a "strange home," but it remains home. Unlike Wright, Baldwin returns home from France and without having made any kind of visit to Africa. The students and emigrés whom he befriends in France represent, one might say, the kind of Africans—those on the road to civilization—with whom Baldwin would prefer to associate.

If Wright belongs to a no-man's land between Black and White and Baldwin is ambivalent about blackness, the writers of the Black Power–Black Consciousness–Black Aesthetic movement of the 1960s and 1970s certainly belong to everything Black. Their work is geared towards validating the glorious past (Africa) and building a solid, autonomous base in the present (America). Among the artists of this period are: Nikki Giovanni, Ameer Baraka, Don L. Lee, and Sonia Sanchez.

Much of the work of these Black aestheticians is poetry. They use free verse and down-to-earth, popular Black English; they refer to African deities; the artists wear African clothes and natural (Afro) hairstyles; they change their names to show their Africanness. These symbols are supposed to give the revolution a cultural base. The setting of this activism is America. The Pan-Africanist position of this period does not lessen the sense of struggle in America; rather, it complements it. The artist now believes in Frantz Fanon's notion of Third World solidarity. For the first time, Blacks in America fully believe that they are victims of a colonial conditioning and cultural imperialism. Askia Muhammad Touré, one of the Black aestheticians, declares: "We are cultural slaves!"[20]

I think the popular base remains the most valid aspect of this revolutionary literature—no intellectual hang-ups, no reservations regarding Africa and Africans, no confusion about the quality of black color. Unfortunately, the Black Aesthetic has been forgotten as another footnote in the upward march towards civilization. The dilemma of committed artists seems so horrifyingly similar in Africa and America.

Dudley Randall's poem, "The Intellectuals" (Alhamisi and Wangara, *Black Arts*, 112), paints a picture of what direct action could do, and also the ambiguity of it all, leaving one to wonder about the definition of commitment and the very identity of the committed. Randall paints a rather disturbing picture of Blacks trying to move forward. The intellectuals are mostly talkers, individuals full of themselves, ego-trippers breathing fiery words and nothing else, posing and positing meaningless ideologies while millions are dying for direct action. While the self-aggrandizing intellectuals are discussing principles, debating how to formulate and establish a rationale, the others, those who believe in action, storm the hall, shoot the leaders and arrest the remainder whom they then hang. Thus ends the useless talking! It is significant that the instant-action militants believe that "they should be up and all others down," which means that they are no less absolutist and self-centered than those they have condemned to die. In essence, therefore, the poet shows no way forward.

The overall message of the Black Arts Movement (Hughes calls it "truculent negritude" in the essay "The Twenties: Harlem and Its Negritude," 20) is still relevant today as the Black masses in Africa and America are bleeding in "the wasteland of a prostituted society" (Eugene Perkins, in Alhamisi and Wangara, *Black Arts*, 99).

Alice Walker is one of those that has followed in her fiction the advice of

Booker T. Washington, that Negroes go to Africa to enlighten the Africans. Her ideas on Africa resemble those expressed in Jean Toomer's *Cane*. In *The Color Purple*, Nellie, the "missionary," goes to Africa by accident. As the story of her sojourn unfolds, she comes across as one who herself needs to be saved. One is angered by her ridiculously ignorant opinions on African culture. And, oddly enough, Nellie, Sam, and Corrine, being Black, are supposed to have an advantage over White missionaries on the scene: "We are not white. We are not Europeans. We are black like the Africans themselves" (127).

The irony cannot be lost upon the African reader: these Black missionaries are White inside (cf. Fanon's nation of "black skin, white masks" that underlines black alienation). Instead of trying to understand African culture, Walker's characters are bent upon occidentalizing their hosts. By the time of their departure, Nellie writes to Celie: "The Olinka know we can leave, they must stay. And, of course, none of this has to do with color" (228). Here, indeed, is a strange statement, implying that the missionaries are privileged to be able to return home to civilization while the Olinka have no choice but to stay in their jungle. Finally, when Tashi, the Olinka girl with tribal marks, refuses to marry the American young man, Adam, for fear that the "Americans would look down on her as a savage and shun her" (243), Adam himself gets scarification marks. What a happy ending! what love! what civilized magnanimity! Tashi, already marginalized from her culture with the help of her missionary mentors, must, of course, be mentally prepared for life in America. Without understanding the cultural significance of facial marks, Adam is doing no more than ridiculing himself and that culture.

Another best-selling novelist, Charles Johnson, in *Middle Passage* (1990), relates the story of a freed slave, Rutherford Calhoun, who, drifting from southern Illinois to New Orleans, is forced to run from his creditors and a harassing, ugly lover seeking marriage, Isadora, into a slave-trading ship, the *Republic*, sailing for Africa. As he goes to Africa and returns to America, Rutherford undergoes the full turnaround of fortune. The dichotomy between Africa and America is well laid out by Johnson: from rags to riches; from grass to grace; from savagery to civilization; from hate to love. Rutherford succeeds in overcoming his nemesis, the mulatto slave-dealer, Papa Zeringue, "a black lord in ruins, a fallen angel like Lucifer" (13) from whom he finally snatches the now sweet and pretty Isadora.

Walker and Johnson take a stand similar to that visible in the poetry of Robert Hayden in "Middle Passage," Bruce McM. Wright in "The African Affair," and Bob Kaufman in "African Dream" (see Bontemps, 113–18; 144–45; 188–89). In each case, dream of Africa constitutes a nightmare that haunts the memory and continues to build a wedge between African Americans and Africans. Since literary reviews use a patently Eurocentric perspective, no one sees anything detrimental or derogatory towards Africa in most of these works. Africa, to the Western mind, is secondary, irrelevant. Quite often, Africa is not even considered as part of the world.

However, other writers posit and preserve a positive outlook on Africa. Among the various characters struggling to survive in the dead-end ghetto of Gloria Naylor's *The Women of Brewster Place* is Kiswana, mulatto daughter of bourgeois parents, who, at age twenty-three, has decided to move to the ghetto and has changed her name from Melanie to emphasize her African heritage and radical philosophy. In the novel's frontispiece, Naylor quotes Langston Hughes's poignant poem asking about the destiny of "a dream deferred." The answer proffered in her novel is that the dream is too resilient and refuses to die, even though there is not yet a visible end to the tunnel of deprivation.

The work of Paule Marshall is as Afrocentric as that of any writer in America today. For her, the spiritual return to Africa is a necessity. In a 1986 interview, she recounts her most positive experiences in Africa, which she visited for the first time in 1977:

Africa is simultaneously both at the same time—a concrete destination and a spiritual homeland. . . . What was extraordinary for me was the way Africans adopted me. . . . I was adopted as a native daughter. There is an expression of Yoruba or Ibo origin, "Omowale" [critic's note: it is Yoruba] which roughly translates to mean "a native daughter has returned." This expression summarizes the experience of my physical return to Africa.[21]

Each of Marshall's fictional works includes either a spiritual or physical return to Africa as a matter of necessity for rehumanizing and reinvigorating her protagonists. The novel *Praisesong for the Widow* (1984) relates the life of Avery Johnson in the 1940s and her marriage to Jerome (Jay) Johnson, tracing her lineage through Grenada back to Africa. It is the lost awareness, that connection, the most valuable part of themselves that Avery begins to search for, with the medium of dream and a totally unplanned trip to Grenada, the island of her African ancestors.

There Avery meets an old man in a bar, an Ifa (Yoruba religion) priest of sorts with "ways of seeing that went beyond mere sight and ways of knowing that outstripped ordinary intelligence and thus had no need for words" (172). Although unsure of her ethnic background (Arara, Banda, Chamba, Cromanti, Manding, Moko, Temne, Yoruba, all are listed by the old man), Avery is in a position to forge solidarity with her people in the present just as the slaves succeeded in creating new communities despite their different backgrounds and the enslavers' deliberate efforts at total cultural disintegration. With "memories that come down to one in the blood" (178), Avery invites all her brothers and sisters to struggle together. Marshall believes that Africa brings to diasporan Blacks "a sense of unity."[22]

Other contemporary writers have tried with much less success than Paule Marshall to make the connection with Africa. One of them is Marita Golden, whose autobiography, *Migrations of the Heart* (1983), relates her problematic life in America, her emigration to Nigeria with her Nigerian husband, and her *escape* with her son back home to the United States after three and a half years of *adventure*. (The stressed words are vital for understanding Golden's relationship with Africa.) One must first of all realize that fiction and fact, though intertwined, are not interchangeable; therefore, Marshall's novels cannot be critiqued in the same manner as Golden's real return. Nevertheless, what sets apart Marshall's work is not its fictionality, but the author's attitude towards Africa, as well as the conditions and circumstances determining her characters' approximation to Africa. As has been confirmed, Africa is essential for Marshall. It was and remains home. For Golden, the opposite is the case: Africa is an adventure, a foreign, strange land from which she finally escapes. America is the only home she knows. And it cannot be overemphasized that the concept of home is as much psychological (vertical journey) as physical (horizontal).

Golden has no real, genuine notion of Africa—Africa symbolized by an Afro haircut that her father abhors, in any case; Africa known only by name and, later, through contact with the man that she marries, Femi Ajayi, a budding "New African." Those images of Africa are hardly good enough to prepare anyone for life in the ancestral motherland. Deflated by her innumerable sad experiences, Golden equates love to anger. America, one might say, has failed Golden. She is now ready for Africa to rescue her. Golden is so captivated by Femi's confidence that she rubs her fingers across his hand: "I want some of your confidence to rub off on me" (54). None of the cultural problems facing the couple is ever resolved—or addressed.

Femi gives Marita an African definition of love, beyond copulation and the couple and encompassing the family. "Deliverance wiping beads of sweat" from her brow, she accepts "the burden" (57). The question of adaptability and compatibility is left hanging in the air. Optimistic, she claims to be determined to find love in Africa; and love, in this instance, would include a kind of safe house, an escape. Her own words prove the great necessity for hope: "I only wanted to shape a re-birth of hope" (61).

If Marita is guilty, Femi is, indeed, more guilty than she. He does nothing to make her fully aware of the realities of his culture. In fact, he himself is alienated from that culture. The son of a rich chief, a brilliant intellectual, and a man bloated by a superiority complex that Marita misreads as charming confidence, he does not realize his own responsibilities towards the woman he is about to marry and take into a totally new surrounding. Withdrawn, Femi discusses almost nothing with her.

Marita appears pleased with his rigidity. "I realized that I would never see him cry, admit to doubt or error. Say 'I am sorry.' But it was that strength I required to bolster my quicksand foundation" (69). Unfortunately, Marita views Africa with civilized blinkers.

An avowed "explorer looking for the end of [her] personal rainbow" (90), Marita has no intention of making Nigeria home. The closest she gets to involvement in popular culture is the University of Ife. She remarks in passing on "Ile-Ife, an ancient Yoruba town" (92), showing no recognition of the importance of the home of the ethnic group that has given to the African diaspora a great deal of the heritage kept alive there today. Golden's visit to Africa reinforces the wall separating her from African culture. Surprisingly enough, she claims a victory: "I had snatched the shroud from the bowed head of my past. Now at night I would sleep fitfully, and a tribal marked face and the sound of a drum would haunt my waking hours until I returned" (92).

There is ambiguity in that rhetoric. The shroud remains unclear. The haunting tribal-marked face, the drum, "the jungle of startling emotions" (93), rather than bring to mind thoughts of peace and harmony, would elicit fear and mystery, thus confirming the continuing cleavage or, at best, a confused affinity. And when Marita mentions her feeling free "to become [in Africa] whatever *else* there was" (93) inside her, one may perceive that in a positive light, even though the problem is that the ground has not been prepared for such optimism. Femi is a catalyst, a means of carrying to fruition her "crusade to regain the courage to be" (93). He is her Africa, which is still confused with America.

Marita's failure to settle down in Nigeria is therefore not unexpected. After spending three and a half tumultuous years, she ends up escaping back to America with her one-year-old baby boy with the help of her American lover in Lagos, who drives them across the border. Marita is clearsighted enough to admit: "because of my need, I had denied or ignored" the incompatibilities between her and Femi (220).

One is impressed by Marita Golden's honesty and feels sympathetic towards her dilemma. Maybe Africa has helped her to find herself in America. Maybe now she will find happiness. The fact remains that, without real effort to comprehend Africa in her own terms, individuals like Marita will continue to run away after their *adventure*. They will need therapists to help rid them of hate. Marita's son, Tunde, will grow up American; barely able to stand, he already shows interest in the printed word. Meanwhile, Femi, finally in the money but forever ignorant of his wife's needs, writes in vain, trying to get her to return to Africa.[23]

Marita Golden's subsequent work of fiction, *A Woman's Place*, also pursues an African dream, but with more positive results than she did in her autobiography. One of the characters of *A Woman's Place* (1986), Serena, settles in Kenya in the 1970s. A respected, politically aware landowner, she works with Kenyan women and is witness to the spurting gropings of that country towards nationhood. Serena's comments on Africa are gripping and tragic: Africa of the aborted revolution. Africa enslaved by the International Monetary Fund and myriad multinationals. Africa of dictators decreeing death to progressive elements. Africa aping America. When Serena visits the United States, she says she feels like a foreigner. That feeling, ostensibly a declaration of her attachment to Africa, does not however dissipate the dilemma of Blacks on both sides of the big sea: while Serena feels foreign in America, Africans are dying to become Americanized.

If Africans dream of America while Black Americans dream of Africa, with both unable until now to take the best out of each other, how do we harmonize the cross-currents to guide the cultural ship safely ashore? And which shore are we seeking? Serena (the name makes one think of serene, peaceful) finds her woman's place in an Africa making possible a superior status; she becomes a chief in Kenya. She is in control. She is the equal of men and independent in everything, in love and in life. Her success does not, however, equate Africa's. She thus takes us back to Marita Golden's aborted aspirations in the autobiography, underscoring once again the basic individualism of Euro-American civilization. The search for woman's place, the dream of empowerment mangled by male hegemony in America materializes in Black Africa, leaving millions of people as victims. Serena, the individual, is saved, but the society is caught in the clutch of imperialism and neocolonialism. The success story symbolized by Serena would perhaps have been more pertinent in an American setting, not in Africa. Of course, only in Africa could it have been realistic, which is a sad comment on the life of Blacks in America.

The persistent racism in the United States means that Blacks cannot, even if they want to, detach themselves from Africa. The feel-all-right attitude expressed in some poems, for example, Horace Julian Bond's "The Bishop of Atlanta: Ray Charles" (in Bontemps, 184), is only a fleeting consolation from age-old frustrations. Such consolation "molded on Africa's anvil" (Bond), however, is still to be preferred to the mainstream pipe dreams of writers like James Baldwin, who think that Blacks can partake of the American Dream by renouncing or minimizing African heritage.

Before concluding, no meaningful study of African-American literature can be complete without making mention of Alex Haley's bestseller *Roots*. Magubane (232–34) makes very incisive comments on the great effect of Haley's work on the whole of American society; it is the television series, not the written text, that had the greatest impact. While *Roots* no doubt affirmed in the strongest terms that Blacks have a heritage in Africa, the irony remains that this heritage was stolen away from them by the larger society, thereby lessening the particularity of Black Africanity. The television series turned the serious personal drama into a public melodrama, or another fad—it was time for everyone to go in search of his or her roots! In other words, *Roots* ended up emphasizing the American Dream, instead of the Africanity of the African American.

At the inauguration of Bill Clinton, the U.S. forty-second President, on January 20, 1993, the highly acclaimed African-American poet, Maya Angelou, was commissioned to read a poem. "The Horizon Leans Forward" is a powerful celebration of the American nation formed of diverse peoples. The poet places particular emphasis on the African component, enslaved, forced across the Atlantic, "praying for a dream." Angelou acts as a symbol for rooting that dream, a reference for making it meaningful, concrete, solid, tenacious, and indestructible. She captures the trauma of slavery but strips it of the opprobrium that has often made it a shameful history to be forgotten. She makes it an experience marked by courage to continue and construct, a re-affirmation of a people's humanity and their attachment to a viable culture within a multicultural nation. Thus, from the nightmare of slavery, African Americans have moved into the dawn of freedom, with their ever-present Africanity.

The poet becomes the Rock, the River, the Tree, all of which are like totems (compare with the *iroko* and baobab trees and the Rivers Congo, Niger, Nile, all of which are used as symbols in poetry) relieved of their restrictive Africanity and converted into the common symbols of Americanity. The particularity remains strong, nonetheless: the Ashanti, the Yoruba, the Kru cannot afford to forget their heritage. Returning to America from Africa years ago, the traveling Angelou informs us in *All God's Children Need Traveling Shoes*:

Now I know my people had never completely left Africa. We had changed its color, modified its rhythms, yet it was Africa which rode in the bulges of our high calves, shook in our protruding behinds and crackled in our wide open laughter. (208)

Here we are back in the ineluctable embrace of Negritude. Maya Angelou is reminding us that, whether we Blacks like it or not, there is something basic, beautiful, overwhelming that is exclusively ours and that has helped us to survive as a people, in spite of all odds visited upon us from within and without. On both sides of the great divide, we need understanding and cooperation. Patronizing attitudes cannot be productive.

Now, it is not enough to blame African Americans for the gorge separating us. If we Africans have forgotten the trauma of slavery, it is time to dust off our memory and remember. The South African writer Es'kia Mphahlele, in *The African Image*, opines: "We must create a climate that will help us understand what it is we expect of each other" (122).

If we sit down to talk, we shall discover bases for solidarity, not schism. In *Migrations of the Heart*, Marita Golden astonishes her boyfriend's brother with her unusual interest in Africa. Babatope tells her:

"It's whites who invite me to their homes, who are eager to know about my country and not make fun of it."

"I believe you," I agreed lamely. "But it's a long, complicated story, why we're this way." I told him about Tarzan movies, Africa jokes, slavery, and a past I'd dug to find like a determined, driven prospector.

"But we do not know these things," he said wondrously. "We cannot know how you have suffered." (55)

Given such "sparks of revelation and admission of sin" (56), it would still be preposterous to precipitously proclaim that we have, indeed, succeeded in understanding each other. In the Africa of 1996, Blacks from abroad are still considered foreigners; and, in America, Africans are still hated for their pride. Current socioeconomic and political conditions and circumstances do not help matters. If slavery has been abolished, enslavement is alive and well. Culture, no matter how beautiful and essential, cannot live without bread on the table, without economic development of the countries claiming to be its repositories. Today, Africa, the New Africa of messiahs best named murderers, is being bled to the bones and its best daughters and sons are scurrying abroad to Civilization.

Africa's tragedy is in our lack of focus and foresight. And we owe it all to independence and the patriots that led us into neocolonialism. W.E.B. Du Bois warned many years ago: "A body of local private capitalists, even if they are black, can never free Africa; they will simply sell it into new slavery to old masters overseas" (*The World and Africa*, 309).

Du Bois foresaw a time when the future of Blacks in the world would be safe as a result of cooperation. If Africa has retrogressed into New Colonialism, Black America is also in bad shape and Harlem, mecca of the legendary Renaissance, is today a symbol of a bad, bitter dream (call it a nightmare). Harlem, the same Harlem that meant heaven to the masses moving up from the South, the same Harlem that Langston Hughes and others describe so beautifully as a land of hope, has become a real hell and does not seem about to undergo any transformation for the better.

NOTES

1. Langston Hughes, "Negro," in *Selected Poems of Langston Hughes* (New York: Knopf, 1975), 8.

2. Frank Harris, a white editor, to Claude McKay, in McKay, *A Long Way from Home* (New York: Arno Press, 1969), 21.

3. Everett Goodwin, "Africa and Afro-American Identity: Problems and Possibilities," *Black World* 22, no. 7 (May 1973): 78.

4. Paule Marshall, in *SAGE* 3, no. 2 (Fall 1986): 53.

5. See "Guinée," in *La Montagne ensorcelée* (Paris: Les Editeurs Français Réunis, 1972), 253.

6. Francis and Val Gray Ward, "The Black Artist—His Role in the Struggle," *The Black Scholar* January 1971, 24. See Femi Ojo-Ade, "Of Culture, Commitment and Construction: Reflections on African Literature," *Transition*, no. 53 (1991): 4–24.

7. Note that, as part of the determination to discourage miscegenation, Blacks were encouraged to return to Africa. And Black emigrationists who accepted the idea were sure that equality could never be attained with Whites in America. For example, see John David Smith, "Out of Sight, Out of Mind: Robert Stein's 1904 'Deafricanization' Scheme to 'Hopeland,' " *Phylon* 46, no. 1 (Spring 1985); 1–15.

8. Renfro, *Life and Works of Phyllis Wheatley* (1916), p. 48. Wheatley's poem is a forerunner to the poetry of Countee Cullen, who takes pains to prove that he is a Christian.

9. Quoted in Magubane, 97. Claude McKay, a Jamaican like Garvey, actually hated Garvey. A chapter in this book is devoted to McKay.

10. *Journal of Negro History* 25, no. 40: 590–92.

11. Irele, "Negritude or Black Cultural Nationalism," *The Journal of Modern African Studies* 3, no. 3 (1965): 327.

12. Langston Hughes, "The Negro Artist and the Racial Mountain," *Nation* 122 (June 1926): 692.

13. "The Twenties: Harlem and Its Negritude," *African Forum* 1 (Spring 1966): 18.

14. Ibid., p. 12.

15. Another novel of that period in which color-shade is a major issue, is Wallace Thurman's *The Blacker the Berry* (1929). The protagonist's (Emma Lou's) family descends from original Africans and that "primitive heritage" stalks her throughout life. Episodes of wild dancing by "darkies" are the usual fare. Jean Toomer's novel *Cane* (1923) also dwells on the theme of primitiveness, instinct, and Black animalism. A confused line of distinction is drawn between the forces of civilization and savagery.

16. Examples of those not insisting on "blackness" include Georgia Johnson ("The True American," in Honey, *Shadowed Dreams*, 121), who paints her ideal American as "the cosmopolitan," free of prejudice. Mae Cowdery, in "A Brown Aesthete Speaks" (Honey, 88), posits an American beauty with Black and White acting as "mutual teachers." Actually, the poet is pleading for acceptance in the circle of aesthetes who appreciate Keats and Poe.

17. Cullen, "Poet on Poet," *Opportunity* no. 4 (1926): 74.

18. These ideas are expressed in his speech at the 1956 Paris Congress of Black Writers and Artists; see Femi Ojo-Ade, "Black Burden, White Ways," *ALA Bulletin* 14, no. 3 (Summer 1988): 17–23.

19. *Presence Africaine*, no. 34–35 (1961): 238. A cynical reader might say that this homage is gratuitous and one more example of that journal's ambiguity. On the other hand, it would be proof of solidarity and tradition: you honor your dead, out of love and magnanimity.

20. Quoted in Ahmed Alhamisi and H. Wangara, eds., *Black Arts* (Detroit: Black Arts Publications, 1969), 34.

21. *SAGE* 3, no. 2 (1986): 52–53.

22. Ibid., 53. In an interview Marshall, Ama Ata Aidoo, and Es'kia Mphahlele were kind enough to grant me at University of Richmond, Virginia, in the spring of 1989, Paule Marshall emphasized her belief in the "unbroken circle" of African culture. I have often wondered why Marshall's Africanity is so much more pronounced than that of many others, such as Ralph Ellison for whom the American matrix is absolute and any thought of an African connection is anathema. Marshall's Caribbean roots may be a reason; but then Claude McKay also had Caribbean roots and he was far from matching Marshall's Africanity. For other positive concepts of Africanity, consult the works of Toni Cade Bambara (language), Toni Morrison (sense of community), and Eugene Redmond (the language and message of the drum: his chosen name is "Ilugangan," Yoruba for "talking drum"). The difference in McKay and Marshall's generations would provide some explanation, but only partially.

23. Maya Angelou's *All God's Children Need Traveling Shoes* (1986) comes to mind when we think of other autobiographies dealing with African experience.

BIBLIOGRAPHY

Alhamisi, Ahmed, and H. Wangara. *Black Arts: An Anthology of Black Creations.* Detroit: Black Arts Publications, 1969.

Angelou, Maya. *All God's Children Need Traveling Shoes*. New York: Vintage Books, 1991.

Baldwin, James. *The Price of the Ticket*. New York: St. Martin's/Marek, 1985.

Berghahn, Marion. *Images of Africa in Black American Literature*. London: MacMillan, 1977.

Bontemps, Arna, ed. *American Negro Poetry*. New York: Hill and Wang, 1974.

————. *The Harlem Renaissance Remembered*. New York: Dodd, Mead and Co., 1972.

Brent, Linda. *Incidents in the Life of a Slave-Girl*. New York: Harcourt Brace Jovanovich, 1973.

Chapman, Abraham, ed. *Black Voices*. New York: Mentor, 1968.

Cobb, Martha. *Harlem, Haiti and Havana*. Washington, D.C.: Three Continents Press, 1979.

Cullen, Countee. *Color*. New York: Arno Press, 1969.

Du Bois, W.E.B. *An A.B.C. of Color*. Berlin: Seven Seas Books, 1964.

————. *Dusk of Dawn*. New York: Harcourt, Brace, 1940.

————. *The Souls of Black Folk*. New York: New American Library, 1969.

————. *The World and Africa*. New York: International Publishers, 1965.

Emanuel, James A. *Langston Hughes*. New York: Twayne Publishers, 1967.

Fanon, Frantz. *Black Skin White Masks*. Trans. Charles Lam Markmann. New York: Grove Press, 1967.

Fredrickson, George. *The Black Image in the White Mind*. 1971.

Golden, Marita. *Migrations of the Heart*. New York: Ballantine Books, 1983.

————. *A Woman's Place*. New York: Ballantine Books, 1986.

Hemenway, Robert. *Zora Neale Hurston: A Literary Biography*. Urbana: University of Illinois Press, 1977.

Honey, Maureen, ed. *Shadowed Dreams*. New Brunswick, N.J.: Rutgers University Press, 1989.

Hughes, Langston. *The Big Sea*. New York: Hill and Wang, 1940. Reprint, 1981.

————. *Selected Poems*. New York: Knopf, 1965.

Hurston, Zora Neale. *Jonah's Gourd Vine*. Philadelphia: J.B. Lippincott, 1934. Reprint, 1971.

————. *Tell My Horse*. Philadelphia: J.B. Lippincott, 1938.

————. "Harlem and Its Negritude." *African Forum* 1 (Spring 1966): 11–20.

Isaacs, Harold. *The New World of the Negro American*. New York: Viking Press, 1964.

Johnson, Charles. *Middle Passage*. New York: Penguin, 1990.

King, Woodie, and Earl Anthony, eds. *Black Poets and Prophets*. New York: New American Library, 1972.

Larsen, Nella. *Quicksand*. New York: Collier, 1928. Reprint, 1971.

Logan, Rayford. "The American Negro's View of Africa." In *Africa from the Point of View of American Negro Scholars*. Paris: Présence Africaine, 1958. Pp. 217–27.

Magubane, Bernard Makhosezwe. *The Ties that Bind: African-American Consciousness of Africa*. Trenton, N.J.: Africa World Press, 1987.

Marshall, Paule. *Praisesong for the Widow*. New York: E.P. Dutton, 1983.

Mphahlele, Es'kia. *The African Image*. New York: Praeger, 1974.

Naylor, Gloria. *The Women of Brewster Place*. New York: Penguin, 1982.

Ngugi wa Thiong'o. *Writers in Politics*. London: Heinemann, 1981.

Ojo-Ade, Femi. *On Black Culture*. Ile-Ife: Obafemi Awolowo University Press, 1989.

Senghor, Léopold-Sédar. *Anthologie de la nouvelle poésie nègre et malgacher.* Paris: Presses Universitaires de France, 1948. Reprint, 1969.

Smyth, Hon. J. H. "The African in Africa and the African in America." In *Africa and the American Negro.* 1985 Atlanta Congress on Africa. Miami: Mnemosyne Publishing Co., 1969.

Thurman, Wallace. *The Blacker the Berry.* New York: Macaulay, 1929. Rev. ed., Collier, 1970.

Walker, Alice. *The Color Purple.* New York: Washington Square Press, 1982.

Ward, Francis, and Val Gray Ward. "The Black Artist—His Role in the Struggle." *The Black Scholar.* January 1971, 24–26.

Wilson, Harriet. *Our Nig.* New York: Random House, 1983. London: Allison & Busby, 1984.

Wright, Richard. *Black Boy.* New York: Harper, 1945.

———. *Black Power.* New York: Harper, 1945.

———. *Native Son.* New York: Harper, 1940.

———. *The Outsider.* New York: Harper, 1953.

2

W.E.B. Du Bois: The Man and His Vision of Africa for Africans

F. UGBOAJA OHAEGBULAM

This is not a biography of William Edward Burghardt Du Bois. Deep insights into the man's life can be obtained from both his series of autobiographical recollections and the several accounts of his life produced by other writers.[1] Rather, this essay attempts to provide an account of W.E.B. Du Bois' vision of Africa as the "Motherland" of Black people; his attachment to, and vision for, the continent and for all peoples of African descent.

W.E.B. Du Bois, widely known as the "intellectual and spiritual father of Pan-Africanism," a leading educator, a major social critic, philosopher and scientist, an uncompromising political journalist of Black America for over sixty years, was an undaunted advocate of African independence. In 1890, at the age of twenty-two, Du Bois declared that he sincerely believed he had something to say to the world. Accordingly, he contributed in no small measure, through his works, to shape the twentieth century from an African-centered perspective.

On July 9, 1868, barely three months after Du Bois' birth, the Fourteenth Amendment to the U.S. Constitution was ratified. It defined an American citizen and included African people in America who met the conditions of the definition as U.S. citizens. Before Du Bois was two years old, the Fifteenth Amendment to the Constitution was ratified, extending suffrage to Blacks.

In spite of the major constitutional guarantees of these amendments, African Americans generally were subjected to vicious political, social, and racial injustice throughout the land during and after the most formative years of Du Bois's life. He learned early that some human beings considered his brown skin a misfortune, a crime[2] and that to be a Black in a White-dominated world was to be despised and rejected. Du Bois was very insightful when, in 1903, he asserted in *The Souls of Black Folk*: "The problem of the twentieth century is the problem of the color-line,—the relation of the darker to the lighter races of men in Asia and Africa, in America and the islands of the sea."[3]

Racial or color prejudice remains alive and is a major problem of modern times. In the waning decades of the twentieth century, politicians win victories at the poll by appealing to racial prejudice. As we witnessed, for example, in the 1988 U.S. presidential election campaigns, the release from prison of Willie Horton, a convict who happened to be Black, served as a major negative campaign advertisement that rallied electoral support to the eventual victorious Republican candidate. Again, appealing to racial prejudice in the 1990 U.S. senatorial election campaign, another Republican candidate in North Carolina, Jesse Helms, trumpeted allegations of legalized quotas to benefit African Americans. This negative campaign turned the scales against his Black political opponent, who had been leading in the polls, and won him the victory.

DU BOIS AND EUROPEAN IMPERIAL OCCUPATION OF AFRICA

Du Bois's birth and childhood coincided also with the marauding activities of European nations in Africa. Earlier, European Christian missionaries, explorers, and traders had employed a variety of strategies to prepare the way for European imperialism in Africa. In November 1884, five months after Du Bois's graduation from high school, European nations held a conference in Berlin where they concluded a treaty (The Berlin Act, February 26, 1885) dividing the African continent into colonial possessions among themselves. Thus, both in Africa, the ancestral homeland, and in the diaspora in North America, African peoples became subjected to political domination, economic exploitation, and social subjugation with racist overtones.

These events and developments experienced by African peoples helped to awaken Du Bois's racial consciousness and, perhaps more importantly, his racial obligations, especially after he enrolled at Fisk University (1885–1888) and shared with Black southerners the experience of rejection, discrimination, and white racism.[4] Significantly, the catalog of Fisk University listed Africa as one of the institution's principal objectives. Authors of the catalog urged and prayed those who labor in the university to recognize and be guided by the objective that the institution's ultimate and best work would be that of redeeming Africa.

Du Bois dutifully embraced this proclaimed objective of his alma mater. Concerns with Africa, the ancestry and culture of African Americans, and the elevation of the Black race became central themes of his thought and writings. To this end, he devoted his entire life to the cause of freeing Black people from the political and social oppression and degradation of racism. A proud and outspoken man, he became a fervid defender of the race as a whole.

DU BOIS'S STRATEGIES FOR THE LIBERATION OF BLACK PEOPLE

As a graduate student at the University of Berlin (1892–1894), Du Bois said to himself on his twenty-fifth birthday: ''These are my plans: to make a name in science, to make a name in literature and thus to raise my race."[5] He employed a variety of strategies to enhance the dignity and liberation of Black people. As he saw them, published contemporary historical and sociological studies and doctrines in the Western world were defective, lacking objectivity and accuracy in their portrayal, interpretation, and treatment of Black people. A major objective of his research and writings, most of them empirical, was to produce an interpretation of historical and sociological facts that would at the same time provide a deeper insight into the Black experience and enhance the morale and confidence of Black people. His assumption was that the world would act in accordance with the truth or the knowledge of the facts about Black people and racial oppression to bring about social justice for all.

Much of Du Bois's writings, whether about himself or a historical narrative of the Black race, was autobiographical. The works reveal the soul of black folk—the essence of Black people's being, their "immortal or nonmaterial part," and the "sensitive feeling component" of their personality.[6] They also illustrate personal or generalized experience of Black people, and provide deep insights into the Black condition. In them, Du Bois reveals with passion, shrewdness, honesty, and artistic sophistication a meaning of Black existence never known before.

In *The World and Africa* (1965), an unusually penetrating and far-sighted statement for its time, Du Bois attempted to reconstruct the mutilated story of the African past, while emphasizing the historic presence, achievements, and artistic and social history of Africa. By a masterful marshalling of facts, he also refuted the misinformation of Eurocentric scholarship that Africa had no history prior to its colonial occupation by European nations. In *Color and Democracy* (1975), Du Bois, who was already lobbying the United Nations for the representation of African colonial peoples in the emerging international organization, sought to link Africa's future with that of the rest of the world, and to clothe African nationalism with Socialist thought. Without mincing words, he called for the liquidation of British and French colonial empires in Africa.

Collectively, Du Bois's works endeavored to dispel the Eurocentric notion of the innate inferiority of Black people, to inspire all peoples of African descent, to nourish and advance the will of Black people to achieve full political and social equality of which the international slave trade and Western European colonial occupation had robbed them. Du Bois believed and required that the art and literature of Black people should play a central role in their struggle for political empowerment and advancement. His dedication to promoting an understanding of the Black experience and the liberation of Black people through research and writing was total. He authored about forty books and hundreds of articles and pamphlets on these concerns. At the invitation of President Kwame Nkrumah, Du Bois emigrated to Ghana in 1961 to begin editing *Encyclopedia Africana*, for many years his cherished desire, which no foundation had been willing to fund on the scale he had envisioned. The text was never published, although an *Encyclopedia of the Negro* had been published by the Phelps-Stokes

Fund in 1945. Already an old man, Du Bois died in Ghana on August 27, 1963, while editing the encyclopedia.

Convinced of White Euro-America's determination to keep Black people down, he declared that only Black people, "bound and welded together" as a race and "inspired by one great ideal," can develop the Black genius and "work out in its fullness the great message they have for humanity."[7]

Furthermore, Du Bois asserted: "Where separation of mankind into races, groups and classes is compulsory, either by law or custom, and whether that compulsion be temporary or permanent, the only effective defense that the segregated and despised group has against complete spiritual and physical disaster, is internal self-organization for self-respect and self-defense."[8] His espousal of Black voluntary self-segregation is akin to the Igbo philosophical concept of *Onye ajuru ajula onwe ya*: A person rejected and despised by others should not reject himself. He should, rather, so develop himself that he becomes a force to reckon with.

At first Du Bois regarded Black people in America as "the advance guard" of the Black race who should provide the leadership for the conservation and solidarity of the race. (By the 1950s, he conceded that role to continental Africans.) It was therefore incumbent upon them not to undertake "a servile imitation of the Anglo-Saxon culture, but [to conserve] a stalwart originality which shall unswervingly follow [Black] ideals."[9] This, he held, could be accomplished through collective self-help or communality. While Du Bois was writing in America, in West Africa, Edward Wilmot Blyden and J. E. Casely Hayford, pioneer African cultural nationalists, were similarly admonishing the educated elite of Africa against race suicide through uncritical adoption of European values, customs, and institutions.[10]

According to his writings, Du Bois's espoused race conservation required self-knowledge and mutual understanding among peoples of African descent. His belief in race conservation through communality led him to organize Pan-African congresses between 1900 and 1945. He used these congresses also as a forum to appeal to the great powers of the world and the leading international organizations, such as the League of Nations and the United Nations, to accord all peoples of African descent under their control improved educational opportunities, the right of self-determination and opportunity to participate in their own governance, and equitable economic treatment.

The theme of his book *Color and Democracy: Colonies and Peace* was that the Dumbarton Oaks Conference of 1944, which sought to ensure world peace and eventually culminated in the establishment of the United Nations, left a danger and a recurring cause of war in its failure to emphasize the rights of colonial peoples. Du Bois stressed that there could be neither peace nor security unless the interests, the wishes, and the cultural freedom of the darker races, which comprised the overwhelming majority of the peoples of the world, were considered in any post-World War II peace plan.[11]

Du Bois's approach in demanding self-determination for Black people was nonviolent because he recognized the magnitude of the weight and power of White people who controlled the contemporary world. The advancement and dignity of Africans at home and in the diaspora, as he envisaged it, would best be promoted not through race war and opposition but, rather, through peaceful cooperation with "the white rulers of the world." In spite of his nonviolent approach, Du Bois's activities, including the Pan-African congresses, were continually under surveillance by the United States and the colonial powers. For example, the Woodrow Wilson administration in the United States sought to prevent the holding of the 1919 congress in Paris,[12] while the colonial powers restricted Du Bois's movement during his visit to Africa in 1923.

Du Bois also called for economic nationalism as a cornerstone of race conservation and solidarity. A self-segregated economy, Du Bois asserted, was a step in the formation of institutions that would bolster Black morale and solidarity. It was one way Black people in America could face the fact of enforced segregation and turn it to their advantage. To the rest of the Black world, Du Bois said that it was imperative that

they should begin to concentrate upon this problem of economic survival, the best of their brains and education. Pan-Africa means intellectual understanding and cooperation among groups of [African] descent in order to bring about at the earliest possible time the industrial and spiritual emancipation of [African] peoples.[13]

Our final example of Du Bois's strategies for the liberation of Black people is his call for the training and liberal education of the "Talented Tenth" among Black folk, those who would provide the critical leadership Black people needed. "The [Black] race, like all races, is going to be saved by its exceptional men,— the 'Talented Tenth.' . . . It is they who would guide the mass away from the contamination and death of the Worst in their own and other races. No others can do this work."[14] Du Bois's advocacy of a liberal arts education and training of a Black leadership cadre ran counter to Booker T. Washington's espousal of industrial education for Black people as the major tool of Black liberation. Du Bois never denied the necessity of providing industrial education for Black people, but he insisted that it was "industrialism drunk with its vision of success, to imagine that its own work can be accomplished without providing for the training of broadly cultured men and women to teach its own teachers, and to teach the teachers of the public schools."[15]

From Du Bois's perspective, the struggle for equality in America was irrevocably tied to the fight for African independence, while self-government in Africa and the regeneration and uplift of all Black people required racial solidarity and economic independence. Therefore, the "Talented Tenth" of the race were to be liberally educated to appreciate the essence of these prerequisites and their responsibilities to the race.

WHAT WAS AFRICA TO DU BOIS?

At this stage, it is pertinent to raise the question, What was Africa to Du Bois? especially regarding his racial consciousness, devoted to the continent and all peoples of its descent, and the use of, and respect for, African norms and traditions. Of all the Black intellectuals of the period 1880 to 1935 in North America, Du Bois was, unquestionably, the one who most deeply identified with Africa. Most of his predecessors, and many of his contemporaries as well, accepted prevailing White stereotypical views about Africa—its alleged barbarism, the assumed backwardness, idolatriousness, ignorance, and backwardness of its inhabitants—and were ambivalent towards their ancestral homeland. Frequently, they exhibited anger, bitterness, and remorse over the weaknesses that permitted the dispersion of Africans to occur and vehemently opposed any ideas for physical or spiritual return to the continent.[16] In the view of critics, Du Bois's articulated concept of the Black American's double consciousness of Africa and America in two of his works, *The Conservation of Races* (1897) and *The Souls of Black Folk* (1903), was a manifestation of his own ambivalence about his race. Du Bois had written:

The history of the American Negro is the history of this strife—this longing to attain self-conscious manhood, to merge his double self into a better and truer self. In this merging he wishes neither of the older selves to be lost. He would not Africanize America, for America has too much to teach the world and Africa. He would not bleach his Negro soul in a flood of white Americanism, for he knows that Negro blood has a message for the world. He simply wishes to make it possible for a man to be both a Negro and an American, without being cursed and spit upon by his fellows, without having the doors of Opportunity closed roughly in his face.[17]

What appears here as ambivalence about Africa was a product of historical circumstances and environment. Du Bois's environment was one that stressed and practiced White/European values and supremacy and Black/African inferiority, an environment in which white was beautiful and ideal and black was regarded as dirty and ugly, one in which Black people were treated at worst as subhuman and at best as inferior. Du Bois wrote in 1947, just as Henry Highland Garnett had written about one hundred years earlier, that, due to White miseducation, Black Americans denied their Africanity and accepted in part the color line. The impact of the partial acceptance of the color line was brought to the fore in August 1963 when the Reverend Martin Luther King, Jr., eloquently told a huge crowd of Black and White people in Washington, D.C., of his dreaming of a time when his children would be judged on the content of their character and not on the color of their skin, implying that the black skin was somehow evil.

It seems also that the classic dialectical dilemma of the African American, as articulated by Du Bois, was the concern that the coexistence of the ideals of the

White race and those of Black folks among Black intellectuals, the vanguard of the race, might, through assimilation, undermine the particular genius of the African race. This concern was legitimate, given the domination of the White race and its values and institutions in the contemporary world. However, Du Bois believed that the dogged strength of the Black race alone would prevent this from happening and would ultimately enable Black folks to win their freedom to develop their own racial soul and humanize the whiteness of Teutonic values. Thus, the notion expressed by Du Bois that the African American would not Africanize America was not, strictly speaking, correct. For the African American was already, in a variety of ways, adding his specific stamp on America, enriching its culture, economics, science, religion, arts, dance, and music and modifying its constitutional and political process and development. Du Bois himself questioned whether America would be America without its Black citizens.

Du Bois obviously overcame the historically and environmentally-induced ambivalence about his race. Addressing the All-African People's Conference at Accra, Ghana, on December 22, 1958, he informed his "Fellow Africans," how, about 1735, his great-great grandfather had been kidnapped on the coast of West Africa and taken by the Dutch to the colony of New York in America where he was sold into slavery. Yet, Du Bois told his audience that, as a boy, he

knew little of Africa save legends and some music in my family. The books which we studied in the public school had almost no information about Africa, save Egypt, which we were told was not Negroid. I heard of few great men of Negro blood, but I built up in my mind a dream of what Negroes would do in the future even though they had no past.[18]

His feelings for Africa, he insisted, were real and a large determinant of his life and character. "I felt myself an African by 'race,' and by that token was African and an integral member of the group of dark Americans who were called Negroes." He then stated: "Africa is, of course, my fatherland . . . my tie to Africa is strong. . . . The real essence of this kinship is its social heritage of slavery; the discrimination and insult; and this heritage binds together . . . the children of Africa. . . . It is this unity that draws me to Africa."[19]

In his autobiography, Du Bois paid tribute to another aspect of his African cultural heritage. "In my family," he wrote, "old folks found a home with relatives; but in the surrounding community the first worry of the average citizen was for provision for his old age."[20] He acquired a comprehensive and in-depth knowledge of Africa through his scientific studies of the continent. In several of his writings he sought to document the African origin of several aspects of civilization in order to demolish the myth of African/Black inferiority; to awaken in Black people pride in the land of their birth and ancestry and in themselves; to provide a fully comprehensive and positive image of Africa and Black life;

and to promote closer ties and linkages between Africa and Black people in North America.

In his first book primarily devoted to African history, *The Negro* (1915), Du Bois emphasized the authenticity and wholesomeness of African history and culture. He asserted that African history and culture influenced Black communities in the diaspora; that there was historical proof that Black peoples began civilization along the Ganges, the Euphrates, and the Nile. Further, he stressed that it was through Africa that Christianity became the religion of the world and that Islam came to play its great role of conqueror and civilizer.

Du Bois initiated a scientific study of Africa in the Soviet Union. In his discussions with the Soviet premier, Nikita Khrushchev, and professors at Leningrad University during a visit in 1958, Du Bois suggested that the Soviet Union should establish an institute for the study of Africa as an integral part of the Soviet Academy of Sciences. As a consequence of the discussions, an Institute on Africa was established in October of that year.

Du Bois's studies and writings on Africa and its role in the world, past as well as contemporary, served his Black readers worldwide as an antidote for the poisoned pictures and distorted stories of Africa in written and oral literature. Horace Mann Bond, one of Du Bois's readers wrote:

And Africa! For an American child growing up between 1910 and 1920, there was scarcely an antidote anywhere for the poisonous picture of Africa, and of Africans, painted in the school geographies, the newspapers and magazines, and by the movies. From the earliest days of *The Crisis*, Africans were revealed as intelligent human beings. I have long counted it as one of my great blessings that I read Du Bois on Africa when I was very young.[21]

African nationalist leaders acknowledged that Du Bois's writings on Africa contributed to their historical knowledge of the continent and stimulated their nationalist struggle for independence from Western European colonial occupation.

DU BOIS AND THE CONCEPT OF PAN-AFRICANISM

Another major avenue through which Du Bois inspired the African nationalist drive for independence was his pursuit of the concept and movement of Pan-Africanism. A direct reaction against White racist oppression and colonialist domination and exploitation, the concept is a belief that the continent of Africa is a Black people's national homeland, which should be independent and free under African leadership. The idea is older than Du Bois. It is rooted in back-to-Africa movements undertaken by such individuals as Paul Cuffee, a New England shipping merchant, who settled thirty-eight free Blacks in Freetown, Sierra Leone, in 1815 at his own expense; John B. Russworm, one of the founders of Liberia; Martin Delany, whose attempts at settlement of Black Americans on the Niger Valley were preempted by the American Civil War; and the activities of the cultural nationalist Edward Wilmot Blyden in West Africa. The concept blossomed at the dawn of the twentieth century with the activities of Du Bois, amidst other developments.

In pursuit of his Pan-African beliefs, Du Bois led five Pan-African Congresses and served as chairman of a sixth. He served as the recording secretary of the 1900 conference in London and organized the 1919 Congress in Paris with the help of Blaise Diagne, a Senegalese deputy in the French National Assembly, and Clemenceau, the French prime minister, despite the opposition of the United States and Britain. Other Du Boisian congresses were held as follows: 1921 in London, Paris, and Brussels; 1923 in London and Lisbon; and 1927 in New York, under the auspices of the National Association of Colored Women. The Depression and World War II prevented further congresses until one held in Manchester, England, in 1945, in which the leadership was passed to continental Africans.

Du Bois encountered institutional, ideological, and other forms of difficulties and opposition that dampened the impact of his Pan-African movement. The hostility of the European colonial powers to the goals of his Pan-Africanist activities persisted and militated against his contact with continental Africans.[22] The colonizers were bent upon having complete control in their exploitation of Africa.

The international aspects of Du Bois's thought were hardly noticed by the masses of Black Americans. The Black American intelligentsia, on whom Du Bois had counted so much to spearhead the struggle for African liberation, was lukewarm to his extensive efforts to popularize Pan-Africanism among them. They displayed repugnance towards Africa and agreed with the leaders of the National Association for the Advancement of Colored People (NAACP) that Du Bois's fervent interest in Africa was irrelevant to the immediate conditions of Black Americans.[23] In addition, cleavages that occurred between Du Bois and other Black leaders blurred the issues of the movement and consequently contributed to minimize its impact on both America and Africa.

The split between Du Bois and Booker T. Washington over approaches to the education and civil and political rights of African Americans prevented a coordination of effort by the two foremost leaders of Black people in America and made Du Bois suspect to the powerful philanthropist supporters of Booker T. Washington. Du Bois's views stirred up resentment in such philanthropic circles and made him totally unacceptable and unworthy of their generosity. This hurt, especially in view of the fact that the movement had no U.S. political backing, no revenue-generating sources or organs and no dues paying membership. The NAACP, which had supported Du Bois's efforts in the 1919 Congress, withdrew its support for subsequent congresses. Its leaders felt that its mission of policing the American scene was a full-time job and they could not allow the dissipation of limited resources outside the scene fighting for the advancement of Africans.

Furthermore, the quarrels between Du Bois and Marcus Garvey over the shade of skin pigmentation and aims and methods of operation of the movement for Black liberation weakened the movement and denied it mass support. Du Bois asserted that "the unfortunate words and career of Marcus Garvey dampened" the interest of Black Americans in African affairs and thus the appeal of his Pan-Africanism.[24]

Across the oceans, in Europe and Africa, Du Bois's movement encountered additional difficulties. At the 1921 congress in London, Paris, and Brussels a split developed between Du Bois and Blaise Diagne over the aims and direction of the movement. Du Bois's Pan-Africanist goals were viewed as too radical and menacing to the European colonial powers by Diagne, who espoused, and was strongly attached to, French rule in Africa. In addition, the immediate post–World War I West African nationalists had no direct rapport with Du Bois's Pan-Africanism. One of these nationalists, J. E. Casely Hayford, criticized Du Bois's concentration on the "Negro problem" and double consciousness. It is evident, however, from Casely Hayford's *Ethiopia Unbound* (1911), published eleven years after the first Pan-African Conference, that his criticism of Du Bois was not directed at the Pan-Africanist movement. The Black man, Casely Hayford believed, ought not to attempt to develop intellectually and materially along the lines of progress of the White man but should engage upon the sublimer task of discovering his true self and place along "natural and national lines." Hayford was actually preaching a return to traditional institutions, which Du Bois had already articulated in *The Conservation of Races* (1897).

On the African continent also, Du Bois's Pan-Africanism was unable to establish any effective propaganda base and apparatus because of lack of resources and the pathological suspicions of the colonial powers. Neither of the two independent tropical African states, Ethiopia and Liberia, hemmed in by European colonial territories and often intimidated by the colonial powers, was powerful enough to capitalize on the Du Boisian movement or to go to its aid with effective national leadership. There is no evidence, however, that Du Bois made any overtures for collaboration with either of the governments. Finally, the most important goal of Pan-Africanism, African independence, for all practical purposes was one that only insiders, rather than overseas Africans, could tackle head on—though with the indirect but critical support of their external brethren. The insiders took on the task in the fullness of time after World War II and paid glowing tribute to Du Bois for his pioneering work and for the inspiration and insight he had provided them.

MAJOR ELEMENTS OF DU BOIS'S VISION FOR AFRICA

Despite the difficulties encountered by his movement, Du Bois sustained his vision for Africa, which, in his view, was the keystone to the liberation and advancement of all peoples of African descent. As we can see from the foregoing pages the major elements of that vision were sixfold:

1. Unity and solidarity of all Black people for their liberation through collective action. Du Bois asked independent African states to make sacrifices in the interest of African unity and for the good of the whole of Africa and its diaspora including the yielding of much-loved local languages "to the few world tongues which serve the largest number of people and promote understanding and world literature."[25] This idea has merits and demerits that need discussion elsewhere.

2. The conservation of the race and authentic African values. The Black intelligentsia were to lead the effort for the conservation of the race and the preservation of authentic values of Black people, especially by avoiding servile imitation of the White man's ways.

3. Reconstruction and preservation of the African past through a scientific study of African people and objective presentation of the findings in publications. Du Bois thus called for a Pan-Africa that would seek "to preserve its own past history, and write the contemporary account, erasing from literature the lies and distortions about black folk which have disgraced the last centuries of European and American literature."[26]

4. Education of the race, including provision of training and liberal education for the "Talented Tenth" of the race and industrial education for others. In 1957, Du Bois envisioned a Pan-African education whose end was to make Africans not simply profitable workers for industry nor stool pigeons for propaganda, but modern, intelligent, responsible men of vision.[27]

5. Economic and political empowerment of Black people. This was to be accomplished through self-help and the promotion and patronizing of Black-owned businesses, including the services provided by Black professional classes.

6. Pan-African socialism. Du Bois's vision of Pan-African socialism was one that "seeks the welfare state in . . . Africa"; refuses "to be exploited by people of other continents for their own benefit and not for the benefit of the peoples of Africa"; no longer consents "to permitting the African majority of any African country to be governed against its will by a minority of invaders who claim racial superiority or the right to [become] rich at African expense"; seeks "not only to raise but to process [Africa's] raw material and to trade it freely with all the world on just and equal terms and prices."[28] Du Bois believed that Africa had no choice between private capitalism and socialism. Private capitalism, in his view, was doomed, whereas the "communistic" system of traditional African societies had a future. He insisted that a "body of local private capitalists, even if they are black, can never free Africa; they will simply sell it into new slavery to old masters overseas" and further warned Africans against the dangers of prolonging "fatal colonial imperialism."[29] While Du Bois proved to be wrong in his view that private capitalism was doomed, his other predictions have largely been vindicated by economic developments in postcolonial Africa.

CONCLUSION

The record of achievements of Du Bois's vision for Africa is a mixed one. In the short term, his Pan-Africanism accomplished very little. The periodic conferences facilitated personal contacts and exchanges of information among the leading elites of the various communities of the African world. To them, the congresses comprised the recognition of a racial fountain that, unfortunately, was devoid of the masses of the race, a group critical to the achievement of the goals and vision of the movement. For, as manifested by the Du Boisian congresses, the concept of Pan-African unity hardly appealed to or impacted the lives of the masses of African people in continental Africa. Moreover, it did not inspire Black people in the Americas. The movement was essentially an elitist one that was so remote from the Black American's concrete day-to-day struggle for existence that it commanded neither his attention nor support and to which well-to-do Black Americans were indifferent.

It became apparent also that, in the short term, masses of Black people and Black educated elite in America and Africa ignored Du Bois's vision of conserving the race and authentic Black values as they imitated the Anglo-Saxon culture. Black Americans disregarded his view that they could rediscover and reaffirm themselves through political and spiritual identification with the ideal of Pan-Africanism. However, the concepts of Negritude, African personality, Black is beautiful, Black power, and Afrocentricity, which are currently in vogue in postcolonial Africa as well as post–civil rights America, are deeply imbedded in his scholarship and writings. They mark him as a pioneer of these concepts and of Africana studies.

In addition, both of Africa's premier international organization, the Organization of African Unity, founded in 1963, and Malcolm X's Organization of Afro-American Unity, are products of Du Bois's Pan-African vision. The National Congress of British West Africa (1920–1930), led by J. E. Casely Hayford, also received some inspiration from Du Bois's 1919 Paris congress. More importantly, Du Bois's Pan-Africanist vision definitely influenced such African nationalist elites as Kwame Nkrumah, Nnamdi Azikiwe, and Jomo Kenyatta, who came in contact with him and his writings and were later to play leading roles in the political liberation of their countries from European colonial domination.

Post-colonial Africa has faced a menace predicted by Du Bois and similar to the one he had decried when he asserted that the autocratic power White America bestowed upon Booker T. Washington endangered Black American advancement. It was the same danger posed to postcolonial Africa by the departing imperial powers, who used various strategies of neocolonialism to install indigenous political successors beholden to them so as to perpetuate their interests in Africa.

Du Bois's Pan-African vision has been vindicated in another way. There is now widespread consensus that he was essentially correct when he asserted that an improvement in the future of African Americans would be conditioned by developments in Africa. John Hope Franklin has suggested that it was critical international factors, among them the political evolution of Africa, and not merely either the U.S. presidential advocacy or the mounting pressure of civil rights movements that induced the U.S. Congress to enact the civil and voting rights acts of 1964 and 1965. The "emergence into independence of the sub-Saharan [African] nations," he affirms,

enormously changed the world-wide significance of the American race problem and provided a considerable stimulus to the movement for racial equality in the United States. As Congress began to debate the proposed civil rights bill in the summer of 1957, the diplomatic representatives from Ghana had taken up residence at the United Nations and in Washington. This important fact could not be ignored by responsible members of Congress. It seemed that black men from the Old World had arrived just in time to help redress the racial balance in the New.[30]

The civil and voting rights acts, to which John Hope Franklin refers, empowered Black America to send representatives to the United States Congress. A product of that political empowerment, the Congressional Black Caucus, in 1977 established an agency, TransAfrica, to lobby the U.S. national government in the interest of African and Caribbean states. In this we see another vindication of Du Bois's Pan-African vision. Additional long-term products of this vision can be seen in the emergence of African Studies in various educational institutions in America, Africa, and other parts of the world; and in the implementation of the December 1988 agreement by the Reverend Jesse Jackson and coethnic leaders that people of African descent in America officially should be christened African Americans, among other reasons, to embellish their cultural anchor.

NOTES

1. See, for example, *The Autobiography of W.E.B. Du Bois: A Soliloquy on Viewing My Life from the Last Decade of Its First Century* (New York: International Publishers, 1968); and his *Dusk of Dawn* (New York: Harcourt, Brace, 1940); *Darkwater: Voices from within the Veil* (New York: Harcourt, Brace, 1969); and *In Battle for Peace: The Story of My 83d Birthday* (Millwood, N.Y.: Kraus-Thomson Organization, 1976). Edited collections and sources by other writers include Herbert Aptheker, ed., *Against Racism: Unpublished Essays, Papers, Addresses, 1887–1961* (Amherst, Mass.: University of Massachusetts Press, 1985); Aptheker, *W.E.B. Du Bois: The Education of Black People, Ten Critiques, 1906–1960* (New York: Monthly Review Press, 1963); John Henrik Clark et al., *Black Titan: W.E.B. Du Bois* (Boston: Beacon Press, 1970); and Shirley Graham Du Bois, *His Day Is Marching On: A Memoir of W.E.B. Du Bois* (Philadelphia: Lippincott, 1971).

2. See Du Bois, *Darkwater*, 11–20.

3. W.E.B. Du Bois, *The Souls of Black Folk* (orig. published, 1903; 1969, p. 54).

4. Du Bois, *Dusk of Dawn*, 114–15.

5. *The Autobiography of W.E.B. Du Bois*, 170–71; Herbert Aptheker, *Afro-American History: The Modern Era* (New York: The Citadel Press, 1973), 48.

6. Du Bois, *The Souls of Black Folk*, introduction by Donald B. Gibson, lx.

7. Julius, Lester, ed., *The Thought and Writings of W.E.B. Du Bois*, vol. 1 (New York: Random House, 1971), 181.

8. Ibid., vol. 2, 237.

9. Ibid., vol. 1, 181.

10. See, e.g., Blyden, *The African Problem and Methods for Its Solution* (Washington, D.C., 1890); J. E. Casely Hayford, *Ethiopia Unbound: Studies in Race Emancipation*, 2d ed. (London: Frank Cass Ltd., 1969).

11. Du Bois, *Color and Democracy: Colonies and Peace* (Millwood, N.Y.: Kraus-Thompson, 1975), 3–6, 19–26, 100–103.

12. Du Bois, *The World and Africa* (New York: Viking, 1947), 237–42.

13. Quoted in Mary Frances Berry and John W. Blassingame, *Long Memory: The Black Experience in America* (New York: Oxford University Press, 1982), 412.

14. Du Bois, "The Talented Tenth," in Lester, *The Thought*, vol. 1, 385–406.

15. Ibid., 385–86.

16. Joseph Harris, ed., *Global Dimensions of the African Diaspora* (Washington, D.C.: Howard University Press, 1982), 27–29.

17. Du Bois, *The Souls of Black Folk*, 5.

18. Du Bois, *The World and Africa*, 395.

19. Du Bois, *Dusk of Dawn*, 116–17.

20. *The Autobiography of W.E.B. Du Bois*, 13.

21. Quoted in Philip J. Foner, ed., *W.E.B. Du Bois Speaks: Speeches and Addresses 1890–1919*, 5–6.

22. Du Bois, *Color and Democracy: Colonies and Peace* (New York: Harcourt, Brace, 1945), 20–21.

23. Du Bois, *Dusk of Dawn*, 275.

24. Du Bois, "Pan Africa," *Crisis* 36 (December 1929): 423–24.

25. Du Bois, *The World and Africa*, 309.

26. Du Bois, "Letter to Nkrumah," in Lester, ed., *The Thought*, vol. 2, 649.

27. Ibid.

28. Ibid.

29. *The World and Africa*, 309.

30. John Hope Franklin, *From Slavery to Freedom: A History of Negro Americans*, 6th ed. (New York: Alfred A. Knopf, 1985), 438.

3

Langston Hughes and Africa

EDDIE OMOTAYO ASGILL

When Langston Hughes at age twenty-one sailed for Africa the first time, it was accidental: he desperately needed to escape all the sad memories of his youth at the time. His mother and stepfather were caught in a vise of poverty and the constant search for better jobs; his father, though he was himself Black, intensely resented Blacks for their social and economic circumstances and pursued wealth with a vengeance that left no room for the sentimental predispositions of his son. Langston, for his part, could no longer cope with the racist attitudes on the campus of Columbia University and in the United States in general; and he did not relish an academic program intended only to please his father. As an act of rebellion at the end of his disappointing first year at Columbia, Langston Hughes joined a ship that he later discovered went nowhere and jumped at another opportunity in one that went somewhere—of all places, Africa! The first thing he did once on board was to throw away all his books that had come to symbolize his despair.

Thus, the fascination with Africa at this stage was not informed by any rehearsed, intellectual purpose or political consciousness. Hughes was steeped in the fashionable image of Africa that was stereotypical, naive, and romantic. Thus, the Africa perceived by the writer was "wild and lovely,"[1] that is, savage and exotic, with its Black and beautiful people, its palm trees, its shining sun and deep rivers. But no sooner did he land on the soil of Africa than reality began to set in. Beyond the "bare, pointed breasts of women in the market places" and the "rippling muscles of men loading palm oil and cocoa beans and mahogany on ships which brought machinery and tools, canned goods, and Hollywood films" and "took away riches out of the earth, loaded by human hands," Hughes had begun a transformation that left a lasting and beneficial relationship with Africa.

Like most American intellectuals, he was not particularly enamored of the agenda of Marcus Garvey's return to the motherland; however, he found to his dismay that Africans already knew about Garvey and regarded him very highly. Hughes's initial efforts to identify with Africans were rebuffed: when he asserted he was not a White, he was informed he was not a Black man either. His initial political education began when a Kru seaman from Liberia explained the political dynamics of color in Africa: the Africans call all colored colonial officers "white men."

Indeed, any persons who in any conceivable way operated in collusion with imperial powers were categorized as White, regardless of the color of their skin. This enlightenment allowed Hughes to reflect more sympathetically on a tragic experience of a young man he met at an African port. This young man's European father had returned to Europe on retirement and abandoned him and his African mother to the ostracism of both the colonial and the local community.

Capturing this intriguing experience in a short story, "African Morning" (*Laughing to Keep Myself*, 15), Hughes intensifies the tragedy of the boy. His mother is now dead, and he is in the indifferent care of his father, still the president of the only bank in the area. The father now has a younger African woman as his mistress. As a twelve-year-old boy, Murai is the unwitting courier of his father's collusive transactions with all foreign companies shipping gold, which the Africans, under severe penalty, are not permitted to own. He is abused on both sides, by White sailors and other Europeans on the one hand and by the Africans who distrust his proximity to their foreign overlords. At the end of the story, we find him naked and alone in the pool waters of a lagoon on the outskirts of the town, bleeding from the attack of a bunch of resentful African boys and contemplating suicide. He has taken off his European clothes, a gesture that is symbolic of his desire to renounce his European parentage. Yet he cannot reclaim an African identity either.

This predicament brought about painful memories of the experience of Langston Hughes's relationship with his father. Thus, the initial encounter with Africa for Hughes was disturbing and ambivalent but at the same time profound and irrevocable. Africa brought to the center "the tragic mulatto" theme (Bullock, 78, and Davis, 195) in much of Hughes's writing and raised his consciousness of the social, political, and economic conditions of Blacks on both sides of the Atlantic. Besides the common ancestry African Americans and Africans share, Africa had become for Hughes a symbol of those aspirations that African Americans cherished in the country of their birth where Jim Crow laws, human indignity, and political deprivations abound. The idea of the Negritude movement was already present in the work of Hughes and others of the Harlem Renaissance. Léopold Senghor, Léon Damas, and Aimé Césaire (see Chapter 1 of this collection) took up the cry and developed more fully the concepts of the pioneers of the Renaissance.

Hughes was no doubt the dominant voice of Harlem Renaissance, and his writings of the 1920s and 1930s later became widely available in anthologies and individual books. He was also one of the first anthologizers of African writers, publishing *An African Treasury* in 1960. This anthology came about after Hughes was invited to be a judge in a writing contest for Africans sponsored by *Drum*, a South African magazine targeted at an African readership. His purpose in this anthology was to present a balanced picture of Africa to counter the negative images depicted in European writings. In 1963, Hughes anthologized another collection, *Poems from Black Africa, Ethiopia and Other Countries*, in an effort to stress the growing cultural unity of Black societies in Africa, the Caribbean, and Latin America.

Hughes's menial work experiences also helped to promote his interest in the welfare of African nations. His sea adventures as a mess boy, his work as a dishwasher in the night clubs of France, and the variety of low-skilled jobs he held in the United States made him more sensitive to the exploitation of Blacks everywhere and deeply appreciative of the life lived by the poor. Not surprisingly, he was first labeled a proletarian poet when *Fine Clothes to the Jew* came out in 1927. A number of his major works return to the endearing theme of the "blues"—the plight, the joys, and the pathos of the oppressed of the diaspora and of Africa. His anger is often directed against those who are the agents or beneficiaries of this oppression. *Not without Laughter* and the "Simple" series of short stories reiterate with humor, passion, and understanding of the life of folk characters in Jim Crow America.

This state of mind in Hughes coincided with the resurgence of Black consciousness during the period of the 1920s and 1930s now regarded as the Harlem Renaissance, when, as he put it, "the Negro was in vogue." Many Harlem Renaissance writers embraced Africa romantically, and a host of White patrons encouraged Black writers to pander to creative exercises that evoked an African milieu or celebrated a psyche or a mentality that explored motifs of the noble savage.

Socially ambitious and educated Blacks were scandalized by this primeval indulgence, the use of Black dialect and the perceived exposé of Black despair in all its stark reality in Hughes's work. His second book of poems was assailed: "Langston Hughes' Book of Poems Trash; Langston Hughes—The Sewer Dweller; The Poet Lowrate of Harlem" (*Big Sea*, 266). Charles Glicksberg titled his attack on this preoccupation with Africa in the *Antioch Review*, "The Negro Cult of the Primitive" (47), and went on to deride this embarrassing evocation of Africa and the poor intellectual and creative quality of the poetic discourse. But Hughes was aware of this misguided fascination of White America for the exotic and the Negro whose affinity to the African is taken as an axiom. For example, "Slave on the Block" and "Rejuvenation through Joy" (*Ways of White Folks*, 19–31, 66–95) are brilliant satires on the White American belief that Negroes were the closest link to the primitive, uncorrupted state of innocence that Africans still enjoy. This belief was held by the woman patron who put Hughes on an allowance so he could complete his first novel, *Not without Laughter*, and to write in the same vein thereafter, believing as she did, that there was mystery and mysticism and spontaneous harmony in Black writers' souls, but that many of them had let the White world pollute and contaminate that mystery and turn it into something cheap, ugly, commercial and, as she said, "white" (*Big Sea*, 316).

Disconcerted, Hughes disavowed "the rhythms of the primitive"; he declared his love for Africa "but [he] was not Africa" (*Big Sea*, 325). In Hughes's ironic presentation, "Slave on the Block" (*The Ways of White Folks*), the Carraways, collectors of Negro art and music, see no use in helping "a race that was already charming and naive and lovely for words" (19). They discover Luther, who is "so utterly Negro" (22) that Mrs. Carraway decides to paint a picture of him standing on a block. To her, this scene should recapture the image of the slave on his arrival in the United States and just about to be auctioned off to a prospective buyer. Gushing over their Negro servant, who by now is virtually a collector's item for them, the Carraways are blithely insensitive to his human needs. They even take slight offense that Luther allowed himself a liaison with their maid. The husband's more expedient and racist mother takes matters in hand to protest the familiarity they have allowed a servant and insists they fire him immediately—much to Luther's own relief. In "Rejuvenation Through Joy" (*The Ways of White Folks*), Hughes similarly lampoons a coterie of rich, vacuous, bored White women who are duped by two rogues who promise them rejuvenated joy on the example of Negroes, "the happiest people on earth" (70).

Indeed, much of Africa, as Pat Ryan phrases it, was "exotically synthesized, but seldom actualized" (235). But, inasmuch as many writers produced works whose merits resided solely in their evocation of things African to gratify an unbridled and unintelligent fascination with Africa—and quite a few of Hughes's poems did not quite rise above this inanity—it would be correct to state that Hughes's espousal of Africa was more convincing than that of others; it was symbolic, functional, and integrated to the purposes of Hughes's poetic statement.

Of all the Black writers during the period of the Harlem Renaissance, only Hughes had actually visited Africa. He was fully aware that his connections were not as familiar as he would have wished, but his references to Africa remain genuine efforts and sincere expressions of a reality he experienced. Some of his poems, such as "Sun Song" and "Natcha" (*Selected Poems*, 5; 72), bear only oblique, evocative references to Africa, or they reinforce recurring symbols that Hughes associates with Africa. The sun, the drum, the dance, the stormy weather or dark night—all positive images of a mysterious, virile, and imposing continent on the threshold of a great reawakening.

In "Afro-American Fragment," significantly the first poem of his choice of "selected poems" first published in 1959 (*Selected Poems*, 3), we recognize the plaintive cry of one longing for an identity that can only be vaguely or intuitively realized; yet the poem is redolent of hope that a closer and more meaningful union awaits a persistent effort to reestablish the old residual ties that are still submerged just below the surface. This deep, desperate notion of something essential but not clearly understood is found in several other Hughesean poems as well. Africa is so far away that the poet has no memories of it except those depicted in history books, which, one is fully aware, are largely a pack of lies. He also has memories of strange songs subdued and lost in time. Yet all hope is not lost; for, Hughes hears another, particular song through the inexplicable, but inextricable, matrix of racial bond. It is this relentless sound, pounding at his ears and his whole being, that makes possible a future understanding and oneness with Africa. The African American, according to Hughes, refused human space in America, has no choice but to fight for it through an establishment of his African heritage and humanity. The bitter yearnings for Africa will continue as long as the dilemma of rejection and refusal of place in America continues.

"The Negro Speaks of Rivers" (*Selected Poems*, 4) was composed even before Hughes dreamed of ever visiting Africa, but it remains one of his most endearing poems, attesting to pride in his African ancestry. "Rivers" is a symbol of great civilizations of the past, and the persona in the poem is the African who has been a part of the earliest civilization and continues, in spite of a checkered history, to be centrally involved in other notable civilizations of the world—along the Euphrates, the Nile, the Congo, and the Mississippi. Hughes draws an analogy between the river flowing relentlessly and the Black's blood, as well as between the river's depth and the depth of the Black soul. He also deftly compares the long history of those ancient and ever present rivers with African civilization, indicating that its superior qualities have been denied while constantly being borrowed from by those very people condemning African "savagery." Hughes reminds us that it is Blacks who built the Egyptian pyramids; today, the Afrocentric ideology based on this assertion has become widespread.

In another poem, "Africa," Hughes exults in the strident nationalistic struggles of African nations and at the prospects of their becoming independent of colonial rule. The images of thunder and lightning reinforce the idea of triumph, power, and strength of a youthful nation eager to meet the challenges of independence. Africa is described as a sleeping giant that is now awake; she is "young," "new," ready to deal with the realities of the so-called modern world.

> Your every step reveals
> The new stride
> In your thighs.
> (*Selected Poems*, 284)

The sexual metaphor of "In your thighs" in the final stanza appropriately suggests the status of a continent at birth (or rebirth), eager and ready to seize control of its own destiny.

Nevertheless, Hughes was more concerned with the plight of his fellow African Americans under the yoke of racial injustices; and his persistence in writing poems expressing this view lost him the patronage of his benefactor, who clearly saw him as a dangerous, ungrateful rabble rouser. Examples of such poems include "Advertisement for the Waldorf-Astoria," which betrays the blatantine quality of Blacks living in Harlem and the lavish lifestyles of many Whites even at the height of the Great Depression; "Park Avenue"; "Harlem"; "A Dream Deferred"; and a host of others published in *Panther and the Lash* which contain the veiled threat that the cozy world of Whites will soon be invaded by poor, inconsiderate Blacks (whom Gwendolyn Brooks more eloquently described in her fascinating poem, "Riot").

As Faith Berry has argued, Langston Hughes was not just a folk poet of Negro life, a poet of the blues and jazz; a major corpus of his work is militant in nature, especially his later poems that related to Africa. Section 5 of *Panther and the Lash* is titled "African Question Mark." In this series of poems, Hughes expressed his revolutionary views on the iniquitous involvement of European nations in the affairs of Africa. "Oppression" sympathizes with the conditions of Blacks under apartheid rule in South Africa. In "Angola Question Mark" (64), Hughes preaches the necessity of armed struggle for freedom in one's own land, even though the consequences may be woeful. "Lumumba's Grave" comments on the unmarked grave of the assassinated first President of the Congo (now Zaire) and asserts that because he died in defense of freedom and truth, his grave is marked for posterity in our hearts. "Final Call" (20) is also a dedication to Lumumba written when rumors first came of his death. Hughes hopes that his memory will help keep alive the fight for freedom; for, in the poet's opinion, Lumumba symbolizes "Freedom now." He calls for the piper to get rid of the rats in our midst. In "Color" (67) Hughes urges independent nations to wear their national colors with pride, not like a shroud, even though the future might seem grim.

In Berry's *Langston Hughes: Before and Beyond Harlem*, "Negro" (29) is a militant statement that catalogs the abuses the African has suffered in history while it romantically records some of his achievements in spite of this oppression. The African built the pyramids. He has sung his songs of sorrow all over the world, particularly in America, where his music has become essential to the whole civilization. He has been a victim of slavery and colonialism exemplified by the maimings carried out by the Belgian masters in the Congo and the lynchings in Texas. All those items constitute a history that can never be forgotten, most importantly because such practices have not stopped; they have only been "modernized." Hughes's poem very subtly affirms that history is not only the past but the present: the simple word, *now*, calls one's attention to the fact. When Hughes cries out his negroness, his blackness, black as the night, black like his Africa, he is combining a complex set of emotions that culminate in the resilience and defiance and determination to survive that have made for the African continuum in the diaspora.

Another poem with a similar historical context is "Lament for Dark People" (Berry, *Before and Beyond Harlem*) in which Hughes repines the loss that Africa has had to accommodate as a result of that fateful contact with Europeans, who proffered a touted superior civilization that has proved a hoax. Hughes sees an affinity between Black and Native American due to their shared history of victimization at the hands of the White man, who did everything in his power to debase and destroy African American and Native American civilizations, to cage both "in the circus of [white] civilization" (48), to drive the latter away from the land while enslaving the former and using him to exploit the stolen land.

In "Broadcast on Ethiopia" (*Good Morning Revolution*), Hughes's monitoring of political events in Africa focuses on the gratuitous attack of Ethiopia by Italy in a desperate bid to acquire a colony in Africa. Again, the civilization that Europe pretends to introduce through colonization is an illusion for those who dare to place their faith in such promises.

In the foreword to Faith Berry's edition of *Good Morning Revolution*, Saunders Redding reveals that Langston Hughes was subjected to the harassments of McCarthyism because he had spent some time in the Soviet Union and produced some works in praise of communism. This witch-hunt was devastating for one of the most celebrated Black poets of this time; many of his speaking engagements were unceremoniously canceled, and some of his books were removed from libraries and school texts. Consequently, Hughes did not allow many of his revolutionary writings, which had been published in obscure magazines, to be anthologized in any of his popular collections.

In 1962, therefore, when he participated in an "All-African Writers Conference" in Kampala, Uganda, he shocked his African audience by not reading any revolutionary pieces. They had access to these works, especially those related to African nationalism, and had expected to hear them. When confronted on this matter, Hughes claimed that the occasion was inappropriate for those poems! Many of these revolutionary poems have been collected by Faith Berry in *Good Morning Revolution*. In this collection, which decries the exploitation of Blacks in the "Third World" (Africa and the Caribbean) and in the United States, the tone adopted by Hughes is quite often caustic, angry, and almost hysterical.

"The Same" (9) jabs at the atrocities committed by Europeans against Africans, all for the sake of accumulating inordinate wealth that did not belong to them. The poem concludes that the time has come for the oppressed to reclaim their destiny. In Sierra Leone, in Albama, in South Africa, in Haiti, in Central America, in Morocco, in Harlem, the common denominator is oppression and exploitation. Millions and billions of dollars, pounds, francs, pesetas, and lire are made from the blood and sweat of the hapless proletariat, working in the diamond mines; picking cotton, coffee and bananas; slaving at the docks; buying finished goods at exhorbitant prices; making life an earthly paradise for the master, while they are living in hell. Most of those victims are "Black: Exploited, beaten, and robbed, shot and killed." Hughes then calls for "the red armies of the International proletariat" made up of all colors and nationalities, to rise and seize power. Here the poet reminds us of the works of other Black revolutionaries, such as Frantz Fanon and Jacques Roumain.

"English" (10) is very reminiscent of Hughes's experiences on his first African trip. (Earlier, in *The Big Sea*, he condemns the whole process of exploitation through which European colonialism and imperialism have thrived in Africa. The White man completely dominates, taking everything away to Europe and America. The Africans, cowed and Christianized, "bow down before the Lord, but they bow much lower before the traders, who carry whips and guns and are protected by white laws, made in Europe for the black colonies" [102].) In "English," Hughes, with great irony, juxtaposes the contrast between the Englishman's meticulous attentions to his grooming, a semblance of his refined culturation, and the unconscionable greed that deprives other people of all their produce. Using the pun of the English "combing" their hair for dinner and combing the access routes to the resources of others, together with the repetition of "load," Hughes exquisitely captures the image of the insatiable appetite and thoroughness that mark the exploitation of the unsuspecting colonized nations. The latter are mesmerized by the invader's "civilized" manners, totally unaware that he is actually a savage ready to eliminate them, to "buy, sell, or rob" in order to attain his great objectives.

This acrimonious vein characterizes the poems pertaining to Africa in *Good Morning Revolution* and bespeaks the depth of Hughes's passionate sympathy with the welfare of Africa. While "Johannesburg Mines" (10) laments the exploitation of African labor, "Merry Christmas" (26) calls attention to the incongruity of a Christian Europe that professes to convert others to Christianity yet ends up with the gross mistreatment of subjected nations.

"Cubes" (11) examines the plight of the Senegalese student who is invited to visit France for the amusement of the French government. The hospitality he receives is tainted, and he returns to his motherland taking with him diseases he picked up in France (and by extension, perverted ideas to compound the social and political climate of his country). The title is an appropriate symbol of the fragmented style of Picasso's paintings; the encounter with French culture augurs a fragmentation of the African's home community. According to the poet, all that France has to offer the African is a group of "three sick, old prostitutes [named] Liberty, Equality, Fraternity," and the vaunted "Civilization" that does nothing more than corrupt and alienate Africans, spreading unnamable diseases among the youths. Hughes's acerbic irony is brought into excellent use in the imagery, mental configurations, and play on words. The basic concept is that of the supposed superiority and supremacy of White (Europe) over Black (Africa). Ever laughing to keep from crying, Hughes turns round the relationship as he implies that the superior society is the very one passing down diseases, corruption, and beastliness to the inferior one. Thus, light comes to represent darkness, and darkness, light. Paris, reputedly the center of civilization, is described as the city of Picasso's cubes, and Hughes emphasizes the element of unwholesomeness, fragmentation, and "DISEASE."

As we continue to witness and marvel at the civilized debate on the origin of AIDS and other devastating diseases, we cannot help recalling Langston Hughes's poetry: Africa, victim of all sorts of opprobrium; Africa, dumping ground for all forms of despicable products of Western genius, not excluding formidable diseases that the master in his wisdom has created but now finds impossible to control.

CONCLUSION

The espousal of Africa in the works of Langston Hughes goes beyond the fashionable statements that have marked many African-American artists and others who seek to connect with the motherland. Hughes met the African *in Africa*, shared his human aspirations, and observed the uniqueness and validity of his way of life. Africa opened his eyes to the inextricable link between the fates of the African American and the African as common victims of discrimination and economic exploitation in a Western-dominated world.

His contemporaries, such as Jean Toomer and Wallace Thurman, full of optimism, were ecstatic about White American patronage of Black artistic expressions and the dreamy setting of northern metropoles such as Harlem. Many, therefore, were miffed by Hughes's preoccupation with Africa and his chipping away at the blatant inequalities and the reckless uses of privilege at the expense of a Black underclass. Eventually, Hughes paid a heavy price for his expressions of solidarity with exploited Africa and with the Communist government of the Soviet Union. And though he tried to defuse some of the anger of the politically correct in the fifties by renouncing some of his earlier poems on religion and would not include his radical verses in anthologies or at poetry reading sessions, he was for a long time a sole, strong voice among Black leaders in the United States who stood up for Africa against the despotism of a colonial hegemony.

NOTE

1. This and succeeding quotations in this and the following paragraph are from *Big Sea*, 103.

BIBLIOGRAPHY

Berry, Faith. *Langston Hughes: Before and Beyond Harlem.* Westport, Conn.: L. Hill, 1983.
Bullock, Penelope. "The Mulatto in American Fiction." *Phylon* 6 (1945): 78–82.
Davis, Arthur P. "The Tragic Mulatto Theme in Six Works of Langston Hughes." *Phylon* 16 (1955): 195–204.
Glicksberg, Charles. "The Negro Cult of the Primitive." *Antioch Review* 4, no. 1 (1944): 47–55.
Hughes, Langston. *An African Treasury.* New York: Crown, 1960.
———. *The Best of Simple.* New York: Hill and Wang, 1961.
———. *The Big Sea.* New York: Thunder Mouth, 1986.
———. *Fine Clothes to the Jew.* New York: Knopf, 1927.
———. *Good Morning Revolution.* Ed. Faith Berry. New York: Hill and Wang, 1973.

————. *Laughing to Keep Myself from Crying*. New York: Aeonian, 1976.

————. *Not without Laughter*. London: Collier, 1969.

————. *Panther and the Lash*. New York: Knopf, 1967.

————. *Poems from Black Africa, Ethiopia and Other Countries*. Bloomington: University of Indiana Press, 1963.

————. *Selected Poems*. New York: Vintage, 1974.

————. *The Ways of White Folks*. New York: Vintage, 1990.

Ryan, Pat. "African Continuities/Discontinuities in Black Writing." *Afro-American Studies* 3 (1975): 235–44.

4

Richard Wright: A Dubious Legacy

CHIMALUM NWANKWO

A reflection on Richard Wright must perforce begin where the writer began his life—with escape. Before that beginning I must preempt hasty repartees by insisting immediately that escaping to philosophical safety is not peculiar to Wright alone or to the African American who thinks like Wright, but also to continental Africans; this is something that many African writers must learn to deal with. The cliché about the grass being greener on the other side applies strongly to many who become very vocal about the failings of the Black world only after successfully escaping from the perils of life in that Black world, especially in cases where poverty was the chief peril. In the case of Richard Wright, who also knew poverty, added to the very grave peril of American racism, his escape involved running from the most salient aspects of Black culture, from its humanness and expansive fellowship with its wealth of an optimistic and dynamic eschatology to the very arid extreme of Western philosophy—that alien wilderness of existentialism, despair, and spiritual loneliness.

Richard Wright's courage and justifiable anger have been highly praised because "he successfully transformed rage into art."[1] His literary reputation is by no means lean. He is still admired for his ability to rise from the murk of Deep South American racism to become one of the most outstanding names in American literature. The great question that has not been clearly and finally settled remains: if his name is now unassailable, what of his mind? Yes, the mind, that quality which should radiate and perpetuate that penumbra of authority, the stimulus for compassionate followership or even radical activity. Personally, for instance, I feel terrified by his Gothic frescoes of macabre violence in works like *Native Son*, but I am not moved to contemplate any other kind of action. I would sooner be moved to more positive reflection by Langston Hughes, Ralph Ellison, James Baldwin, Claude McKay, and some of Wright's other, "lesser" contemporaries. Wright's concerns cannot in any way be considered to enjoy any kind of distinction over the concerns of these other writers.

Deep down, somewhere in the lungs of Wright's art, there is a shortness of air, the root of his peripatetic predilection, of his chronic inability to hold firm to any ideology or any philosophically lasting friendships. Many Wright readers consider him a revolutionary. I hope those readers understand the implication in that position, because a mind constantly on the move offers no pegs for followers, no stable anchor of ideas. Beacons for lost seamen are mounted on lighthouses, not on the shoulders of a formless wind.

No writer in the history of any culture is remembered and studied because of his or her temper. Tempers appear in the footnotes after the works. For this reason alone, the legacy of Richard Wright, and any writers who follow him, is likely to grow more dubious with time. The latest historical signpost is the title of a book on him by his own friend, Margaret Walker, *Richard Wright: A Daemonic Genius*. Walker equivocates about the intention of that title, probably to palliate the sting in the inescapable implication of the demonic as a force encompassing the negative and destructive.

Human society has never preserved the path of demons, whether in the imaginary realm of art or in the real world. To be a genius, needless to say, is very desirable. To be a demonic genius is another story. The genius creates with overwhelming spiritual power, but the demonic vitiates with malevolent distraction. Such, unfortunately, is the dual nature of Wright's art. As a critic of the failings of American society (which was where he began), as a Marxist writer and critic of American capitalism (which was where he ran to next), as an existentialist proudly renouncing all loyalties human and spiritual (which was where he ended), he had his way like a hurricane. And, like a hurricane, his anger blew everything down—those he was fighting for and those he fought against. Wright was a victim of the tragedy of the Black experience, but his criticism of the failings of Blacks failed woefully to take real stock of the agony of slavery, the trauma of colonialism, the marginalization and dependency of the Black world on the hegemonic forces of Western technology and spiritual scarification and psychological disorientation. In his hindsight criticisms of his family, of Black America and of Africa, he failed to see the limits of Communist atheism and Western rationalism, in the fallacy of universalism in a world in which various cultures at different points in time in history cannibalized each other ungratuitously. So he raved at the Black world and acted as if there were no racial secrets. Finally to turn away from that world and pretend to be its oracular defender when convenient must have been a strange role.

Vanishing into the White world is, of course, the logical climax of a race Wright began in childhood, from Natchez, Mississippi, where he was born in 1908, to Paris, where he died in 1960. The corollary of that flight is expressed very clearly in the conduct of virtually all the major characters in his works. He has presented to his readers not the rationalized revolutionary violence of the slave revolts from Nat Turner to Malcolm X, nor the rationalized and firm pacificism from Frederick Douglass to Martin Luther King, Jr. His banner was one of heroes on the run. And, to run is to counter-produce by irrational violence or irrational silence, whether such is verbal or physical. To demonstrate that this matter rises far above aesthetics, we must make a crucial link between the writer Richard Wright, as the man who ran like his characters, and a most significant and unequivocal statement: his book called *Black Power*. It is easier to come to a clearer understanding of Wright's other works in relation to his attitude to the Black World through *Black Power*.

With the flexibility and stylistic freedom offered by what must be seen as docu-fiction, Wright's descriptive genius is there at its best—so much so that, as recently as 1978, Ellen Wright and Wright's fervid devotee Michel Fabre are deceived into concurring that a book so treacherous and shameless "appears to have been written with a humor and an understanding not well appreciated at the time"![2] Happily there are other voices, like Robert Felgar's, which unmask many things. Felgar emphasizes that "the bourgeois values he [Wright] eschews in *Black Boy* are everywhere present in *Black Power*." So also are Wright's other "hasty generalizations,"[3] and penchant for substituting ready-made theories for empiricism.[4] The truth in Felgar's insights becomes quite frightening when, with *Native Son* in mind, he analogically decides that, in *Black Power*, "[t]he 350-year history of the black man in America is the history of black Africa for the last 2,000 years. Bigger Thomas has reappeared as the whole of Africa; the European-American West represents the Daltons and the Buckleys; the opportunistic communists play themselves; and the essential relationship among those protagonists in both scenarios is identical."[5]

In the relationship between the transposable character of such nightmarish analogs and the real world lies the danger of Wright's art, especially to young Black readers. *Black Power* is, therefore, a very useful fulcrum for lifting in order to view a lot of the dead weight in Wright's work, especially that personal dross that gets so neatly concealed in the phony interstices of Marxism and the fitful recourse to Black nationalism which Black writers like him occasionally retreat into to assuage the anguish in the tragedy of race.

Why then did Wright write a book like *Black Power*? For the same reasons that he wrote *Black Boy*, *Native Son*, *The Long Dream*, and others: The circumstances are the same. A brilliant mind has a herculean problem to solve. Anger and impatience pressure him into a half-baked solution, which he insists is the full and final solution.

David Bakish kindly informs us that, like all tourists, especially the Africabound, "in preparation for this trip, Wright did read about the country, its past, and projected future."[6] *Black Power*, this book about Ghana, is not very vocal about the rights of the people to self-determine the complex of their historical and cultural choices. If it did, the whole thing would obviously have distorted the answers to Richard Wright's ultimate question: "What is Africa to me?"[7] If it was positively vocal, it would also not legitimize the basis of Wright's consistent dismissal of the values and mores of his own Black American roots. It is safe to be consistent because investing superiority or inferiority to either the continental African Black or the Black American will neutralize one wing of his earlier thesis, especially in *Native Son*.

Remember the well-known scene in which Bigger Thomas is watching films: "He looked and saw *Trader Horn* unfold and saw pictures of naked black men and women whirling in wild dances and heard drums beating and then gradually the African scene changed."[8] *Native Son* was written nearly fifteen years before *Black Power*, yet the writer's imaging and choice of images are the same. In order to understand the Black man, in Wright's modus operandi, one picks the lowest from the ranks: Only cheerless idiots in cheerless environments can make tragedy. So when Bigger's mind moves on, it picks "white men and women dressed in black and white clothes laughing, talking, drinking and dancing."[9]

When, late in his career, Wright undertakes a major excursion into the psychology of White behavior in *Savage Holiday* (1965), he picks on a hardworking insurance man, Erskine Fowler, who is vacationing after a forced retirement. He does not go, like John Steinbeck, into the jails and poor rural lands of the White world. For Wright, especially in *Black Power*, his African tour guide, his selective Marxism finds grist in salesmen, electricians, cooks, and so forth. (Non-African readers may not understand those terms and their socioeconomic implications.) But for Wright, who read about Africa before going to Ghana, he was certain that the opinions of these men were as valid as any researcher's; hence, the manner he gloated after his record of "discoveries" such as in this encounter with a salesman:

"Haven't you tried to find out where you came from, Sir?"

"Well," I said softly, "you know, you fellows who sold us and the white men who bought us didn't keep any records."

Silence stood between us. *We avoided each other's eyes.*[10] (emphasis mine)

This little exchange is important for one or two reasons. First, the salesman's question was innocuous. If he had been trained in the mask-wearing of Western civility, it is not likely that he would have raised that question. Wright, who obviously read offense into the man's "uncivil behaviour," is unnecessarily quick to truculence. Secondly, the act of avoiding eyes is neither an expression of guilt, cowardice, or weakness, or whatever meanings Western psychology reads into it. Africans mostly show respect in that manner. Thirdly, this kind of report reveals a latent problem in African and African-American relationships, a problem which Wright's claims to understanding Black problems ought to have imposed some delicacy in handling. Finally, the ecclecticism of his readings and observations ought to have enabled him to wonder whether descendants of European slaves and indentured servants in America greet their European cousins as Wright greeted this salesman. If he ever contemplated that intelligent victims of similar historical experiences would serve each other better, he would have edited that encounter and similar useless internecine encounters out of his records. After all the preaching about the brotherhood of White and Black in

America, which he once said was predicated on commonalities, Wright's conduct is part of the trouble in the Black world; but he does not see it: he is only capable of seeing it in others.

Below is another exemplary encounter much later in the book, and I must repeat that there is serious doubt whether Wright knew what words like "electrician" mean in Africa:

"Now, look—you are an electrician. Why don't you invent that stuff?"

His mouth dropped open and he stared at me, and he tossed back his head and laughed.[11]

Whether talking to a porter or to Ghana's president Kwame Nkrumah, whose friendship he often abused, Wright always found everyone a fool. His descriptions and choice of vocabulary attest to that. Such conduct must shock and perplex those who have read Wright's life and death struggle with racism and brutal oppression. One would have expected humility and sympathetic understanding of the differences in people. Can you imagine any foreigner stopping by a roadside in America to ask a construction worker: "Now, look—you are a construction worker. Why don't you invent a tractor?" The Ghanaian electrician merely "tossed back his head and laughed." I leave it to the reader, especially the American reader, to imagine the response of such a worker in America.

Perhaps it is one of the demands of Wright's special Marxist methodology that answers to the questions of Ghana's problems should to be sought always from salesmen, electricians, cooks, taxi drivers, and sometimes children. Perhaps there are other reasons why crucial problems in history, especially slavery, are solved in *Black Power* by such sources. What is even more remarkable is Wright's consistent triumphant air. After another such encounter with a cook, Wright beams:

The illiterate cook had given me, by implication, answers to many questions. It was now obvious why Africans had sold many millions of their black brothers into slavery. To be a slave was proof that one had done something bad, that one was being punished, that one was guilty, one was a slave; if one was not guilty one would not be in the position of a slave.[12]

It is to such many historical and social analyses that Felgar responds that "the generalizations, he makes about the 'African' are testy and unacceptable."[13] Who knows, Wright may have also been at the very brink of discovering why General Cromwell ordered the so-called plantation of Ulster and the carrying off of the Irish to slavery. Nonetheless, there are those whose eyes read differently, for Addison Gayle refers to *Black Power* as "the product of a sophisticated Westerner."[14]

The sophistication of *Black Power* does not stop with ordinary Ghanaians. It extends to poor village women and beggars. Even mourners are ridiculed. The "elongated breasts" of women are "flopping loosely and grotesquely in the sun. . . . There are women with breasts so long that they do not bother to give the baby the teat in front of them, but simply toss it over the shoulder to the child on their back."[15] The genius of the writer takes wings with beggars:

So deformed were some that it was painful to look at them. Monstrously swollen legs, running sores, limbs broken so that jagged ends of the healed bones jutted out like blackened sticks, blind men whose empty eye sockets yawned wetly, palsied palms extended and waiting, a mammoth wen suspended from a skinny neck gleaming blackly in the hot sun. . . . *I wondered* if they were professional beggars, if they had deliberately deformed themselves to make these heart-wracking appeals? *If they had, they had surely over done it in terms of Western sensibilities for I was moved not to compassion but to revulsion.*[16] (emphasis mine)

So much for Wright's Western sophistication and its humanism. If Wright was submitting this report to the United Nations, what is the use of his wonderings and speculations about those images? And what, other than to express superiority and disdain, is the use of his Western sensibilities in this situation? This attitude is very strange from a man who was sent running all his lifetime by the West. And only a strange intelligence would leave one blind to such glaring contradictions and pathetic soulless expression of superiority. An insightful critic, Robert Bone, observes: "There is in Wright's late manner a stilted quality, a pompousness, a lack of observation, an absence of the smells and savors and juices of existence. The style becomes gradiose, abstract. It is Wright's surrender to abstraction that betrays his spiritual sickness."[17]

In a book copious with racial insults at his own race perhaps it is this spiritual sickness that Ellen Wright and Michel Fabre find humorous. I find the whole book an obscene travelogue. A funeral is "more like the advertisement to a circus,"[18] naked children are "gripped with disease" (154), classrooms are "evil-looking" (155), Kumasi market is "a vast masterpiece of disorder" (294), the Atlantic is "misty and gray" (254), the laughter of the people is a "howl" (247), their religiosity fetish-worship. The people are "trained to a cryptic servility" (278). More annoying are the writer's occasional efforts at redefinitions of objects: simple things like the chewing stick he calls "the African toothpick" (295). Perhaps in moments of blind and inexplicable anger the language of redefinition becomes more vicious diatribe.

I am constantly amazed at the rapidity with which Wright leaps from empty flourish to the armchair philosopher's conclusion. Note that the writer could speak none of the languages of his hosts; that is a matter which an omniscient intellect can deal with: hence, the encyclopedic and many-sided cynical picture we have of the "preposterous chiefs," their "godlike positions," and "thirst for blood and alcohol and women. . . . Their justice is barbaric, their interpretations of life are contrary to commonsense" (307).

The above confessional with the hasty repudiation somewhat summarizes Wright's problem with Africa. There is some kind of kinship, but Wright would not be caught napping with *natives*. Any kind of common sense that does not fit the straitjackets of Wright's superior Western model is totally askew. Thus, the Gold Coast (now Ghana) intellectuals, with the exception of Nkrumah, are pitied for being locked out "from the currents of modern thought" (135). Wright's final verdict is that he would never feel an identification with Africans on a racial basis.

Wright, crusader for a new world of justice and harmony, made this discovery about Africans (all his ideas are discoveries!) less than ten years after *Black Boy* started speaking to the world about the evils of White racism. It need be emphasized that the author's claim as champion of Black American liberty remains as gratuitous as his reasons for hating Africa. One must come to that unhappy conclusion based on the fact that, among other things, *12 Million Black Voices* (1941) could not have been written by the same man who wrote *Black Power*. *Voices* is too sedate. If it was written by the same writer, it was probably a mercenary and selfish enterprise. That would be the only way to explain the gulf between all those dreadful and shameful disavowals of Africa and the affinity and spiritual sobriety of the earlier book especially evident in the following: "We had our own literature, our own systems of law, religion, medicine, science and education. . . . in short, centuries before the Romans ruled, we lived as men."[19] One thing is noteworthy: Wright seems to need to impress the White man, to prove something to him, to make the White man listen!

Black Power was published in 1954, seventeen years after *Black Boy*. After the cathartic cleansing from the boy's experience at the hands of the racist society, one expects to see the boy begin to grow into manhood. Sadly, this does not happen. Disappointing selfishness has been the result; for, what critics fancifully call self-hatred in Wright is a mere projection of selfishness.

Even though Wright rejects affinity with Africa and Africans, the dominant family consciousness in *Black Boy* is that of the African extended family: the configuration of relatives extending from Wright's grandmother, with whom he lived at one time, to his distant uncles and aunts, who appear every now and then in the autobiography to deal with one family crisis or the other. Let us look at Wright in a few crucial incidents in the relationship with key family members.

In the early pages of *Black Boy*, a cat comes in meowing annoyingly, and Richard's sleepy father angrily directs the kids to send it away: " 'Kill that damn thing!' my father exploded. 'Do anything, but get it away from here!' "[20] Despite Richard's younger brother's explanation, Richard interprets his father's instructions literally and kills the cat. Upon escaping punishment after a hot debate involving his mother, the author declares his happiness: "I have made him [his father] know that I felt he was cruel and I had done it without his punishing me" (19). No one knows whether a four-year-old is capable of that kind of reflection. My concern here is with Wright's delight in hurting or demonstrating triumphantly the capability to hurt his father.

Thanks to certain female African-American writers, it is needless to waste print on the character of Wright's father. We cannot blame the author for the lecherous and irresponsible image of his father because that is now an immortal stereotype. What we can do is to draw further attention to irreverent descriptions. Some are Falstaffian: "He was quite fat and his bloated stomach always lapped over his belt" (17). All this comes before his confessed reasons for hating the old man. It is from other sources that one reads of the frustrations of the father, Nathaniel Wright, in that age of the boll weevil disaster and unemployment in Mississippi. As for Wright, psychosociologist, there is more space for indicting than for extenuating circumstances.

Twenty-five years later, *Black Boy* reintroduces the same old man on the plantation, in a tone of victorious clangor conferred by growing confidence and independence. He is astonished at how his father's memories were fastened to a raw past and how his actions and emotions were tightly linked to the animalistic impulse of his shriveling body. Wright concludes by mentioning his spirit of forgiveness and pity for his father. As an African, I initially feared that it might be a cultural risk to comment on Wright's attitude to his father, until I read Michel Fabre's comment on the above passages: "What a proud, God-like stance on the part of Wright!"[21]

Wright's attitude to his grandmother was no less scornful than that to everyone else. "Now no one can be as puritanical as a Southern grandmother, particularly at that time in history,"[22] rings the understanding voice of John A. Williams in *The Most Native of Sons*. On the contrary, Wright's impression is that of a mean, ascetic and almost wicked witch. His insensitivity and lack of observation, which, according to Robert Bone, were developed later in his life, were probably congenital and habitual traits. For example, in the detailed description of the scene in which his grandmother gives him a bath, Wright is the poor, innocent child mistreated and abused by the uncaring woman. Here is one more situation where he is right and everyone else, wrong.

The most regrettable charge made by Wright against Blacks in general is the much quoted passage where he indelicately and fatuously relates how he used to reflect over "the strange absence of real kindness in Negroes, how unstable was our tenderness, how lacking in genuine passion we were, how void of great hope, how timid our joy, how bare our traditions" (45). These are very strange words from the author of *Black Boy*, which details the very circumstances that made normal life for Blacks well nigh impossible. Weighed against the situation in which Wright presents the Black world beleaguered by the terrorism of White supremacy, his charge makes no sense. Rather, it further comments on his selfishness and deep spiritual crisis, especially when his glib declarations are followed by contradictions, such as the extended family response of community and solidarity to his mother's ill health (97).

If Wright could look at the African American with such vengeful bitterness, why should anyone expect him to be more sympathetic towards nebulous cousins in Black Africa, whom he disdainfully addresses as "you fellows who sold us"?

Commenting on Wright's attitude toward Africa in *Black Power*, Kwame Anthony Appiah has argued about Wright's need "to punish Africa for failing him" and about his response to Africa "with the fury of the lover spurned."[23] Appiah's reading notwithstanding, the writer's attitude must be placed in the context of his constant personal crisis. To see Wright as punishing Africa alone is to shrink the canvas of the action of his one-man global police force. To see him as punishing or endeavoring to punish the world for the misfortune of all human quirks and the additional misfortune of his having been born Black appears to me to be a most fitting context for looking at Wright's works and life. There is no better way to explain the following, for example.

His life, as detailed in *Black Boy*, contains no clear references of closeness to any member of his family, immediate or extended. His services to his mother read like the payment of material debts and nothing else. His activities up North, whether in the service of the Federal Writers Project or the Communist party, appear to be escapist ventures discarded as soon as those associations outlived their usefulness. His later sojourn in Paris and his contact with the Africans associated with *Présence Africaine* were irritations he quickly eliminated. The cultivation of the friendship of men such as George Padmore, one of the then Gold Coast's Pan-Africanists, and Kwame Nkrumah, independent Ghana's first President, was probably ego-boosting more than anything really genuine.

The books about Spain and the Ban-dung conference, as well as the journalistic and populist treatises like *Twelve Million Black Voices* (1941) and *American Hunger* (1944), are no less revealing. *Pagan Spain* (1957) is full of words from a secure alien observatory, the beatitudes of an angelic plenipotentiary whose role is sheltered from the dirt of reality. In the case of Africa in *Black Power*, it appears that he probably felt he had nothing to lose. After all, when he wrote the text, he had come to a point in his life when he could declare to a student in Paris: "You see the difference between the two of us is that I am completely free, I have no roots whereas you are bound to European history and the tyranny of place."[24] *Black Power* is the culmination of a pattern of responses to the problem of being Black, which finds early expression in *Uncle Tom's Children* (1936). The major question arising from those stories and, indeed, the rest of Wright's work is: Why is his world so full of heroes on the run?

Abdul Jan Mohammed has constructed an elaborate defense of Wright's unconscious rationale for presenting these heroes on the run. From the writer-critic Orlando Patterson's view of slavery as social death, Jan Mohammed strives to evince something positive by insisting ostensibly that Wright's running-hero syndrome is "an adamant desire for liberation" and that "the willing acceptance of death functions as the most viable form of liberation in the fiction of Richard Wright."[25] Here, I think, one must be very careful to draw a clear line between liberation and escape, between a canalized and transformative action and an action that is merely a remove from one unsafe dead end to another.

In order to understand this point, let us reconsider the pattern of action in the story "Big Boy Leaves Home" (*Uncle Tom's Children*). The protagonist offers neither the suggestion of any glimpse into a new future derived from a temporary liminal energy nor a methodical engagement with the conventional restrictions of any threshold. When two of Big Boy's friends are killed for what could be interpreted as the violation of a sacred White world, he engages in a struggle with the White gunman for the latter's rifle, which explodes and kills the man. Big Boy flees and so does his friend Bobo. This conflict is not articulated as rationalized revolutionary action by any whit. It is instinctual and selfish. The northbound flight itself is not premeditated nor conceived as part of the process of a larger political action.

The brightness of another story, "Bright and Morning Star" (*Uncle Tom's Children*), rests in an assertive and spiritually triumphant heroine, Aunt Sue, whose commitment to the rescue of her son redeems a narrative that would probably have suffered the fate of Wright's Communist poems. Stripped of its Communist activism and the sociopolitical ethos of the Depression years from which it derives its impetus, the story could have stood as one of the few nonescapist works of Wright's. Unfortunately, the rhetoric of workers and masses becomes a lodestone hardly mitigated when the author ceded the royalties from its publication to the American Marxists in 1941. In short, engagement with reality is largely absent from these stories. Instead of an adamant desire for liberation, there is rather a desire to run, and where that is not possible, there is an irrational and violent expression of rebellion. The same problem is seen in the celebrated *Native Son*.

In a recent article, Jane Davis extensively pleads Wright's case with references to *Native Son*, *Lawd Today* (1963), and *The Long Dream* (1958). Against the strong negative score cards handed in on Wright's works by Du Bois, Robert Stepto, Ellison, Walker and numerous other critics, Davis presents the defense of Houston Baker, claiming that "Wright's works are generally celebrations of life, particularly the complex life lived by black Americans. Wright repeatedly declares that blacks are affirmers."[26] One is hard pressed to discover what is being affirmed and celebrated in several Wrightian characters, including Bigger (*Native Son*), Fish (*The Long Dream*), and Cross Damon (*The Outsider*).

All in all, we must always return to the inevitable picture Wright presents of the Black American and raise a pedagogical question: If, as he suggests in "Blue Print for Negro Writing," the writer is responsible for the welfare of his people, what charts of progress do Wright's works really leave for Black Americans to follow? The irrational rebellion of Bigger Thomas? The existential flight, despair, and loneliness of the rest of his characters? Or, communism, in America? I would like to suggest above all that, as an artist, Wright without doubt was touched by the gift of dreams for humanity, but, once on the writing table, the nightmares of the terrible conditions of growing up in American society took over. Even though it might be difficult to forgive or forget the demons behind those nightmares, one must be truthful about the quality of his mind so that Black writers after him may clearly take what is good and leave the dross where it belongs.

Let us not fear the question broached by Harold Bloom in his introduction to *Richard Wright: Modern Critical Interpretations*: "What remains of Richard Wright's work if we apply to it only aesthetic standards of judgment?"[27] Very much remains. "His importance," suggests Bloom, "transcends the concerns of a strictly literary criticism, and reminds the critic of the claims of history, society, political economy and the larger records of oppression and injustice that history continues to scout" (Introduction). A critical Black reader would still find in Wright's uncontrolled insistence on the validity and urgency of those claims fresh questions tied to the grave dichotomy between ideal and practice. Questions about the Black crusader's honesty and caution regarding his responsibility; about his understanding of his community and his art; about our own estimation of the power of his art and the clouds of his vatic anger. Finally and above all, one wonders whether one could ignore the hauteur of *Black Power* and what that book means in relation to Wright's life and works.

Questions of this nature must continue to haunt the minds of readers of Wright, and the discomfort created by the search for safe answers is what will probably continue to stigmatize his legacy as a dubious one.

NOTES

1. Harold Bloom, *Richard Wright: Modern Critical Interpretations* (New York: Chelsea House, 1988), 51.

2. Ellen Wright and Michel Fabre, *The Richard Wright Reader* (New York: Harper & Row, 1978), preface.

3. Robert Felgar, *Richard Wright* (Boston: Twayne Publishers, 1980), 140.

4. Ibid., 140.

5. Ibid., 141.

6. David Bakish, *Richard Wright* (New York: Ungar, 1973), 75.

7. One of the lines of Countee Cullen's "Heritage" used to epigraph Wright's *Black Power*.

8. Wright, *Native Son* (New York: Harper & Row, 1940), 35.

9. Ibid., 35–36.

10. Wright, *Black Power* (New York: Harper & Row, 1954), 36.

11. Ibid., 146.

12. Ibid., 194.

13. Felgar, *Richard Wright* 140.

14. Addison Gayle, *Ordeal of a Native Son* (New York: Anchor Press, 1980), 81.

15. Wright, *Black Power*, 129.

16. Ibid., 51.

17. Robert Bone, *Richard Wright* (Minneapolis: University of Minnesota Press, 1969), 44.

18. Wright, *Black Power*, 329. Succeeding page references are to this text.

19. Richard Wright, *12 Million Black Voices* (New York: Viking, 1941), 13.

20. Wright, *Black Boy* (New York: Harper & Row, 1966), 19. Succeeding page references are to this text.

21. Michel Fabre, *The World of Richard Wright* (Jackson: University Press of Mississippi, 1985), 80.

22. John A. Williams, *The Most of Native Sons* (New York: Doubleday, 1970), 21.

23. Anthony Kwame Appiah, in Bloom, *Richard Wright*, 190.

24. Fabre, *The World of Richard Wright*, 77.

25. Jan Mohammed, in Bloom, *Richard Wright*, 203.

26. Quoted by Jane Davis in *The Literary Griot* 1, no. 1 (1988): 76.

27. Bloom, *Richard Wright*, Introduction.

5

Claude McKay: The Tragic Solitude of an Exiled Son of Africa

FEMI OJO-ADE

McKay might be termed the first of the New Negroes, of whom Dr. W.E.B. Du Bois, Alain Locke, and James Weldon Johnson were the deans.[1]

Be not deceived, for every
    deed you do
I could match—out-match: am I
    not Afric's son,
Black of that black land where
    black deeds are done![2]

If this renaissance we're talking about is going to be more than a sporadic and scabby thing, we'll have to get down to our racial roots to create it.[3]

If we don't respect ourselves as a race we can't expect white people to respect us.[4]

Autobiography, a common art among many African-American writers, is used to find out why dreams have remained at best a mesmerizing mirage. The truth is, that no one seems to have succeeded in finding peace of mind in a setting that is supposed to be perfect for making dreams come true.

It is with this truth in mind that I have approached the work of Claude McKay. Contrary to widespread opinion, there are in this Jamaican-turned-American writer myriad manifestations of the schizophrenia and alienation resulting from that first, forced deportation from the motherland and the tantalizing, confused, deferred dreams of a new paradise in Western civilization. In order to understand McKay's creative work, one must study his autobiography, *A Long Way from Home*. McKay's Jamaican origin is significant because, on the hierarchical Black ladder propped up by Western civilization, the West Indian is symbolically caught in the "middle passage" between "savagery" (Africa) and "civilization" (United States). Although already a successful poet in Jamaica, McKay found it imperative to leave his island: "Jamaica was too small for high achievement" (*A Long Way from Home*, 20); further references, when sequential, will be made to pages only). McKay wanted "to achieve something new, something in the spirit and accent of America" (4). It took him but two years at Kansas State College (1912–14) to experience the stunning impact of American racism. He decided to drop out and begin his life of vagabondage.

There was also another side to McKay: he was Britain's foster child, imbued with a superiority complex that made him constantly draw a line of distinction between himself and Black Americans. While he is viewed as part of the Harlem Renaissance, McKay never thought he belonged. He often derided the movement, ridiculing Harlemites and castigating fellow writers for their bourgeois uptightness and uprightness. He always mentions his alienation in Harlem, particularly when invited to recite his poems before audiences of "ladies and gentlemen in *tenue de rigueur*."[5] By the time the self-declared "troubadour wanderer" decided to leave America on his first voyage abroad (1922), he had affirmed and confirmed that being Black was problematic and that the solution was no less problematic. When he returned to America in 1924 and became more acquainted with his fellow Blacks, McKay did not understand them any better.

During his travels with his White friends and mentors, he experienced many moments of racism. In New Jersey, no restaurant would serve him or his White friends Eugene Boissevan and Max Eastman because he was Black; hence, they all had to eat together in the kitchen. About Europe, he expressed "the instinctive and animal and purely physical pride of a black person resolute in being himself and yet living a simple civilized life like themselves" (that is, Whites; *A Long Way*, 245).

McKay's problem stemmed from his attempt to combine two contradictions, the "savage" and the "civilized," two stereotypes to which he appeared to give absolute characteristics. One also notices the writer's ambivalent rapport with Africa. McKay hated Marcus Garvey,[6] a true African of the diaspora. It is remarkable that Whites were among McKay's best friends and mentors. As Nathan Huggins states: "Throughout his life, McKay was strangely tied to some white patron" (*Harlem Renaissance*, 127). That dependency, of course, was ultimately on civilization, a monster yet a mentor; a fiend, but a friend; an ally that McKay needed desperately to define himself positively in the world. The question of color-consciousness was only the physical manifestation of a deeper, psychological malady, that of being condemned to the verge of a civilization that he loved. Were racism to be removed from the American landscape, McKay would probably not have run for cover in an Africa of his dreams that edified an ethos of primitivism. McKay said he was drawn to Harlem's "precipitous gorges" (*A Long Way*, 95). He expressed his preference for the proletariat and condemned the Black bourgeoisie and its corrosive, conservative culture that catered to the comforts of the privileged. One wonders, however, whether McKay's attacks on the middle class did not emanate from his own failure to be allowed to settle down and blend into civilization.

Whether Whites liked it or not, McKay, as "Blackface" (*A Long Way*, 145), was determined to haunt them forever. To console himself in his misery, the "ghost of Civilization" would dream of jungles, "revel in the rare scents and riotous colors, croon a plantation melody, be a real original Negro in spite of all the crackers" (146).

McKay's African sojourn is an eye-opener. He visited Morocco in 1929 and chose to lodge in the popular sections of the cities. He claimed to have "experienced a feeling that must be akin to the physical well-being of a dumb animal among kindred animals, who lives instinctively and by sensations only, without thinking" (300). However, that "dumb animal" sooner than later was forced to find reason and to flee the company of the "kindred animals." McKay wrote in a letter describing his Moroccan visit:

I did not want to leave it were it not that the French are masters there. . . . The French are the cleverest propagandists in the world. They hate colored people, yet they pretend they are liberal because they have a liberal tradition to live up to. (quoted in Cooper, *The Passion of Claude McKay*, 148)

There, loud and clear, is the lesson of his African travel: America is better than France. Commenting on colonialism on another occasion, McKay even said that America would most likely have done better than others had it been involved in the enterprise. An incident recounted in his autobiography is symbolic of his alienation from, and ignorance of, Black African culture. In Casablanca, his Martinican friend, whom he had met in Barcelona and who had told him that Morocco was the best place to visit in Africa, took him to his house in the "native" quarter where "some Guinean sorcerors were performing a magic rite." McKay noticed the remarkable resemblance between their performance and that of some peasants in Jamaica. His description, fraught with "civilized" ignorance before an exotic (that is, "savage") occurrence, could have come out of the travel memoirs of Frobenius!:

The Gueanoua were exorcising a sick woman and they danced and whirled like devils. . . . But I did not see the end . . . because a dancing woman frightened me by throwing herself in a frenzy upon me. They said I was a strange spirit and a hindrance to the magic working. So I had to get out. (*A Long Way From Home*, 296–97)

Not only France and Africa were inadequate; England, too cold and too White, with a culture "formidable like an iceberg, . . . was not built to accommodate Negros" (304). "The white hound of [American] Civilization" (304), criticized and cussed out by McKay, nonetheless remained implacable and inescapable, forever.

THE POETRY OF PRIMITIVISM AND ENSLAVEMENT TO CIVILIZATION

Before *Banjo* (1929), the novel for which McKay became most famous among Blacks all over the world, he had written poetry; and that poetry was a response to racism: "From the fullness of my heart I poured myself out with passion of love and hate, of sorrow and joy, writing out of myself" (*A Long Way*, 4).

A misfit in Alabama and Kansas, McKay moved north to New York. That earliest period gave birth to the poem "To the White Friends" (quoted from in this essay's epigraph), in which the enraged poet defiantly boasts of matching, and actually outmatching, the savagery and fiendishness of his powerful enemies. He brings into play the supreme power of Almighty God, who has drawn him from the darkness of hell, just like one of those few chosen to go to paradise, and to prove himself to be of higher quality than the White racist establishment ever expected.

Marion Berghahn mentions the particularity of the word "savage" in the above poem and in others by McKay: "The word 'savage' . . . is an expression of the black's determination to survive and to voice his protest against an inhuman civilisation" (*Images of Africa*, 137). Berghahn's assessment that the West, and not Africa, is barbaric, is largely correct. Where he goes wrong is in coalescing into one unit Africa and Blacks; for McKay does not make such absolute complementarity in his poem.

For McKay, the source of Black savagery is Africa. Of course, there is also the idea of a mysterious, implacable power able to destroy the enemy; yet we cannot shed the Black burden of barbarity. Is the poet's soul, drawn from the darkness by the Almighty as a unique entity, chosen to serve as light for dark Africa? Or for White, dark-hearted America? Is he meant to lead his people, the Africans, or to serve as an example of their humanism among the diabolically evil enemy? The latter, one would say. The final movement of the poem proves it. The poet informs us that his dark face is made to confront, and compete against, the Whites, so that he may prove himself as being superior: that is, to his own people. Thus, one sees the break between McKay and Africa, whose dark deeds can serve the man caught in the ancestral darkness in moments of need (the ability to pounce like a tiger upon the enemy?), but a savage Africa which remains in repose (see "To the White Fiends," in *Selected Poems of Claude McKay*, 38).

The African critic Es'kia Mphahlele also brings to our attention the element of posturing and lack of authentic emotions visible in McKay's sonnets:

[In "Outcast"] You cannot help but feel that he is striking a posture; he is on some bandwagon. And we do not *feel* the "white man's menace," the distance between him and his "native clime," that he talks about; nor do we appreciate the "vital thing" that he says has gone out of his heart. Always his emotion ends up in a straightjacket. But then again McKay really thought that Africa and primitivism were a *cul de sac*. (*The African Image*, 112)

In "Outcast" McKay laments the fact that his enslavement to White culture and civilization is more or less absolute; that something in him is lost forever; that, like a ghost, he is condemned to walking the earth without roots, without a shadow, an outcast. It probably would have been more acceptable if his life as outcast had been blessed with some form of freedom. Pity that this is not so: the White man, owner of the great Western world, is ever present, ever menacing, ever staring, always in control, keeping his Black victim in a timeless mode, without space, without speech, without a sense of humanity. And we note that the poet's humanity is inextricably linked to his belonging to a particular place, Africa. Born far from his native land, he has lost that chance to retain his humanity and, in addition, the Western world has worked hard, through psychological genocide, to make sure he can never attain it. (see "Outcast," in *Selected Poems*, 41).

We have a double tragedy here. America, the civilized, is hard to reach. Africa, the savage, though easily accessible, is repulsive. The poet would love to keep that savagery in the lost past. As a victim of dehumanization in racist civilization, he is compelled to remember the past. Note that this memory is *not* active, but reactive. The master acts, the slave reacts; hence, images of Africa cannot but be negative even as they seemingly serve useful purposes; they can only be contrived as a superficial source of strength even as they supposedly express consciousness of one's humanity and heritage.

A ghost, McKay is not able—he is not allowed to—be a human being like others, because he is Black, because his forefathers came from Africa. There is a certain ambiguity in the identity of what McKay has lost. What is not ambiguous is his attachment, absolutely, to the "great" West, which implies its opposite, the "small" Africa.

McKay's hunger for the old ways, hypothetical and hypocritical, never matched the hunger for America. It could probably have been different, because McKay did pen a poem tracing the times of glory of African civilization and lamenting its loss. In "Africa," written in 1921 (*Selected Poems*, 40), he describes the continent as the ancient land of treasures that modern society has stripped naked. He mentions the marvelous monuments, such as the pyramids. He calls attention to the sphinx, symbol of mystery but also of inaction—righteous but rigid, unable to influence the destructive actions of Africa's denigrators. With that image comes another, that of the harlot, raped and reviled, dehumanized by her treacherous customers. Here we perceive McKay's despair at the destruction and pillage of African civilization, at the despoliation of its treasures. Africa's evolution has come full circle, from power to powerlessness and prostitution, from grace to grass.

The shortcoming of this poem is that the change in Africa's fortunes is detailed almost without emotion. The sonnet is like scientific data, with firm figures devoid of the heartbeat of human beings. If any valuation exists in McKay's poem, it would be in the mythical power of the sphinx, that enigmatic, mysterious Egyptian figure, that fearful monster, watching, waiting for the right moment to rise from the ashes and destroy its enemies.

The titles of McKay's poems enunciate his ineluctable attachment to America: "Enslaved," "In Bondage," "The White House," "The Lynching," "The White City," "Baptism," "Mulatto," "America." In "Enslaved" (*Selected Poems*, 42), McKay prays for the angel, an avenger, to destroy the White man's wonderful world and to liberate his people enslaved by that world. However, he forgets that the angel is White; or maybe he knows and is only hoping that the angel would let him rise from the depth upward into White heaven.[7] McKay knew that racism would not subside soon, but he was searching for the strength to keep his love for America even while steely, blue-eyed lynchers continued their heinous activities ("The Lynching," *Selected Poems*, 37). If hate remains, it would be because the Black man is not permitted to share in the privileges of White society.

The barriers of the sealed-off city of privileged Whites would, hopefully, be brought down some day and the cowardly monsters would regain their human sanity. Meanwhile, McKay insists that Blacks fight back, with dignity, to claim their rights within civilization, and to transform hell into heaven. The struggle, violent in response to the victimizers' own violence, would no longer be out of hate but out of the desire for life. The fire of hate would be approximated to that of love ("Baptism," *Selected Poems*, 35).

The publication of his poetry collection *Harlem Shadows* (1922) saw the realization of McKay's obsessive pursuit of "one object: the publication of an American book of verse" (*A Long Way*, 147). "I love this cultured hell," he declared. His America-based poetry thus marks the cultural ascent from Jamaica to America. The White editor, Frank Harris, encouraged him, however, to write prose (*A Long Way*, 20).

That encouragement led to McKay's series of novels on primitivism and civilization. The novels would be cathartic in the individual's painful search for self within an unfriendly civilization. His desire for the light of civilization is irrevocable. The particularity of his plight becomes paramount: "So what I write is urged out of my blood. There is no white man who could write my book" ("The Negro's Tragedy," in Abraham Chapman, ed., *Black Voices*, 373–74).

MCKAY'S NOVELS AND THE TRAGEDY OF A CIVILIZED NEGRO

McKay is perhaps expressing the idea of being the voice of the voiceless, a controversial standpoint in the West, to say the least. For, the act of writing in Western society often reduces commitment to one's community to that of self. Self-survival, individualism—indeed, selfishness—such are the pivotal interests of the writer placed by double-consciousness on the verge of the (White-dominated) community. The writer, epitome of the middle class, may love Harlem's night life, the spontaneity and instinctive joy of living of the common people. He, however, is always aware that, in the final analysis, there is a big psychological space, almost palpable in its profundity, between him and "those people." McKay's dilemma is poignantly explicated in the character of Ray, a Haitian intellectual of sorts, in *Home to Harlem* (1928; henceforth referred to as *Home*) and *Banjo* (1929).

The confusion already noticed in McKay's poetry is more glaring in his fiction: the superiority of civilization is shown as improvement of the individual's head, but with it comes a depreciation of his heart, an inferiorization of the soul into superficiality of actions and attitudes. Only "some savage culture in the jungles of Africa" (*Home*, 274) could restore to him the lost estate. The problem is, Ray goes to Europe in search of Africa! Indeed, what irks the man is American racism.

In *Banjo*, Ray surfaces in Marseilles and finds Banjo whose character, to a large extent, complements that of *Home*'s Jake. Ray, now a writer, focuses on the art of writing and once again reveals McKay's Eurocentric viewpoint about commitment to art, universalism, and proletarianism. Present on the fictionalized scene are McKay's proletarian protagonists: Banjo, the vagabond American hero; Goosey, his compatriot; Dengel; Senegalese; and others, as well as Ray. Goosey, an avowed Garveyist, questions Ray's plan to write a story on the unsavory lives of the Ditch boys, convinced that "the crackers" would use Ray's work against the race. Ray's response, that he is telling stories just for the fun of it, that it does not matter who is listening, that "a good story is like good ore" found anywhere in the world (*Banjo*, 115), immediately reminds us of Langston Hughes's famous declaration about Negro artists wishing to "express [their] individual dark-skinned selves without fear or shame" (see chapter 1 of this volume). Ray rejects Goosey's suggestion to write about "the race men and women who are making it good in Paris." He sneers at such "society" bourgeois Blacks everywhere (*Banjo*, 115).

The galling gratuitousness of Ray's argument cannot be over-emphasized. By writing about the Ditch boys, Ray wishes to prove his affinity to them as an instinctive, primitive person. But he forgets that his very position as writer—of which he is very proud—makes him also a "misfit." Besides, his audience cannot be the proletariat, who hardly read. In fact, what Ray does is to display his broad knowledge of European literature, culture, and philosophy; and the novel ends with his thoughts on the philosophies of H. G. Wells, Bernard Shaw, and Bertrand Russell; the ultimate triumph, one might say, of Civilization.

Among the audience that zealously welcomed *Banjo* onto the literary scene were French West African and West Indian students living in France in the 1930s. The Belgian critic Lilyan Kesteloot (*Les Ecrivains noirs de langue française*, 63–82) writes at length on the great influence that *Banjo* and other Negro-American works had on Black intellectuals. Although enjoying modest success in the United States, *Banjo* quickly became a bible of inspiration for such aspiring writers as the Negritude leaders, Léopold Senghor, Césaire and Damas, among others.

The euphoria of African students regarding *Banjo* was due to McKay's condemnation of French racism and colonialism. It is noteworthy that Blacks in America were not as enthusiastic. McKay's generalizations on Black primitive vitality were compared by one critic to that of "his brothers of the Klan"! McKay "knows he is slurring his people to please white readers" (quoted in Cooper, *Claude McKay*, 258). W.E.B. Du Bois said that, upon reading *Home*, he felt the need to take a bath! Meanwhile, White radicals, imbued with the vogue of exoticism, were praising it condescendingly. McKay's reaction is worth quoting: "We must leave the appreciation of what we are doing to the emancipated Negro intelligentsia of the future, while we are sardonically aware now that only the intelligentsia of the superior race is developed enough to afford artistic truth" (in Cooper, 247).

McKay's notion of "development" seems to mean the integration of Blacks into the mainstream of Western civilization. Of course, that remains a dream. Neither McKay nor his contemporaries ever made mention of his Africanity. Current assessments simply claim that his novels demonstrate that he held Africa in high esteem. In Berghahn's opinion, for example, the process of identification with Africa reaches a very high point in *Banjo*, in which McKay "certainly included Africa much more directly and openly in his concept of the New Negro than did Toomer" in *Cane* (Berghahn, 146). Berghahn believes that McKay's destination in his search for identity is Africa. McKay's autobiography definitely reveals no such proof. One simply needs to read *Banjo* attentively.

This "story without plot" (McKay's subtitle) introduces us to the lives of Black vagabonds from Africa, America, and the Caribbean "bumming" in the port city of Marseilles, a sort of microcosm of European civilized society. It takes only the appearance of Banjo for the serious reader to realize that there is, indeed, a plot hidden behind the mask of hedonistic vagabondage preached and relentlessly pursued by the hero and the supporting cast around him.

The most important of the supporting players called "the Ditch boys," are led by Malty, a West Indian sailor whose mother chose her son's Christian names from the labels of her missionary master's case goods, for which she had taken a fondness. There is also Ginger, an old, philosophizing Black American ex-seaman marooned in Marseilles. Bugsy, another American Negro, is aggressive, belligerent, hard-fisted, and doomed to die in Marseilles. The group is rounded out by the Senegalese Dengel, who is filthy, always drunk, and too lazy for any exertion. From the first, we are informed that drinking is the focus of their group life; hence, we are not surprised to see them always in bars and brothels. That fact could catch the unwary reader in a trap of revelry and ribaldry, because, as they drink and dance and drift, our "scavengers of proletarian life" (7) are seeking the truth about themselves and society; in essence, they are serving as medium for McKay's own search.

The Ditch boys are joined on the stage of life by other players, who, at times, come out of the shadow and share the front stage with Banjo; they stand up to and against him, but, by so doing, show Banjo's superiority. First comes Ray, the wandering Haitian intellectual, full of self-doubt and a paralyzing ambivalence, continuing from where he left off in *Home to Harlem*. He is the son of a member of the entourage of Haiti's president exiled to Jamaica; his father followed the president and took the child, Ray, along. Now, as Ray travels in Europe in search of his identity, he reveals his dilemma: uncertain of his ancestry—he wonders whether he has East African or West African Fulah heritage—he also hates wearing the badge of writer in public and prefers to be "one of the boys" even though he enjoys his intellectualism and, unlike the Ditch boys, he has a discerning mind that helps him analyze and therefore appreciate the "cruel beauty" of Marseilles (68).

Goosey, a Garveyist often clashing with Banjo and Ray over racial matters, ends up returning to the "United Snakes" that he once vowed to abandon forever. The Senegalese bar owner, a former seaman who made his money in America, provides a meeting point for the Negroes and propounds his own brand of Negritude. Taloufa, who "came from the Nigerian bush," represents Africa's affinity to Garveyism. Latnah, a mixture of Arabian, Persian, and Indian, introduced as a friend of the boys by Malty, is soon sleeping with the irresistible Banjo.

Ray compares America to Europe and shows his preference for America, the land of romance. In all the comparisons in the novel, that choice is very clear. Among the Negroes, McKay distinguishes between African *dialects* and the Martinique *dialect* on the one hand and, on the other, the civilized *tongues*. Marseilles' *barbarous* romance is attractive because it brings Ray close to his primitive roots. Its "white-fanged vileness" (69) at once attracts and repulses the Negro, who has a love-hate relationship with Civilization. Although McKay throws in French words and expressions throughout his novel, he nonetheless affirms the superiority of the English language. Most of the characters are complimented for their ability to speak English, including the francophone Africans who are not seen using their African "dialects" at any time during the story.

McKay makes no attempt to valuate African languages; they are simply incomprehensible, exotic "dialects." He makes one striking exception as far as the choice of English over French is concerned: an article on a Senegalese rifleman condemned for murder appears in the newspaper, and Ray cuts it out because it shows what he calls civilized logic (African savages ought not to be taught to use a gun!) with which he agrees, although not with the author's manner of presentation (277).

We must note here that McKay uses language in the Western way, as a tool to depict the superiority of civilization over savagery. Certain key words are present in his vocabulary, which, this author maintains, is not much different from the stock language of the enslaver-colonizer—words such as *native*, *savage*, and *brute*; and the primary people and places thus described are African. Of a Black girl dancing in the Senegalese bar, we read: "her full lips were a savage challenge"; of the Senegalese, "happy brutes dance . . . more natively, more savagely" (48). Two Africans dance "like a ram goat and a ram kid."

Black dancers are always "in a wild heat of movement . . . rearing up and down" (53); and, of course, well in line with the myth, Whites, bad dancers that they are, when they dance at all, cannot keep up with Negroes.

One might claim that such examples are proof of McKay's pride in Black natural qualities. Yet, there is the subtle implication that Civilization knows that drinking and dancing do not matter in the struggle for survival and progress. As McKay himself confirms in an episode relating the success of a French taxi driver, one of Ray's many White friends, who uses his part in a prostitution ring in the Ditch to pile up cash to build himself a house in the countryside, "bawdiness was only a means toward the ultimate purpose of respectability" (248). So, if White man cannot dance in the bar, he can dance on the social stage with a controlled rhythm that regulates the existence of Negroes, who, all bombed out, come out to "bum" for the essentials that the White man has been accumulating while they were busy getting drunk!

France is roundly condemned for its racism. Ray stresses the failings of French colonialism and the civilization propagating the lie that Blacks are better off under French rule than any other on earth.

A discussion in the Senegalese bar further dismantles the myth of French liberalism and underscores the superiority of American civilization. The bar owner argues with a compatriot, a francophile seaman convinced that there is no racism in France. The bar owner expresses the notion that America is better every time for a colored man. He praises America as the land of progress and opportunity, as well as honesty and forthrightness, and contrasts it with French hypocrisy.

As the arguments continue throughout the novel, the Africans reveal their own prejudices and class conflicts, which is ironic, given the fact that Ray lends credence to the opinion of one of the budding bourgeois, Senghor. That irony carries over to the position of Ray himself: Ray, the man with a missionary fervor to bridge the gap between him and the Black proletariat, constantly (subconsciously?) favors bourgeois positions. Besides, the real-life Senghor has not been the committed anti-French-colonialism stalwart that McKay and many others believed.

In Ray's opinion, Germany comes closest to America in quality of life: It has something American, even though it lacks the dynamic confusion of America. America is specifically Harlem. Ray compares Harlem to Marseilles: "Harlem's smell is like animals brought in from the fields to stable. Here it's rotten-stinking" (299). The simile vividly confirms a point already made in this essay, that, for the Negro, going to America is a movement upwards from the savagery symbolized by Africa. Animals, uncouth, instinctive, exposed to the unfriendly elements in the jungle (Africa), are brought into the stable where they find civilization as they are domesticated, adapted to shelter and the sweet smells of human society (America). Once, Ray, feeling nostalgia for his Caribbean tropical shores, smokes drugs with Banjo's woman, Latnah; but, instead of dreaming of the tropics, he dreams of Harlem (284), one more proof that, all the vagabondage notwithstanding and no matter how many ancestry-inducing stimuli, the magnetic pull of Civilization would remain uncontrollable and unequaled. Harlem, in essence, would always be home. McKay's characters will, not surprisingly, head back *"home to Harlem."*

Banjo, the character propped up as the perfect portrait of primitivism, is no less assertive of American superiority than Ray. From the first, Banjo is presented as a unique character, a kind of honorary member of the vagabond band. Although he is a deportee from America, America is always a part of him, no matter where he goes. We know that in real life, McKay himself never lost that connection. America casts a long shadow impossible to shake, even as the novelist deals with the myriad problems posed by life in America. If one were to believe many a critical analysis of *Banjo*, one would conclude that American racism is roundly condemned by McKay.

That is not the whole truth, however. Let us look closely at McKay's series of choices. French racism, he tells us, is comparable to, if not more insidious than the American. There is a general preference for Black over White, following the stereotypes of Blacks' physical strength and Whites' weakness (18). In any fight, Whites are always the aggressors. If Whites win at all, it is because the fight is not even (71). Descriptions of White men are invariably negative. The White prostitute who approaches Ray is described as a loathsome white worm, an obscene bird, reminiscent of the white buzzard of the Caribbean. When Whites play music in the Marseilles bars, they do so in a hard, unsmiling, funereal, and execrable way; and they play only for money. In a subtle way, the message is that Blacks have rhythm and Whites lack it. McKay's formula seems so appropriate for the Negro folk saying chosen by Wallace Thurman as the title of his novel *The Blacker the Berry* (1929, same year as *Banjo*): "The blacker the berry, the sweeter the juice."

As one should expect, however, the truth is more complex than a simple choice of Black over White. That, in itself, would be a welcome turn of events. Where Claude McKay fails to convince is in his inability (or, rather, unwillingness) to extricate himself from the very stereotyping that he apparently wishes to downplay in *Banjo*. Black still connotes brute strength. For example, Ray would like to have sex with a woman "with primitive joy"; he explains the notion of Negroes being oversexed as a matter of their being "freer and simpler in their sexual urge" (252) than Whites. Ray cannot individuate and humanize Blacks as people living beyond the prison of race and color; yet he goes a long way in doing exactly that with Whites. He forgives and forgets quite easily, and both he and Banjo recount their experiences with Whites that are as human as one could ever imagine.

One of the most interesting discussions among Blacks in *Banjo* centers on the issue of interracial marriage. It takes place in the Senegalese bar as part of the debate on "a racial renaissance" among Ray, the Senegalese bar owner, an Ivory Coast student, and a Martinique mulatto student whose greatest joy is that Empress Josephine, Napoleon's wife, was born on his home island and who is also proud that René Maran's "naughty book," *Batouala*, was banned in the colonies. Ray speaks, as usual, as the "educated Negro" distinguishing between "savagery" and "culture" (200–201). He preaches a return to roots, a concerted effort to "build up" from our own people. The problem, however, is a lack of precision on the part of the preacher. Further, one remains unconvinced of his commitment to the culture.

For example, Ray advises the Martinique student and others of the Black middle class to, among other things, become interested in "the native African dialects and, though you don't understand, be humble before their simple beauty instead of despising them" (201). A strange position, indeed, because Ray himself shows no appreciation of African culture. His pronouncements on Africanity are superficial and quite lame. One always senses in him a certain disturbing dilettantism that mainly serves the purpose of promoting his superiority over others and hardly hides the man's confusion.

Surprisingly enough, Ray, the one committed to his "native roots," explains away miscegenation as a result of colored women and White men's desire to go together. He thus reverts to his old reliable position of deracialized universal love. "Woman is woman all over the world, no matter what her color is," he asserts. Yet he goes on to say that "an intelligent race-conscious man" should not marry a White woman. Furthermore, he expresses satisfaction with America's policy of keeping Blacks "in their place," claiming that "it may be better for the race in the long run" (206).

If woman is woman all over the world, why blame the Senghors of the Negro race for marrying White women? What exactly does Ray mean by "respectable society"? As the discussion in the Senegalese bar is coming to an end, six distinguished Whites enter; they include a White woman who recognizes Ray as the model who used to pose nude for her White American art student. When the Ivorian student exclaims that this friendly woman is American, Ray sneers at him "in malicious triumph" and asks: "Did you think there were no human relations between white and black in America . . . ?" (208).

IMAGES OF AFRICA AND AFRICANS IN *BANJO:* ANOTHER TRIUMPH OF CIVILIZATION

In *Banjo*, blackness does not equate love or consciousness of African heritage. It is the failure to make that lucid analysis that led to canonization of the novel as bible of the Negritude generation. Contrary to what some critics would have us believe, McKay has given no new meaning to the words used to dehumanize Blacks. The racist's stock language is all over the pages of *Banjo*. References are made to the Negroes' knack for throwing a wild laugh because of their big mouths (251). Blacks in Marseilles are "jungle-like Negroes" (68). The West Indies are "them monkey islands" (158). The only thing that these savages trying to survive in civilization can teach their French hosts is the instinctive spontaneity of primitivism, "the natural animal grace and rhythm of Negroes jazzing" (166).

In this jungle of Negroes, there is a caste system in which Africans and Africa are stuck at the bottom. Dengel, the only African in the main group of "bummers," is one of the least interesting. His image is fixed, stagnant; he is forever in a state of inebriety. While his friends are bathing on the beach, he sits watching out for the police, not bothering to clean himself. Banjo calls Africans "cannibals" (117). Goosey sees them as slow witted and docile. When Banjo is slow in preparing to board the ship leaving for America, Goosey chides him: " 'Get some American pep into you and don't act so African' " (302).

The closest that McKay's alter ego, Ray, gets to Africans is to show towards them the pity of Big Brother. In one of his knowledgeable discussions with Whites (on this occasion, a British panhandler with whom he rides the streets of Marseilles), Ray remarks about White propaganda against French West African troops during the World War. He complains that, rather than mention the exploitation of "primitive and ignorant black conscripts," critics were only interested in the sexuality of Negroes. McKay is right to criticize the exploitation of Africans, but wrong to think that the exploited were simply poor, ignorant nonentities. His attitude replicates that of the enslaver and exploiter. History has documented otherwise: Africans under the governorship of a Black Frenchman from Guyane, Felix Eboué, were, indeed, the very first to heed General Charles de Gaulle's call for the Resistance movement.[8]

According to Ray, Africans are best left in their jungles because they do not adapt easily to civilization. He elicits this very notion after reading the article in the *faits divers* column of a radical French newspaper supporting the government's conscription of Africans into the French army. It relates the story of a crazy Senegalese soldier who went on a shooting spree in Toulon, killing quite a number of people. Ray has kept the article "as an amusing revelation of civilized logic [and because] *he was in agreement with the thesis while loathing the manner of its presentation*" (emphasis mine). McKay quotes the article in its French original; translated excerpts are included here: "Perhaps we should cross our hearts and ask ourselves whether it is wise enough to teach primitives how to use a gun. . . . [There are exceptions] but the majority of these blackskinned 'natives' are big babies unable to grasp the subtleties of our morals and language" (*Banjo*, 277; translation mine). The civilized writer of that article desists from drawing any conclusion, but he well knows that his readers are intelligent enough to draw the expected one, just as Ray does.

In the Ditch, Africans never cease to show that they deserve their place at the bottom. They have specialized in eating garbage gathered from the ships and meant for pigs. When the passengers on deck see the throng of wild, hungry "niggers" scrambling for the rotten food, they scamper for their cameras to take pictures that they would keep for posterity!

Among the exceptions to the rule are Senghor, whose mixed marriage is a subject of Ray's analytical mind, and sailors such as Taloufa, the one that "came from the Nigerian bush'' and was fortunate to be raised by a missionary who saved him from his native jungle. Denied refugee status in Britain, Taloufa has the better fortune of going to America. Before he leaves, his more civilized friends give him quick training. "You ain't in the African jungle with the monkeys in the trees now," chides Goosey (111).

CONCLUSION: THE TRAGEDY OF A CIVILIZED NEGRO

The claim about the Africanity of Claude McKay's work is a result of the repetition of characteristics of (noble?) savagery in his Black stereotypes. Hardly does any critic complain that such savagery is denigrating towards Africa.

As for McKay's ill-defined socialism (his vaunted primitivism and proletarianism), one finds that it is part of the confusion of a man trying to combine socialism and capitalist individualism. Both strands would emanate from McKay's desperate desire to realize the American Dream. The attempted return to roots was not voluntary; it was not authentic; it was never meant to be long lasting. In order to conceptualize Africa in a positive light, McKay would have had to understand its culture and civilization; to do that, he would have followed, not his Western masters (and the combination of Victorian philosophy and the American legacy of slavery and racism with the Jim Crow laws must have been devastating), but Africans aware of the qualities of their ethos. The Africans that McKay met in France were themselves alienated. The significant difference is, that while they could go home again, McKay was an eternal exile seeking a home, caught between two opposing poles, Africa and America, attached to one by heritage but bent upon ascending to the other as a sort of hope for salvation.

McKay's poetry may be considered Afrocentric if one thinks of Africa as offering a source of pride and strength for the Black fighting White racism. On the contrary, McKay's novels are as removed from Africa as Europe, which is ironical when one notes the constant reference to *Banjo* as a Negritude novel. To an African critic, the irony is to be expected: the Negritude generation of bourgeois *arrivistes* was at best acculturated, at worst alienated as far as Africa was concerned.

Berghahn believes that there is a resolution of Ray's dilemma as McKay makes him evolve from *Home to Harlem* to *Banjo* and that, by the time McKay wrote his third novel, *Banana Bottom* (1933), in which the Western educated heroine, Bita, returns to her Jamaican village, McKay had developed "from a total rejection of Africa to a position of approval and admiration for African traditions." He goes on to say that McKay "wanted to generate an understanding for the idea that African cultures had a value of their own and that they were capable of creating more humane living conditions" (*Images of Africa*, 150).

In *Banjo*, Ray's dilemma is definitely not resolved in favor of Africa. At the end of the novel, Banjo scolds Ray for his intellectualism. Ray laments not having the character to enjoy life like Banjo. All that remorse, all that guilt complex, is it meant to show us an image of the honest intellectual feeling unnecessarily hamstrung by his morality and now anxious to take chances like his primitive, natural vagabond friend, Banjo? Is Ray being transformed into an adventurer using his street-smarts to survive? Or could it be that Ray's dilemma is finally resolved in Bita's return to the village as a rejection of civilization and its dehumanizing machinery? Whatever answers may be given to these questions, they can only point to the tragedy of the civilized Negro in Ray, as well as McKay.

What McKay has proclaimed as good qualities in Banjo and others of the primitivist mold, are, to say the least, shocking if not nauseating. The Banjos of McKay's universe would not in any way help ameliorate the conditions of Blacks; they cannot help to reaffirm Black humanity; nor can they combat and conquer the iniquities of racism and imperialism; nor regain respectability and reawaken to a commitment that, even from the euphoric era of Harlem, has too often been difficult to define in a positive fashion.

After reading *Banjo*, one has a feeling that McKay has depicted in both Ray and Banjo aspects of his personal tragedy. Any revolutionary philosophy that one may find in McKay's work[9] is roundly repudiated in his fiction. Ray is a universalist moderate, a liberal expressing "the principle of stressing the exception [the good in Whites] above the average" (*Banjo*, 275). He says he does not believe in the "Negro problem," that "of the highest importance was the problem of the individual." For Ray, "the Negro was one significant and challenging aspect of *the human life of the world as a whole*" (272; emphasis mine). He sees nothing wrong in the colonialist-imperialist arrangement. While Ray condemns Christianity's false morality, McKay himself converted to Catholicism after his illness and final return to the United States. Huggins quotes McKay:

I maintain that since in the United States we are a most special type minority, amid a majority of whites, the real issue for us is Adjustment, and not Segregation. For when we come down to brass tacks, the Negro minority must depend finally on the good-will of white America. We, more than any other people in the New World, need a Good Neighbor Policy. (Huggins, 178–79)

That final confession is not unexpected; for, all his life, McKay depended on the goodwill of Whites. The consolation might be that, before the final capitulation, he struggled to set his soul free. His truly tragic demise makes one think of the mother-land's own descent into neocolonial hell. Several figures and episodes in *Banjo* are relevant to African and African-American realities: Sister Geter, the Pentecostal Fire Baptized Believer from New York preaching in English to French-speaking Marseillais in the certainty that "people heahs what I say and jest gotta understand no matter what lang-idge they speaks" (290); those "students of life" living aimlessly abroad in the "cosmopolitan world of people of different races and colors" (246); leaders of the New Africa preaching progress while selling their people to masters old and new. These and others underscore our tragedy.

McKay's work is an explication of the disastrous consequences of deracination and of the brainwashing brought about by our multiple experiences of slavery, colonialism, racism, and neocolonialism. The fictitious Blacks bumming their way through Europe are more or less doubles of real life Blacks, "harlots of mighty nations" (adapted from McKay's poem, "Africa," in *Selected Poems*; 40), begging or having our brains drained for the profit of Euro-America while Africa is dying from the shows of shame choreographed by self-appointed saviors. When Goosey, the constantly ridiculed Ditch boy, says, "If we don't respect ourselves as a race we can't expect white people to respect us," he is making what would normally be a thought-provoking statement. But nobody listens to Goosey, the supporter of Garvey, the man whom McKay called a charlatan.

It so happens that McKay himself saw "the Negro problem" as a nagging embarrassment. In a letter to a friend, he wrote that *Banjo* "is clogged up with 'the problem of the Negro.' However, I had to get that out of my system. Now I can go on with real creative work" (in Cooper, *The Passion of Claude McKay*, 147). Till the very end, Claude McKay was searching for himself. That, perhaps, is the ultimate tragedy.

NOTES

1. Langston Hughes, "The Twenties: Harlem and Its Negritude," *African Forum* 1 (Spring 1966): 1.

2. Claude McKay, "To the White Fiends," in *Selected Poems*, 38.

3. McKay, *Banjo* (originally published 1929); present essay quotes from Harcourt Brace Jovanovich edition, 1957, p. 200.

4. Ibid., 128.

5. McKay did not really become familiar with Negro intellectuals until his return from Europe in 1924. It is then that he met radicals, "the Black Reds," such as Grace Campbell, pioneer member of the Socialist party, and Cyril Briggs, editor of *The Crusader*. He also met conservative leaders of the NAACP, like W.E.B. Du Bois and his favorite, James Weldon Johnson.

6. See Cooper, *The Passion of Claude McKay*, 65–69; quotes and comments on McKay's essay "Garvey as a Negro Moses."

7. Critics have mentioned McKay's early anti-Christian position and the conversion to Christianity at the end of his life. That does not erase the fact that his poems contain a constant Christian imagery and some messianic expectation: prayers to the Almighty in the hope that a messiah would come down and save the enslaved Black people; a faith in God that would bring about a radical change in the victims' destiny.

8. The exploitation concomitant to colonialism has always been addressed by Africans. Note, nonetheless, that French colonialism was unique: it made "new people" out of the colonized. An excellent example is the much vaunted notion of "francophonie" which, to this critic's mind, is a sanitized form of colonialism. The Francophone African

bourgeoisie believed in the French mystique. Patriots to the core, they were ready to die (and did die) for their adopted motherland. Of course, certain progressive elements opposed such actions. See, for example, Leon-Gontran Damas's poetry-collection, *Pigments* (1937), particularly the poem, "Et caetera" (77–78), in which the poet calls out to the Senegalese riflemen fighting for France to leave the Germans alone and "begin by invading Senegal."

9. For example, Etienne Léro, in the only issue of the Black French West Indian journal *Légitime Défense* (1932), names McKay and Langston Hughes as revolutionary writers whose works would hopefully influence those of West Indians.

BIBLIOGRAPHY

Berghahn, Marion. *Images of Africa in Black American Literature*. London: MacMillan Press, 1977.

Chapman, Abraham, ed. *Black Voices*. New York: Mentor, 1968.

Cooper, Wayne. *Claude McKay, Rebel Sojourner in the Harlem Renaissance*. Baton Rouge: Louisiana University Press, 1987.

———. *The Passion of Claude McKay*. New York: Schocken Books, 1973.

Damas, Léon-Gontran. *Pigments*. Paris: Guy Lévis Mano, 1937.

Du Bois, W.E.B. *The Souls of Black Folk*. Greenwich, Conn.: Fawcett Publications, 1903.

Huggins, Nathan. *Harlem Renaissance*. New York: Oxford University Press, 1971.

Hughes, Langston. "The Negro Artist and the Racial Mountain." *Nation* 122 (June 1926): 692–94.

Kesteloot, Lilyan. *Les Ecrivains noirs de langue française*. Brussels: eds. de l'Université de Bruxelles, 1963.

Légitime Défense (no. 1). Paris, 1932.

Maran, René. *Batouala*. Paris: Albin Michel, 1921.

McKay, Claude. *Banana Bottom*. New York: Harper, 1933.

———. *Banjo*. New York: Harper, 1929; New York: Harcourt Brace Jovanovich, 1957.

———. *Harlem Shadows*. New York: Harcourt, Brace, 1922.

———. *Home to Harlem*. New York: Harper, 1928.

———. *A Long Way from Home*. New York: Lee Furman, 1937.

———. *Selected Poems of Claude McKay*. New York: Bookman, 1953.

Mphahlele, Ezekiel. *The African Image*. New York: Praeger, 1974.

6

Another African Artist's Wayward Thoughts on Eugene Redmond's Poetry

TESS ONWUEME

I write because I can't sing, I can't dance. . . . I write to vent anxieties and tensions, having been boxed in socially, politically, racially, sexually. . . . There are a lot of tensions that build up in us; for example, self hatred—venting frustration about that which is unknown. I also write praise poetry and love poetry. I love deeply and long—my love is comprehensive. I love my family . . . black people. *I love black people!*
—Eugene B. Redmond

It is this sense of urgency, an unusual sense of mission and vision that is structured on the landscape of LOVE that marks Eugene Redmond's voice and poetry as distinct in contemporary African-American literature.[1] Eugene Redmond calls himself the "poet of love," devoting the greater part of his five poetry anthologies to promoting the ideology of love as a therapy and metaphor for healing, self and collective renewal of the "ties that bind"[2] the universal family. This revelation in itself has provoked relevant questions: Is there any such viable concept as "the Black family," especially in a season where Black is not hegemonic and is, in fact, a minority silenced, voiceless, and made up of unattractive fragments? What is the configuration of this Black family, and what is the character of this love for the Black family? Is it universal or simply African American? The poet responds that his love is comprehensive. In the particular interview he kindly gave me on February 17, 1993, Redmond, unlike many others who are yet to resolve the conflicts of "double-consciousness,"[3] defines and affirms repeatedly that his map of the Black family is all inclusive, encompassing all the "peoples of African extraction dispersed all over the world." Quite often, the poet evokes Africa as the motherland without the usual ambivalence that characterizes African-American consciousness of Africa.

Indeed, the centrality of Africa in Redmond's poetry, vision and consciousness readily reminds one of Marcus Garvey and his return-to-Africa politics that once gained currency for the displaced Africans in the New World to reinstate, rehabilitate, and renew themselves in Africa. This theology is currently visible in Molefi Asante's creed of Afrocentricity.[4] The return is posited as a necessary step in the renewal of identity and continuity of the race.

Later in this discussion we will focus on Redmond's constant evocation and adaptation of *Drumvoices*[5] as the mythological mediator between crossroads and opposites, as interpreter and as diviner whose words imbue power and esteem. In addition, Drumvoices in Redmond's poetry echo Léopold-Sédar Senghor's Negritude ideology of the 1930s. Just as the Senghorian drum motif typifies and reaffirms Black-African consciousness, Redmond's Drum persona appears to have been so patterned and intricately woven into the poetic fabric that it assumes the dimension of an archetype.

In many ways, the character of this drum archetype is reminiscent of the various configurations of the West African trickster-god and mediator at the crossroads. In Yorubaland, this trickster is Eshu-Elegbara; in Igboland, it is Uke; and in Ashantiland, Ananse. But having crossed and survived the Middle Passage, this trickster-god reemerges in the New World, renamed the Signifyin(g) Monkey in North America and Legba in Latin America. Specifically, in Redmond's poetry, the drum grows in stages, shifting and crossing boundaries in its mission to communicate and bridge distances between the self and the other, between Africa and the diaspora, with the aim of fortifying, unifying, and reaffirming those tenuous ties that bind Black people, and as a means of ensuring wholeness and continuity of the race.

"Love for black people" is not just recurrent in this poetry, it grows into the taboo religion of "Jazzography" through which the author radically affirms the creed, beauty, and integrity of Blackness as a new article of faith to guide and redeem the Black race in a world in which Blacks are constantly being marginalized, oppressed, and dehumanized. Redmond's religion of Jazzography is heretical to the hegemonic White America because it seems both to assault the foundation of their rule of supremacy and to (re)create and (re)construct the distorted memory and what the poet calls "mis-history" of a nation:

> In my secret soul heroes have always been
> Black.
> But America raised me on
> John Wayne
> Shirley Temple
> And Tarzan.
>
> America gave me distance!
> America gave me distance![6]

In addition to the poet's vehement opposition to these conventional injustices, his mission is to unmask, demystify, and demythologize the supremacy of dominant White constructions of truth and knowledge so Black people can see through the falsehoods in the system and rise into action to recreate and revision their place, history, and destiny with the self (Black race), rather than the other (White race) as the center of their world. This confrontational engagement with history is at the core of Redmond's Afrocentric vision, which is textured on love for Black people and which he expresses in the poem "Love Is Upbringing" (*The Eye*, 120). Ultimately, the love-rhythms intensity into a liberation theology aimed at emancipating peoples of African descent from the confines of oppression, marginalization, and self-destruction.

We note, however, that arriving at this truth was exceedingly difficult for the poet himself, since the mission of reconnecting and empowering Black people across spatial and temporal boundaries of culture and knowledge must first begin within the self, until reinforced to make the necessary transition to link up with the other. In this regard, we note three identifiable stages in both the poet's journey of becoming and reconnecting the ties that bind African peoples in the world. The pivot for accomplishing this desired transition and harmony is the Black family, with the male and female working together.

But this is where the tension begins and persists; for this family, too, is in fragments, and the outside enemy uses the one against the other. In fact, as revealed in Redmond's poetry, it is typically the Black man who loses and is played out of the game of power by White America, which employs its noted infamous politics of divide and rule. For Redmond, therefore, freedom and unity for Black people must begin from within the family, where the enslaved Black male, together with his female counterpart, must first be liberated in order to reconnect proudly with the rest of the African kindred in the world. Therefore, in addition to the recurrent Afrocentric and Pan-Africanist ideology and aesthetic concerns, love occupies a significant space and focus in Redmond's poetry as the panacea for African communal linkages, reunions, and renewals. It is mainly for this reason that Redmond is not only an important voice in Black writing today and an outstanding poet of love, but a major voice for the endangered Black male in White America.

BLACK MAN AND BLACK WOMAN: THE COMPLEMENTARY ROLE OF LOVE

The development of this ethics of love occurs in three identifiable stages. Initially, the love is sporadic, revealing restless, chaotic, unprogrammatic spurts of desire for union, communion, anchor, and identity with the Other that is not just elusive, but exacts an oppressive power to keep the Black male captive, with the result that he finds himself caught in the tension of attraction and repulsion.

On the surface, this oppressive and predatory other is constructed on the image of the Black woman. But on a more symbolic level, Redmond implies that the Black woman serves as an agency for the more malevolent superstructures of racism in White America. This accounts for the poet's ambivalent projection of the Black woman at this stage as victim and as a treacherous benevolent oppressor who conspires with the unjust system to rape the Black male of his manhood and dignity. The image is therefore of the Black man sentenced to the life of exile at home by the Black woman, and outside home by the combined forces of the White male and White female. Consequently, the Black man is an alienated, emasculated "endangered species."[7]

The poet points an accusing finger at the Black woman as the enemy within and as the symbolic obstacle that the Black male must not only pass through but transcend. For him to attain the ultimate goal of his journey, therefore, he must cross the boundaries of yet another Middle Passage symbolized by the Black woman. The first stage of this poet's journey towards becoming thus centers on the impediments, conflicts, and tensions in harmonizing relationships between the Black male and the Black female until it builds up to a reverberating rhetorical question in the poem "On/Again; Off/Again":

> Does a whiteness separate us,
> /Blackwoman/? (*The Eye*, 143)

One goal is clear in his mind: he longs for union with the Black woman, with the world. But he is convinced that even though he cannot really entrust his destiny to the Black woman, who stands in the way of his dream of power and collective renewal with his community, he cannot bypass her, for she is the metaphorical crossroad between self and the other, between here and there. Thus, often in Redmond's poetry, the Black woman is portrayed as a vicarious medium for attaining the ultimate goal of rooting, fulfillment, and belonging for the Black man and the Black family.

Contrary to the popular portrayal of the Black woman at the margin, especially in the writings of Black women scholars and writers, Redmond problematizes and challenges the current notions of the engendering and endangering of women at the margin. Redmond places the Black woman not just at the center of the power problem in America, but also at the center of his projected solution to the human problem. Though frustrated in his constant aborted struggle to win her over and transform and transcend her powers to complement his own ultimate empowerment in a society where he has been dehumanized, the poet makes two abiding resolutions: he will neither resort to the all-too-common misogynistic tendencies, nor wallow in self-pity and self-hatred, all of which are lethal to his life and purpose. Redmond, instead, proposes his anthem of love between the Black man and the Black woman as the healing balm and therapy to seal the cracks in their relationship, family, and race. The poet reaffirms and resounds his commitment in the poem "I Can Never Unlove You":

> To *not want*
> is to *not exist*

Is to be de-minded
Is to be disembodied
Is to be disempersoned
And float like an apparition
Into the non-where
Into the grey whim of limbo
And that is why I can never unlove you.
(*The Eye*, 125)

What is particularly refreshing here is the dogged commitment to love woman in spite of the problematics of the relationship. The man is determined to break the jinx and cross the impeding boundary between him and her, even though he is painfully aware of the sagacious experiences as expressed in "In Love, in Terror," "Love as Enigma: Eye," and "Love as Gnaw" (*The Eye*, 123, 139). And though he approaches love with trepidation, he still believes in the power of the Black woman, intractable as she may seem, and also in the redeeming power of love to heal and mend the sore wounds between him and the Black woman. The insatiable sexual appetite for the Black woman is no longer just physical but a symbolic call for union and harmony and needing urgent, lasting response. Though sometimes he experiences temporary palliatives or relief through sex, this is merely superficial, and the echoes of need for profound and lasting answers intensify into a burning quest, until provoked into a scream: "I am still on fire" / The flames in my veins and heart / Boil blood and burn hissing-hot" (*The Eye*, 62).

Response is urgently being awaited and the uncanny silence accompanying the call, far from closing the door to answer, paradoxically, amplifies the anguish while he anticipates response. And so even at this stage, an antiphonal rhythm, or the call-and-response pattern so typical of African folk tradition and music, is slowly developing in Redmond's poetry. A duet is implied, though the voice of woman, now physically inaudible, invigorates the other with its mysterious powers. This antiphonal rhythm progressively rises into a crescendo and later transforms into the peculiar canons and aesthetics of *Drumvoices, Jazzography*, and *Songs from an Afro/Phone*.

We note the significance of the Drumvoices as trope for unlocking the text and aesthetics of Redmond's poetry. We note too the importance of the Drumvoices in forging a dialectic between the disparate self and the other; between the African and the diaspora. In addition to our earlier observation, we note the importance of Drumvoices in underscoring the artistic message and purpose—that of transcending limitations and failures through courage and heroism and renewed faith in the self and the other. And the Drumvoices suggest a confluence or fusion of voices and peoples. In the interplay, the Black man and the Black woman must be the protagonists in this drama of reunion. They must form the foundation for renewal and reconstruction of the Black family within and without their domestic and ethnic boundaries.

Redmond therefore proposes an alternative vision of power by constructing a new paradigm in the gender relations between the Black male and the Black female in America and also between the African and the African American and other diaspora Blacks as a new vision of power, strength, and hope for the race. In particular, Redmond's poetry is unlike other African-American writings promoting the kind of discord that intensifies the already tenuous relationship between the Black male and the Black female. (See for example, the relationship between Celie and Mr.—in Alice Walker's *The Color Purple* together with one of the virulent reactions to this phenomenon in Ralph Wiley's "Purple with a Purpose" in *Why Black People Tend to Shout*.[8]) But the male voice in Redmond's poetry resolves neither to be embittered nor to be despondent, for he is committed to his dream of freedom and "chainless manhood" (*The Eye*, 121).

In Redmond's poetry, although sexual images abound giving the impression of promiscuity and lust on the part of the man, the sexual escapades also constitute an inevitable process in the poet's journey toward becoming and reaching his desired objective of union with his immediate other, woman, and through whom he can attain a broader, universal union with his universal Black community or family. It is for this reason that the would-be analyst of Redmond's poetry is best advised not to fall into the usual pitfall of feminist discourse in equating sex and female body with mere deification or objectification of woman. Indeed, with respect to Redmond's poetry, sex becomes symbolic, an archetypal passage on the crossroads to the union of opposites—man and woman, and Africa and the diaspora—as a necessary process in the rebirth and reconstruction of the Black psyche, family, and race. (An alternative vision of sex and the body in this context is that they serve as the medium for light, awakening, and the creative liberation of the poet's imagination and consciousness.)

Because the Black woman provides the seeker with the liminal base, opening up the vital, luminous space both for the interjection and projection of his dream of union, she typifies the vicarious, transitory medium or passage for the traveler. It is no wonder, then, that for the Black man to cross the impeding boundaries and enter into the desired stable, harmonious realm of being, he must continue to forge ahead, to undertake the necessary encounters with woman in spite of his incessant failures, frustrations, tensions and conflicts at the threshold of transition. This forms the basis of the poems "In the Fleshflame That Is Her Face" and "Not Rejection: But Complex and Painful Truth" (*The Eye*, 115), "Double Clutch Lover" (141), "On Again, Off Again" (143), "Passion Giant" (148), "Jam Battle" (157), and "Request (if it is not asking too much)" (171).

Of the poems that revisit the poet's tumultuous journeys and struggles of identity and unity through love and women, the most seminal to the concept is "Lady: A Love Named Freedom":

> Freedom
> Last night
> I crept from my cage of color

/the prison of my past/
And made love
To a lady named *Freedom*
She was countless
And, almost, mountless—but I made it!
Made her:
Achieved that voluptuous summit,
Then rode her vertical luxury:
Where I, in birthday nakedness,
Diluted my chant with prayer . . .
   And Aretha appeared in Goddess-Glare
   And Angela came as Lordess of Love
   Roberta with "quiet-fire" to scorch me on, on
   Sojourner appearing with a proclamation of my manhood
Inside a web of *blood-lines*
Inside a fire of *new-youth*—
Inside a flame that licks my testicles
And tells me to leap the roof
Of Chance and mount the charcoal queen . . .
(*The Eye*, 113–4)

In reading between the lines of this intercourse, the significant event for the
man is not that he had sex and made love to a woman. What is memorable and
important for him is the inspirational, liberating force and spiritual empowerment he achieves in the liminal and seminal passage. The intercourse with
woman becomes a journey of rebirth and emancipation, not just from his "cage
of color," but from the shackles of social, cultural, economic, and political
impotence. The man is born again, a *new-youth* with a new self-image, self-
possessed and awakened to cross the boundaries of fear, race, gender, and class
in order to reaffirm his dignity and identity. The result for him is an epiphany.
In the end, he has crossed the threshold and attained wholeness.

In order to underscore the metaphysical importance of this encounter, the poet
stresses the journey motif with the nuances of struggle. Sex becomes a mock
battle as he "draft," "rode," "straddled," and "stretched out" until he became
whole both personally and spiritually. In the complex process of search, the poet
rereads the accepted signs and truths and questions reality to enable him to
redefine and reconstruct his knowledge, his being, and his bearing.

These are fundamental processes in his mission and vision of a new order:
hence, the triumphant cry of joy at the height of ecstasy climatized with the
evocation of names of powerful, Black women who have left unique marks in
the imprints of American or world music or politics, in Civil Rights Movements,
and in emancipation of Black people from slavery. Each of these women, Aretha
(Franklin), Angela (Davis), Roberta (Flack), and Sojourner (Truth) has in her
own unique way contributed and inspired the liberation of the creative energies
and spirits of Black folks. The poet not only alludes to them with passion,

familiarity, and fondness, he evokes them as divinities: "And Aretha appeared in Goddess-Glare / and Angela came as Lordess of Love / Roberta with 'quiet-fire' [like the holy spirit] / Sojourner appearing with a proclamation of my manhood." The allusion here points to the Black woman as path, vehicle, and channel of liberation; hence, the fondness, adoration, and worship of woman. The man becomes the symbolic rider, whose power of winning is enormously vested in the willing power and spirit of the horse. Without the horse, he is metaphorically impotent; hence, his victory chant as he experiences new realms of power.

As in African folk-play, a dance of courtship begins with the man being transfigured by the mysterious power of the goddess, his "charcoal queen." In this state of elation and enchantment, he feels himself becoming a man again, discovering his voice and going into a ritual celebratory chant of her prowess and her exotic blackness that is her beauty. He no longer hears his lone voice bouncing back and forth. A rhythmic pattern of call and response, which Redmond uniquely names "the Drumvoices," has now evolved and is being enacted in this fusion of opposites:

> Where I, in birthday nakedness,
> Diluted my chant with prayer:
> Where the wind made of me a rocking-chair
> /back-and-forth: back-and-forth/ . . .
> (*The Eye*, 113–14)

The Drumvoices become the cumulative congregation and linkages of all the audible, eloquent, and silent voices, here and there, past, present, and future. In Redmond's poetry, this drum is not just a physical instrument, it is empowered with the speaking voice of a persona. Enunciating the principles of the African drum, Ruth Finnegan states that "the instruments communicate through direct representation of spoken language itself, stimulating the tone and rhythm of actual speech."[9] Below, we will explore in detail the character of the drum in Redmond's poetry.

THE CHARACTER OF THE DRUM IN REDMOND'S POETRY

In Redmond's poetry, the Drum persona cracks the walls of silence, shifting in time and space to play mediative, subversive, and persuasive, as well as ritualistic, celebrative roles. The various roles that must be played also call for changes, transformations, and modulations of mood and tone so that the poet and this drum persona grow accordingly. In the first stage of groping and uncertainly, the drum wears the face of darkness and night. In the second phase, marked by the throes of transition and the Middle Passage, the drum persona adopts the archetypal image of the West African trickster-god Esu or Uke, and it is in light of these configurations that the drums must take center stage in the discourse on Redmond's poetry.

Having discovered the unmistakable powers of the drums to "signify" and "songify," Redmond adopts the drum motif for constructing meaning in his life, poetry, and scholarship. For example, his critical study is titled *The Mission of Afro-American Poetry, DRUM VOICES: A Critical History*. He is the current editor of the St. Louis-based journal *Drumvoices Revue*, his own brainchild, which is intended to serve as a critical space for putting Black scholars and creative artists on center stage to dialogue on issues of mutual interest to their world and race.

Above all, Redmond's adopted African name is Ilu Gan Gan (the Yoruba gangan drum). Ishmael Reed acknowledges this factor in his contribution to the dust jacket blurb of Redmond's *The Eye in the Ceiling: Selected Poems*, which won the 1993 American Book Award for poetry: "Eugene Redmond (Ilu Gan Gan) has not only maintained the tones of the Yoruba language in his poetry, but has also maintained the role of worker and healer." The drum is not only a vehicle for transmitting messages in Redmond's poetry, it has become transformed into an interpretative and a mediative persona imbued with the power and aura of connecting distances, especially between the man and woman of African descent.

In a recent interview, Redmond demonstrated his avowed dedication to African drum language and to the tradition of Oriki (in Yorubaland), Itu-Afa (in Igboland), and Izibongo (in Zululand), where the polyrhythmic powers of the drums are often evoked in political, social, ritual, and religious occasions to celebrate, praise, criticize, and divine action and meaning within the context of the performance. Concerning the origin and power of the drums in his poetry, Redmond resorts to drum/praise chant in speaking thus to this critic about Catherine Durham: "my mother to whom I owe so much debt I cannot repay . . . Catherine Durham, my mother who opened up my insights and ears to the enduring powers of the drums."

In that 1993 interview, Redmond emphasized his fascination with "the multiple powers of the drum" and his desire to capture "the polyrhythms of every pageant of the peoples of African extraction." Thus, the drum constitutes a vital link in the continuing "liminal crossroads of culture contact and ensuing difference at which Africa meets Afro-America."[10] In Redmond's poetry, the drum-persona at times plays the role of griot/historian. For example, in the poem "River of Bones and Flesh and Blood," the Mississippi river takes on the image of the ancient mother and Black woman who must bear the womb and burden of the race in spite of her own pain. Despite constant adversities, she thrives with exceptional resilience, dignity, and courage. She is therefore praised for being the "River of time/Vibrant vein/Bent, crooked,/ . . . Ancient as the winds/ that break on your/Serene and shining face;/ . . . River truth" (*The Eye*, 37).

Redmond's association of the river with qualities of Black womanhood and motherhood is noteworthy as he underscores the metaphysical and symbolic signs and meanings of love and womanhood. The drum-persona functions as a lead character, combining the past and the present to provide a synthesis of values as guide and continuity for the race. However, recalling, reinterpreting, and revisioning have their own peculiar pain of memory, fear, and hope. It is in this light that the persona could also be considered as a tragic hero caught in the dilemma of forging order out of the chaos of existence at the crossroads. To reinforce this anguish, the setting of most of Redmond's poetry takes on the face of night and harrowing darkness.

The problem is how the wandering "traveler" can find the voice to tell the story and transcend his condition without being annihilated or submerged forever. Redmond invents the polyvalent voices and polyrhythmic idioms of the drum and its persona to mediate between the self and the other; between man and woman; between the past and the present; between Africa and the diaspora.

For the effective reconstruction of the conflicting signs on the road, impersonation becomes imperative; hence, the Drum persona becomes the trickster-god, whom Henry Louis Gates reconstructs as the figure of "the Signifying Monkey" in his text of the same name.[11] I would suggest that Redmond's adaptation of the African trickster-figure/god has significant implications for our rereading of *Drumvoices*. Apart from the multivalent impact of the music and "double-voicing," the drumvoices function as a linguistic shield to insulate the vulnerable artist from the reprieve of oppressive, racist systems that must be outwitted and transcended.

However, it is on the score of sexuality that Redmond's Drum persona bears close resemblance to the trickster figure, and, in this regard, he reintegrates the signs of the body, sex and love, especially as they concern the Black woman. Once the trickster figure assumes the mediative role, the anguished voice of the seeker that is "still on fire" (*The Eye*, 62) is replaced with the triumphant voice of the initiate who has crossed boundaries and arrived at the desired goal of reaching the other, the community and the race. The resulting linkage does not only empower, but inculcates within the Black race a chorus of drumvoices, singing their distinctive "Songs from an Afro/phone." For Redmond, love signifies and reinscribes idioms of Pan-Africanism, Afrocentricism and Cultural Renaissance for the renewal and linking of the ties that bind the Black race through man and woman.

Reaffirming this new experience of union in the poem "Lady, A Love Named Freedom," the persona admits, "incestuously [I] succumbed to my Siamese twin" (*The Eye*, 114). Redmond's creed of love should be seen as a new trend in the right direction to bridge the widening gap created in the black male-female relationship as a result of the increasing emphasis on feminism and female emancipation. His vision of love is decidedly inclusive and integrative so that the race may survive. Hence, the poet pays homage to womanhood and motherhood. His Mother-Africa is the source of embodiment of freedom and the divine spirit of procreativity, like the Earth-Mother herself who is the source, the end, and the beginning of all human seed and growth.

The poet unequivocally adapts the African myth/tradition of elevating and assigning motherhood a realm of sacredness and supremacy. Just as the Igbo folklore states that "Nneka, Mother is Gold or Mother is Supreme," Redmond eulogizes his grandmother, constantly speaking of her in superlative terms as his "grandwise grandmother." He recalls in particular his deprived and depraved formative years down below in the ghetto of East St. Louis.

It is his grandmother who nurtured him as a child, who gave him strength, who planted in him the seed of love as an essential healing balm for the self, the Black family and the race. Indeed, she laid the foundation for Redmond's ideology, religion, and politics of love, which have come to distinguish his writing in later life. This is why he can speak of love "As Upbringing" (*The Eye*, 120), with all the attendant emphasis of the upliftment and the salutary effects.

In some measure, the images of benevolent but strong women shaped Redmond's Pan-African and Afrocentric ideology as he painfully but proudly recalls:

> My love grew/from a seed/Draped in a tear poised
> in my grand/mother's eye . . .
> In the vision of cotton-dresses
> In my tattered totems of hope
> My grandwise grandmother
> My love grew from blisters
> My love grew from sore rumps.
> (*The Eye*, 121)

The above eulogy brings to mind the African Camara Laye's celebration of his mother, motherhood, and family in *The Dark Child* (1954). Unlike other contemporary writers of African descent, Redmond's consciousness and commitment to Africa is exceptionally strong, bold, and unique, especially in these times when Africa is stigmatized, unfashionable, and threatened by the wave of new technologies and the new world order dictated by and constructed upon the Western model.

In his long search for identity and unity, Redmond affirms a mission and his commitment to achieving it. Although the poet is unsure of actual directions at the beginning, a recognizable pattern emerges as his vision evolves, revealing three major landmarks from which the stages of growth of consciousness could be measured and analyzed. The first stage is defined by darkness marked by indecision. In just one anthology, *The Eye*, the number of poems dedicated to the theme of uncertainty include "Last Night" (8), "City Night Storm" (43), "O! Where Has the Night Flown? O!" (111), and "Night Grows" (155), among others. There is the fear of his becoming permanently trapped in the endless body of the black woman. The urge progressively intensifies for him to cross this boundary of fear and to move toward the desired goal.

The second stage of the search is marked by the tensions and throes of transition affirmed through silence, double-talk, and the polyrhythms of a persona caught in the dilemma of double-consciousness until he finds "a voice" with adequate power to close up distances between the self and the other, to eliminate the current tensions between the dislocation and anguish of exile in the New World while inhabiting a mythological space that is distinctly African in the mind (see "Distance" in *The Eye*, 62).

In the final phase of the search, the verse, "distance Calls" (from "Distance," 53) repeatedly exerts response and action. Informed by a sensibility compellingly Afrocentric, the poet breaks from the jinx of being at the threshold and captures the idiom of the African drums as an enduring agency and instrument for bridging distances and establishing communication. This is the stage of epiphany. From now on, Redmond speaks confidently of *Drumvoices*, distilling and blending African essences with the American and thus producing a peculiarly African-American accent and sensibility that could be identified as *Songs from an Afro/Phone*. His is an anthem of love for Black people. Although he may not have been the first or the only Black poet to write about love or to forge an aesthetic out of the language of the African drums, Redmond has been exceptional and particularly intense in the power he ascribes to the drum, which he builds into a multidimensional persona in his poetry.

NOTES

1. Quote is from this critic's interview with Eugene Redmond, February 17, 1993, East St. Louis, Missouri.

2. Bernard Magubane, *Ties that Bind: African-American Consciousness of Africa* (Trenton, N.J.: Africa World Press, 1987).

3. W.E.B. Du Bois, *The Souls of Black Folk* (New York: Fawcett, 1965).

4. Asante, *African Culture: The Rhythms of Unity* (Trenton, N.J.: Africa World Press, 1990), 3–12.

5. Eugene Redmond, *The Mission of Afro-American Poetry: Drumvoices, A Critical History* (New York: Anchor Books, 1976). Redmond also makes reference to *Drumvoices* in his four books of poems, published by Black River Press, East St. Louis, Mo.: *Songs from an Afro/phone* (1968); *Sentry of the Four Golden Pillars* (1970); *River of Bones and Flesh and Blood* (1971); *In a Time of Rain and Desire* (1973).

6. Eugene Redmond, *The Eye in the Ceiling: Selected Poems* (New York: Harlem River Press, 1991), 63–64.

7. Von Washington, "The Operation," in *Roots and Blossoms: African American Plays for Today*, edited by Daphne Ntiri and Tess Onwueme (Detroit: Bedford Press, 1990), 563–608.

8. Alice Walker, *The Color Purple* (New York: Pocket Books, 1982).

9. Ruth Finnegan, *Oral Literature from Africa* (Nairobi: Oxford University Press, 1970), 481.

10. Henry Louis Gates, *The Signifying Monkey: A Theory of Afro-American Literary Criticism* (New York: Oxford University Press, 1988), 4.

11. Ibid.

BIBLIOGRAPHY

Redmond, Eugene. *The Eye in the Ceiling: Selected Poems.* New York: Harlem River Press, 1991.

7

Branches of the Same Tree: African and African-American Poetry

TANURE OJAIDE

Studies of African-American literary works often draw attention to the African cultural and racial origin. Residues of African culture no doubt exist in Black America, and these apparently show in the creative expression. The indebtedness to African oral culture and folklore was a major feature of early African-American literature. The enslaved Africans in America had to adapt African tales and myths to their new environment. This influence extends through the Harlem Renaissance to contemporary African-American writings.

Henry Louis Gates, in *The Signifying Monkey*, sees the African trickster motif (the Yoruba variant in particular) mediated upon by the American environment in the works of Zora Neale Hurston, Ishmael Reed, and Alice Walker. John W. Roberts's *From Trickster to Badman* also treats the trickster motif in terms of Black folk heroes originating in Africa. Joseph E. Holloway has edited a collection of essays under the title *Africanism in American Culture*, some of which deal with folklore and other artistic expressions. These works, which use African folkloric motifs to interpret African-American literature, no doubt illuminate the works and deepen our understanding of the African-American literary tradition.

However, there seem to be other areas of comparison between African literature and African-American literature that go beyond cultural affinities per se. Even when culture is asserted, both modern Africans and African Americans are using the same strategies to negate absorption into a foreign culture. Thus, there are common experiences, arising from separate but related historical conditions, which bind American Blacks and Africans. Though Black America struggles against being absorbed into the Anglo-Saxon American mainstream in order to retain a Black identity, it is neither African nor American mainstream. Thus, African-American literature needs more than African culture and Western literary aesthetics to interpret it.

It is in this light that Sonia Sanchez's question "Are we not more than color and drums?" (84) is pertinent. Africans and African Americans share experiences that transcend color. I, therefore, want to do a comparative study of modern African and African-American poetry with a view to showing similarities in the works as a result of conditions prevailing in Africa as well as in Black America. Such conditions include poverty, self-assertion, and identity.

I am aware of the "great cultural differences between literatures which are produced by a Black minority in a rich and powerful white country and those produced by the Black majority population of an independent nation" (Ashcroft, Griffiths and Tiffin, 21). While "this is especially so since the latter nations are often still experiencing the residual effects of foreign domination in the political and economic spheres" (Ashcroft et al., 21), the institution of slavery has lasting effects on African-American consciousness. The postindependence status of Africa is comparable to the post-Emancipation of African Americans.

American Blacks have at various times established alliances with African peoples for reasons other than race. As Maulana Karenga puts it, "there are concrete bases for alliances among Third World peoples growing out of their situational similarity in that they are oppressed and exploited on the bases of race and class" (256). It is this "situational similarity" between Africans and African Americans that I want to explore in African-American poetry. African Americans may have a different geographical space—the United States of America—but they share the same consciousness with Africans culturally, historically, and in other ways. As I have indicated earlier, African peoples see the current phase of their history as mainly postindependence, which is analogous to the post–1862 Emancipation Proclamation, or, at best, the post–Civil Rights Act of 1964 for African Americans.

It is not only that Sonia Sanchez was influenced by the Nigerian Christopher Okigbo as in her "elegy," not only that an Ethiopian-owned African World Press published Sanchez's *Under a Soprano Sky*, not only that the poets I am going to discuss are Black, but that they all express an African consciousness in the American environment in their writings. Significantly, on the back of the front cover of Carolyn Rodgers's *Songs of a Black Bird*, published by Third World Press in Chicago (1969), there is a "statement of purpose" by the editors:

The Third World is a liberating concept for people of color, non-europeans—for Black people. That world has an ethos—a black aesthetic if u will—and it is the intent of Third World Press to capture that ethos, that black energy. We publish black . . . for Africans here . . . and Africans abroad.

"Third World" is used here to designate the conditions of Africa, not necessarily its race. However, the emphasis remains Africa and Africans.

I will discuss the poetry of Arna Bontemps, Sonia Sanchez, Carolyn Rodgers, and Audre Lorde as African-American works that express the same consciousness as in modern African poetry. The selection of these poets is based on the availability of their works despite the lack of adequate criticism of these works.

However, many of the qualities I find in their works may also be found in many other African-American poets.

Blacks in the United States face problems that most Africans faced and still face. Their culture is being absorbed by White/Western culture. In elementary schools, high schools, and colleges, Black works are not taught, or at best are taught from a Eurocentric perspective. For a long time, images of Tarzan and other negative myths about the Black person have made African Americans hate themselves for being Black. They were alienated from their African culture, which was presented by the mainstream as primitive. Since the introduction of Black Studies programs in universities in the late 1960s, some attempt has been made to recognize Black culture in the curriculum. The mainstream American culture is White Anglo-Saxon with Hellenistic roots. Many sensitive Blacks have to decolonize their minds like colonized peoples do because they suffer from cultural alienation.

The tension in Gabriel Okara's "Piano and Drums" is comparable to the "double consciousness" that W.E.B. Du Bois highlighted about American Blacks who are torn between remaining Black or getting integrated. African Americans, like the speaker of Okara's poem, are lost, wandering in the mystic rhythm "of jungle drums and the concerto" (*The Fisherman's Invocation*, 20). The same sentiments of conflict of cultures and the need to maintain an African identity is present in Okot p'Bitek's *Song of Lawino*. For American Blacks who want to be their Black selves, resisting White culture leads to cultural assertiveness and liberation.

Since poets generally are cultural standard-bearers of their people, it is not surprising that cultural assertiveness is a predominant preoccupation in African-American poetry. Cultural assertiveness manifests itself in many ways. In no periods has cultural nationalism been so important in African-American literature as in the Harlem Renaissance and the Civil Rights years of the late 1960s and the early 1970s. It is significant that all four poets being discussed here belong to these literary movements: Arna Bontemps was a major figure of the Harlem Renaissance; Carolyn Rodgers, Sonia Sanchez, and Audre Lorde all lived through the Civil Rights Movement period of Black Power. Both the Harlem Renaissance and the Black Power movement were protest periods in which African Americans asserted their Black identity so as not to be absorbed into the White monolith.

Some of the works of the Harlem Renaissance period compare in their protest and cultural assertiveness with Negritude works. In Arna Bontemps's *Personals*, the poet identifies himself as a Black man who is different from the mainstream American. In Bontemps's poem "God Give To Men" (11), there are the yellow men, the blue-eyed men and, particularly, the Black men, whose need for laughter the poet wants God to fulfill. He also prays that the Black man's "cup of tears" be filled afresh, that is, replaced with waters of joy. The poet thus carves a unique identity for Blacks as opposed to other peoples. This identity is based upon the Black race's horrible experiences. In "The Return" (12), Bontemps recollects traditional Africa on a rainy night. Darkness brings "the jungle to our room," as well as the sounds of muffled drums. According to the poet, this is a night of love, a reminder of those nights lived by the African ancestors in their huts. Bontemps emphasizes the role of drums as symbol of a heritage that must not die. Thus, the message of the drum continues to pound on the ears of the diasporan Black.

Throughout the poem, Bontemps passionately evokes images of traditional Africa from which the forebears of African Americans were taken into slavery. His call for a return to the ways of "our fathers" reminds one of the Senegalese Negritude poet Léopold-Sédar Senghor's expression of similar emotions in, among others, "In Memoriam" and "Night of Sine."[1] In both Bontemps and Senghor, there is an idyllic picture of Africa that is generally romanticized. Bontemps's racial consciousness and cultural assertiveness, similar to that of colleagues of the Harlem Renaissance such as Claude McKay and Langston Hughes (see chapters on these writers in this volume), must be specifically understood in light of racial discrimination in America, which has continued a century after Emancipation and decades after different Civil Rights Acts were enacted. In other words, as Africans try to assert themselves culturally and politically after colonialism, so do African Americans after regaining their freedom.

Carolyn Rodgers, who lived through the Civil Rights/Black Power movements, uses her 1975 poetry collection, *how i got ovah*, to affirm her Black heritage as an essential aspect of "the revolution." The poet insists that we must build Black institutions where Black children will call each other sister and brother, where they will be able to grow strong, live, and express their beauty and grace (66).

The Black Power movement made Blacks understand their culture and cultivate pride in their African heritage. Another poet, Audre Lorde, who represents a unique link between Africa and America because of her immediate Caribbean ancestry, defines her blackness in relation to Africa in her collection *Our Dead Behind Us*. There, she alludes to Yoruba and Fon myths of West Africa, the ancestral home of the majority of slaves taken to the diaspora. She defines her gender in terms of African history and folklore as she takes the Amazons, African women warriors of fame, as her ancestors and mentors. In *From a Land Where Other People Live*, Lorde treats the theme of cultural identity in both "Black Mother Woman" and "the Winds of Orisha," among other poems. While identity is a complex issue in Lorde, due to the fact that she is not only Black but also a woman and a lesbian, she continuously harps on her Caribbean and African roots that give her an anchor in the American sea of cultures.

In "Call," the poet invokes Aido Hwedo, symbol of the female warrior and mother:

and I believe in the holy ghost
mother

in your flames beyond our vision
blown light through the fingers of women
enduring warring.
(*Our Dead Behind Us*, 74)

Invocation is a common feature of modern African poetry as shown, for example, in Christopher Okigbo's invocation of "Mother Idoto" in *Labyrinths*
(1971); Wole Soyinka the Nobel laureate's invocation of Ogun in "O Roots!"
(*A Shuttle in the Crypt*, 1971), and this critic-poet's invocation of Aridon in *The
Fate of Vultures* (1990). As African writers take a stand against colonialism,
neocolonialism and other assimilationist tendencies, so do African-American
writers warn against assimilation into the Anglo-Saxon, White-dominated culture. Indeed, according to certain African and Caribbean writers and critics (the
example of the Negritude poet Aimé Césaire immediately comes to mind), the
African American's condition can easily be categorized as a colonial one. This
opinion is quite compelling because it takes into consideration not only the
cultural but also the political and economic realities of this overtly exploited
group.

The history of African Americans is inextricably linked to that of Africans.
As African literature, for instance, reflects African history, so does African-
American literature reflect Black history. Slavery is the ultimate form of domination. The Emancipation Proclamation of 1862 can be compared to the
political independence of African countries that were once colonized. As African
Americans have continued to fight for their rights as free citizens, so do most
Africans fight for freedom and rights even after achieving political independence
in their own countries. It is understandable why African Americans have had
coalitions with African peoples, supported independence movements, and demonstrated an anti-colonial perspective. As an oppressed people who are discriminated against, African Americans have used poetry as a weapon to fight for
freedom. What Evangelista says of Third World literature is true of both African
and African-American literatures in being "history-based, . . . often political and
it *does* carry a call to action" (6).

There is no doubt that much of African-American poetry is political. All four
poets under discussion are political in their expression of the historical experience of Black Americans. Arna Bontemps in "A black man talks of reaping"
expresses the hard labor heritage of Blacks and their exploitation from days of
slavery. Though the poet uses a personal voice, he is expressing the general
Black experience when he says that "my heart has known its winters and carried
gall" (*Personals*, 26). Here the poet is talking symbolically of the harsh Black
experience in America from slavery to his time. Similarly, Carolyn Rodgers
expresses the African-American historical experience in "Non-Poem," published in the collection *Songs of a Black Bird*. Rodgers exhorts fellow Blacks
to "keep on pushin." It is significant that this collection is dedicated to "Love,

Truth, Organization, Discipline and Liberation.'' This shows the decidedly committed philosophy of the poet.

In fact, the Black Art movement of the 1960s influenced both Rodgers and Sanchez. A good number of their poems express protest and Black nationalism in the manner of African writers in colonial and postcolonial times. Sanchez's "Letter to Dr. Martin Luther King," in *homegirls & handgrenades*, is history-based. Sanchez has always been a political poet. In the collection *Home Coming*, "for unborn malcolms" poignantly expresses her radical politics, threatening retaliation ("stone/cold/death") against Whites for any further murders of Black "princes"; declaring categorically that "it is time" to meet violence with violence, to take an eye for an eye, a tooth for a tooth. The language is deliberately incendiary, the images are clearly defamatory of Whites as the poet, enraged, sneers at the White racist as a man without "balls" (28).

While the assassination of Malcolm X was the immediate inspiration of the above poem, the lines bear the entire history of the hostile relationship between Whites and Blacks in America. There is a Black/White conflict that pervades the whole landscape. The relationship is that of the master (White) lording it over his servant/slave (Black). The latter, fed up with his status of being exploited and dehumanized, is passionately calling for retaliation and redress.

The Black/White situation in the United States is in many ways comparable to the conflicts in Africa. In Africa, the conflict once arose out of the colonial experience which, in spite of political independence, has been replaced by, or rather continued in, neocolonialism.

As political scientists have rightly concluded, cultural and racial conflicts are linked to questions of economics, and the African example is proof enough. As the European master physically departed from the colony that attained independence, he was replaced by African leaders, patriots revered by their people who were expecting to be led immediately to a paradise of prosperity and everlasting happiness. Unfortunately, the patriots quickly proved to be selfish and self-centered, and all they did was to replace the former masters who became their allies. Such is the new conflict between these "haves" and "have-nots," a real euphemism for the political elite and the impoverished masses. And one cannot forget the tragic conflict of apartheid in which Africans living in their own land had no basic political rights.

One of the defining features of Africa today is poverty. There is economic and political exploitation on both local and international levels. Basic needs like food, health facilities, and education are not assured; the majority of African people lack basic needs. Many African poets, including Lenrie Peters, Jared Angira, Syl Cheney-Coker, Niyi Osundare, and this writer have expressed concern with the socioeconomic plight of the common people of Africa. Cheney-Coker's "Peasants," in his collection *The Graveyard*, and Angira's "Quiet oratorio," in *Cascades*, are strong indictments of the exploiting ruling class in Africa. Poverty is thus a major concern of African poets, who generally range on the side of the economically disadvantaged masses.

In the United States, the ghettoization of Blacks is a Third World phenomenon in the so-called First World. According to Karenga, the ghetto "not only closes Blacks in the community, but simultaneously shuts them out from the access and various opportunities available in the larger society." With the "general state of political and economic subordination . . . obvious and unarguable" (199), Black Americans suffer from many of the same problems as underdeveloped peoples in Africa. Poor Blacks are hungry and lack health insurance; many are homeless.

African-American poets, mindful of their economic background, write about the poverty of their people. Rodgers reflects on Black poverty in her family experience. In the third section of "For Our Father" in *how i got ovah*, she relates the death of her puppy, which, out of curiosity and what she calls stupidity (the stupidity of an animal), ate the poison that her mother had placed in the house invaded by rats. And the poet, devastated by her people's dead-end destiny, wonders whether the poison was really meant for the rat, or the dog, or "for us . . . the Black niggers caught in the dirty misery constrained ghetto?" (60).

Rodgers's experience is analogous to Arna Bontemps's "bitter fruit" (*Personals*, 36). In subject matter, Rodgers's preoccupation is not different from what many African poets write about, as in Cheney-Coker's "Peasants":

the agony of imagining their squalor but never knowing it
the agony of cramping them in roach infected shacks
(*The Graveyard*, 27)

The rat-infested house in Rodgers's poetry is a manifestation of the abject poverty in Black segments of the American society. As Cheney-Coker's lines show, there is a lot to share at both ends of the Black continuum. African-American poets reflect an experience that Africans also know firsthand.

As a result of the shared experience of history, there is the expression of solidarity and kinship with others who suffer a similar plight of oppression and deprivation. This solidarity is on two levels: internal and external. African Americans express a strong sense of kinship in their common culture and history and also express solidarity with others outside the United States, especially Africans. Sonia Sanchez's "Africa Poem No. 4," in *Under a Soprano Sky*, expresses solidarity with Africa despite the continent's problems. It is because of this shared experience and sense of solidarity that the Kenyan writer Ngugi wa Thiong'o says of Sonia Sanchez:

In her writings I feel at home! In her house I feel at home! In her presence I feel at home! (back cover of *Under a Soprano Sky*)

Audre Lorde also expresses solidarity and kinship with people of Africa and Caribbean people of African descent. Some of her poems talk of the situation in South Africa. Much of African-American poetry expresses a plea for unity and solidarity and the determination to eliminate the injustice against minority groups in America and other oppressed peoples of the world as well as in Africa. African-American literature is history-based as is the experience as a group. The odyssey from slavery through Emancipation and the Civil Rights Movement to the continuing struggle against discrimination is reflected in the poetry.

In the activist role of the African-American poet, he or she becomes a preacher and teacher to instill confidence and faith in the people. Unlike mainstream American poetry, which generally could pass for art for art's sake, African-American poetry is utilitarian and didactic like modern African poetry. There is a call for the human spirit to overcome all difficulties. Reading through most African-American poets of the 1920s, 1930s, 1960s, and 1970s—of the Harlem Renaissance and the Black Power/Black Art movements—is like reading a war cry for cultural, social, and political unity. Claude McKay's "If We Must Die" and Amiri Baraka's "Black Art" are exhortations to Black people in America to resist being victimized by taking actions towards that effect. The title of one of Sanchez's poems, "Masks" (*Under a Soprano Sky*, 28), is itself a symbol of an African identity. This poem treats the same theme as Senghor's poem of the same title. Thus, like African literature, African-American poetry is more community and people-oriented. The poets are like priests and teachers of their people, whom they appeal to for a change in consciousness to act for their group survival.

A common feature of African literature is the moral uprightness of the people in contrast to the immorality and amorality of their colonial exploiters and, later, of the indigenous ruling class. Francophone Negritude writers (for example, Senghor and David Diop) and their Anglophone counterparts (Okot p'Bitek in *Song of Lawino*) present "native values" as superior to the debauched imperialist ones.

In the United States, the White enslavers of Africans bear the guilt of imperialists. African Americans are quick to remind Whites of the travesty of slavery. Arna Bontemps reflects the moral outrage of a spiritual people against an oppressive, godless group. His poem "Southern Mansion" deals with the contrast between the White slave-master and the tortured slave. There is a contrast between the sound of music in the master's house and the sound of chains of bondmen in the cotton field (*Personals*, 16).

Audre Lorde's "Equal Opportunity" satirizes the American system represented by the deputy assistant secretary of defense and American troops in Grenada. Lorde criticizes the militaristic ruling elite in Washington, D.C., in the same manner as many African poets satirize their morally bankrupt governments. In general, African Americans lament the fact that, their long presence in America notwithstanding, they have been relegated to the verge of society.

A further aspect of Africanity in African-American poetry is the style and use of language. As indigenous languages inform the English in Achebe and Soyinka of Nigeria, so do Africanisms inform the African-American variety of

English. Further, many African poets use pidgin English, a blend of African language patterns and English. Mainstream English is probably as much a second language in the African-American community as it is in Africa. The black dialect has its own prosody and semantic register. Popular terms such as "bad" and "dead" show how standard American English has been turned around by African Americans. Folk style is used to reach the largest audience, and, similar to African poets, African-American writers have given English a new freshness and vigor.

Carolyn Rodgers's poetry collection *how i got ovah* is an excellent example of this particular usage of English. Sonia Sanchez's "haiku" in *Under a Soprano Sky* (52) combines wit and humor. Her *We a BaddDDD People* (1970) uses black slang, which not only makes the poetry accessible to most African Americans sharing her experience but also identifies her unconventional attitude toward American society. She uses "BaddDDD" to mean "nice" and "good." At a different level, Audre Lorde uses English modeled on African language patterns. For instance, the incantatory "Call" ends with lines that carry African ritual language patterns. The poet subtly mentions the element of orality and communal apprenticeship in knowledge: one learns by heart things that have "never been taught" and the teachers are not simply individuals, but the ancestors, the deities with fire in their tongues, "Oya Seboulisa Mawu Afrekete":

> and now we are mourning our sisters
> lost to the false hush of sorrow
> to hardness and hatchets and childbirth
> and we are shouting ...
> Mother loosen my tongue.
> (*Our Dead Behind Us*, 74–75)

In this poem, Lorde brings together African and African-American women figures to underline their common origins and aspirations.

In conclusion, African-American poetry, as exemplified by Arna Bontemps, Sonia Sanchez, Carolyn Rodgers and Audre Lorde, shares common thematic and stylistic qualities with African poetry. The poetry is sociopolitically and culturally committed, with emphasis being placed upon the common bond with the disadvantaged Black community. From the experience of slavery, racism, and all forms of discrimination, these poets write militant verses. The experiential, historical, and linguistic aspects of African-American poetry are comparable to those of African poetry, given the shared racial and cultural origins. From the poetry of the Harlem Renaissance (Arna Bontemps) to that of the Civil Rights/Black Power/Black Art movements (Sanchez, Rodgers, and Lorde), we find immense proofs of this Africanity.

NOTE

1. See Ellen Conroy Kennedy, *The Negritude Poets* (New York: Thunder's Mouth Press, 1975), 130.

BIBLIOGRAPHY

Angira, Jared. *Cascades*. London: Longman, 1979.

Ashcroft, Bill, with Gareth Griffiths and Helen Tiffin. *The Empire Writes Back: Theory and Practice in Post-colonial Literatures*. London/New York: Routledge, 1989.

Bontemps, Arna. *Personals*. London: Paul Breman, 1973.

Cheney-Coker, Syl. *The Graveyard Also Has Teeth with Concerto for an Exile*. London: Heinemann, 1980.

Du Bois, W.E.B. *The Souls of Black Folk*. New York: Penguin, 1969.

Evangelista, Susan. "Third World Literature in the First World." Lecture in the English Department Lecture Series, University of Maiduguri (Nigeria), April 1989.

Gates, Henry Louis, Jr. *The Signifying Monkey: A Theory of Afro-American Literary Criticism*. New York/Oxford: Oxford University Press, 1988.

Holloway, Joseph E., ed. *Africanisms in American Culture*. Bloomington: Indiana University Press, 1991.

Karenga, Maulana. *Introduction to Black Studies*. Los Angeles: University of Sankore Press, 1989.

Lewis, David. *When Harlem Was in Vogue*. New York/Oxford: Oxford University Press, 1979.

Lorde, Audre. *From a Land Where Other People Live*. Detroit: Broadside Press, 1973.

———. *Our Dead Behind Us*. New York: Norton, 1986.

Okara, Gabriel. *The Fisherman's Invocation*. Benin, Nigeria: Ethiope Press, 1979.

p'Bitek, Okot. *Song of Lawino*. Nairobi: EAPH, 1966.

Randall, Dudley, ed. *Black Poets*. New York: Bantam, 1971.

Roberts, John W. *From Trickster to Badman: The Black Folk Hero in Slavery and Freedom*. Philadelphia: University of Pennsylvania Press, 1990.

Rodgers, Carolyn. *Songs of a Black Bird*. Chicago: Third World Press, 1969.

———. *how i got ovah; new and selected poems*. Garden City, N.Y.: Anchor, 1975.

Sanchez, Sonia. *homegirls & handgrenades*. New York: Thunder's Mouth Press, 1984.

———. *Under a Soprano Sky*. Trenton, N.J.: Africa World Press, 1987.

———. *We a BaddDDD People*. Detroit: Broadside Press, 1970.

8

Notions and Nuances: Africa in the Works of James Baldwin

EZENWA-OHAETO

The depiction of Africa in the works of African Americans has always constituted a problematic area for responses in the realm of both criticism and creative imagination. The African reader strives to identify the degree to which the work by the African American reflects and is inspired by Africa, while the African-American reader, on the other hand, would not want to be identified as positively responding to a work by an author who seems to be losing faith in the African continent and the African-American struggle.

The relationship between Africa and the African American has, therefore, been rightly observed to be "the subject of a continuing and often lively controversy among writers" (Furay, 32). The African-American writer James Baldwin has been involved in this controversy not only in terms of the time it took him to visit Africa but also in terms of the perception of Africa in his numerous writings. In 1961, when Baldwin was confronted with the fact that he had not visited Africa, he replied in a letter to his literary agent, which has been published as part of "Letters From a Journey," that once he visits Africa he would not "be able to dream anymore" (*Soon, One Morning*, 39). Michael Furay felt that Baldwin's hesitation to visit Africa might be connected with the disillusionment of Richard Wright after his visit, but he opined that "in any case, Baldwin knew he had to confront finally the reality of Africa; he was too honest to continue believing in the old dreams which he felt had assuaged but blinded Negro Americans" (32). That response by Baldwin to his literary agent is justification enough to examine his works closely for the perception of Africa and the depiction of that perception, which is the focus of this study.

James Baldwin was aware of the responsibility and burden of history on him as an African-American writer and also as an American writer. In a memorable meeting with the highly reputed Nigerian novelist Chinua Achebe, at the University of Florida in Gainesville during the African Literature Conference in 1980, Baldwin acknowledged that awareness when he stated that the African and African-American writers have "been divided. We have been dispersed, have been under the control of others for hundreds of years; and economically, and for the most part, politically we still are. One is engaged in an endeavor, which is nothing less than an excavation of a buried and denied history, a history never written down" (Hill-Lubin, 27). This literary excavation of history is linked with Baldwin's perception of Africa because the history of hundreds of years alluded to in that statement has its origin in Africa.

However, one of the early essays by Baldwin on his perception of Africa concerns his comments on the 1956 congress of Black writers in Paris. This essay, first published in *The Encounter*, was collected in the text *Notes of a Native Son* (1955) and, more recently, in *The Price of the Ticket*. The view of Baldwin in that essay shows his initial inability to grasp the essence of the predicament of the African. He describes the Africans as "people whose distrust of the West, however richly justified, also tends to make them dangerously blind and hasty," and he is convinced that a gulf yawns "between the American Negro and all other men of color" (*Price of the Ticket*, 44). At the same time, Baldwin prides himself in his knowledge of the West and his unique position as "the connecting link between Africa and the West" (45).

As a consequence of that attitude, Baldwin has been classified by the African critic Femi Ojo-Ade as a symbol of the Black burden. Ojo-Ade interpreted that Baldwin essay, which is entitled "Princes and Powers," as an illustration of Baldwin's superior attitude toward Africans:

Baldwin affirms that, in spite of their approximation to the West, the African elite remain lower than the American Negro on the ladder leading to civilized paradise. The United States, he states, is a free and open society, affording the Black far greater opportunities than elsewhere. The title of Baldwin's essay thus reveals its ironical and inimical underpinnings. Princes of the savage, mysterious land of Africa engaged in pointless discussions of non-existing power, such is the interpretation. (Ojo-Ade, 20)

It would appear as if that interpretation by Ojo-Ade is too severe, but quite often many of the habits formed and opinions expressed at the commencement of a significant stage of a writer's career prove difficult to dissociate from the corpus of the writer's subsequent products. This idea obviously accounts for the fact that Chinua Achebe has not heard the last concerning his sixties' essay on "The Novelist as a Teacher" (*New Statesman*, January 29, 1965, 161–62), or Wole Soyinka, on his alleged comment concerning the tiger proclaiming its tigritude (*American Scholar* 32, no. 3 [Summer 1963]: 387–96).

All the same, there appears to be a hazy intellectual zone separating the views expressed in fiction. The statements in the essays are definite, but the references to Africa in Baldwin's fiction can only be understood through interpretations that may vary. The African critic, Ezekiel (now Es'kia) Mphahlele, explains this problem when he notes the possibility of change dictated by education in a writer's autobiographical views. "The main reason why we do not find in fiction more intensive self-dramatization concerning Africa and an organic view of it is that the structure of the novel resists it. The best the novelist can do is portray a character's views of Africa" ("Notes from the Black American World," Part 5, 136–37). This limitation notwithstanding, Mphahlele advocates the necessity to keep asking ourselves questions about the writer's tone, feelings, level of consciousness, and meanings whenever he refers to Africa. According to Mphahlele, we must be particularly interested in how convincing the writer is in presenting his dream of Africa to his audience. "Does he feel it as an on-going quest, or is the image an easy way out of emotional and intellectual dilemma?" (Part 4, 113–14).

The analysis of the tone, the feelings, and the views of the characters as references to Africa are made are clearly discernible in James Baldwin's story "This Morning, This Evening, So Soon," one of eight stories in *Going to Meet the Man.* The protagonist is a successful African-American musician living in Paris. He is married to a White French woman, and they have a son known as Pauli. The story opens on the eve of the musician's departure to the United States. He goes on a night out with his producer, who is known as Vidal, and is reminded of his first experiences in Paris. He reminisces:

The Arab cafés are closed—those dark, acrid cafés in which I used to meet with them to drink tea, to get high on hashish, to listen to the obsessive, stringed music which has no relation to any beat, any time, that I have ever known. I once thought of the North Africans as my brothers and that is why I went to their cafés. They were very friendly to me. . . . They seemed to feel that they had every right to [Baldwin's shirts], since I could only have wrested these things from the world by cunning—it meant nothing to say that I had had no choice in the matter; perhaps I had wrested these things from the world by treason, by refusing to be identified with the misery of my people. Perhaps, indeed, I identified myself with those who were responsible for this misery. (*Going to Meet the Man*, 136–37)

The idea that the protagonist is emphasizing here is the problem of identification, which could be termed treason, and also that Africa is diverse, which is why the North African may be more Arabian than African in both culture and perception of reality. The desire of the protagonist to identify with those North Africans and his unacceptance by them makes him wonder. His musing "I once thought of the North Africans as my brothers" illustrates that the African American may not possess as much in common with the African of North Africa as with the West and East African. This incident also magnifies the diversity of Africa and James Baldwin's resentment of the fact that the North Africans find it difficult to identify with non-Arabs as brothers.

However, Baldwin further shows in that story that an understanding of the African American is linked to Africa. Although he did not specify how that understanding could be made, especially in terms of the processes involved, he emphasizes it in a dialogue between the African-American protagonist and his White producer, Vidal:

"And as for Pauli—did it ever occur to you that he might wish one day to see the country in which his father and his father's father was born?"
"To do that, really, he'd have to go to Africa."
"America will always mean more to him than Africa, you know that."
"I don't know. . . . why should he want to cross all that water just to be called a nigger: America never gave him anything."
"It gave him his father."
"You mean his father escaped." (147)

This dialogue illustrates several things, one of which is that Baldwin regards Africa as the root of understanding so long as there is a desire to understand the African American. However, he at the same time insists that the African American must come to terms with the reality of America, which is why the issue of racism is at the core of his works. Mphahlele explains this by saying that "Africa sharpens the sensitive Afro-American's awareness of his relation to the past and the extent to which his Americanness shares his psychological make up" (Part 5, 134). The sensitivity of Baldwin, which emerges in that short story, shows his resentment of the Arabianized North African and also his view that the real Africa is clearly the sub-Saharan zone.

Thus, the image of the North Africans that emerges, especially through Boona, the former boxer, is that they are dishonest and unreliable. The author shows that they identify with the Black race of Africa and elsewhere only when they seek to advance reasons for their misdemeanors. In this regard, Boona's explanation for his perceived dishonesty remains unconvincing, though he insists that he is being blamed because he is an African (*Going to Meet the Man*, 169). We recall that the author has already presented the North African as stealing from other Black people (including the African-American protagonist), which highlights the difference and contradictions between the view of brotherhood by the African American and other Africans on the one hand and the Arabianized North African and other Africans on the other hand.

It is clearly the result of such contradictions that we perceive instances of haziness in the perception of Africa in the works of James Baldwin. There is no doubt that he devoted a lot of time and energy battling racism in America; yet he found it disconcerting to fight the apparent aloofness he noted among his African acquaintances. Perhaps what Baldwin did not realize is that, ironically, the people and the establishment he had been fighting in America had surreptitiously colored his perception of reality. After all, his early opinions concerning even the state of affairs in America depicted by other African-American writers did not illustrate a unanimity of perception between him and those African Americans.

Early in his career, Baldwin had castigated Richard Wright for the slant of his writings, but his view changed as he came to grips with the complexity of the situation. A critic describes that transformation thus: "Even James Baldwin, one of the best writers of his generation, bought the assimilationist philosophy and proceeded to launch a brilliant literary attack against the works of Richard Wright in particular and all 'protest' literature in general." The critic further explained that, "he lived to regret it. He soon discovered as he found fame, that the same critics who had lavished praise on him for his assault on 'protest' literature now lumped his own works under that label. Mr. Baldwin doesn't talk about protest any more" (Fuller, 336).

That observation was made about the early works that could be used in assessing Baldwin's evolutionary perception of Africa, one of which is *The Devil Finds Work*. Despite its disquieting title, *The Devil Finds Work* is Baldwin's study of the Black man's role in the cinema. It is a comprehensive, but personal, interpretation. However, in the midst of this study, Baldwin refers to the Korean War and the forces sent to fight there. He makes a comparison between the sending of Black Americans to Korea and the dispersal of Africans out of Africa, which he labels "an incalculable investment of raw material in what was not yet known as the common market" (84). Thus, Baldwin is aware of the economic and political dimensions to the suffering of the Africans, which he perceives as a corollary of the suffering of the African Americans.

However, though *The Devil Finds Work*, in its brief reference to Africa, appears to indicate that Baldwin had become sensitive to the African reality, he had always expressed disenchantment with Africa. Indeed, in reading Baldwin, there is a certain confusion borne out of his status as one of the oppressed in America. For example, in *No Name in the Street* (1972), he makes a comparison between Africa and America in which he views Africa as a "benighted incompetent" society where, however, "I had never encountered an orphan: the American streets resembled nothing so much as one vast, howling, unprecedented orphanage" (185). Here the author is showing an underhanded appreciation of the age-old attachment to family and community in Africa. We should note at the same time that such appreciation does not lead to love for or desire to be close to the Africans; Baldwin does consider them inferior to him. He highlights their incompetence although, once again, he accuses the West of creating the problem by holding Africa in bondage through colonialism and imperialism.

I mean that in the case of Africa, Africa is still chained to Europe, and exploited by Europe, and Europe and America are chained together and as long as this is so, it is hard to speak of Africa except as a cradle and a potential. Not until the many millions of people on the continent of Africa control their land and their resources will the African personality flower or genuinely African institutions flourish and reveal Africa as she is. (*No Name in the Street*, 192–93)

It is clear from this passage that Baldwin was gradually coming to terms with the African reality and also that he had understood the nature of the exploitation that militated against development in Africa. It is, therefore, this understanding that changed the tone of his later works, as he began to perceive Africa from a sympathetic dimension.

It is clear that unfamiliarity contributed to Baldwin's early attitude toward Africa and his veiled contempt for the abnormal situation in that continent. It could also be stated that his early attitude was influenced by American culture, which surreptitiously attempted to denigrate other cultures in its bid to pronounce itself the prominent culture of the world. James Baldwin bought into the American Dream, while at the same time tried to live down its nightmare. It is the sensitivity emanating from this latter state that makes him relevant to the communal aspirations of the African American and the reality of the African.

The kind of dreams that flourished in the works of Baldwin are not the type he characterizes in *Another Country*, when he says that "the aim of the dreamer, after all, is merely to go on dreaming and not to be molested by the world. His dreams are his protection against the world. But the aims of life are antithetical to those of the dreamer, and the teeth of the world are sharp" (154). It could be inferred that these sharp teeth of the world that prevent the dreamer from merely dreaming in isolation are the problems of racism in America, which engaged much of Baldwin's talent as a writer. Thus, Baldwin even perceived the consequences of racism in America as more problematic than the political or cultural reality in Africa.

In his famous collection of essays *Nobody Knows My Name*, first published in 1961, he acknowledged that "it was clear that our relation to the mysterious continent of Africa would not be clarified until we had found some means of saying, to ourselves and to the world, more about the mysterious American continent than had ever been said before" (29). It is this preoccupation with the "mysterious American continent" that accounted for Baldwin's attention to Africa late in his career when he had used up much of his energy attacking American racism.

Perhaps James Baldwin, who no doubt possesses "great willingness to take on overt social issues" (Iloeje, 187), would have clarified that relationship between the African and the African American if he had come to terms early with his own personal predicament. But this "passionate, angry, but humane voice" (Dennis, 244) could not effectively subdue the racial issues that made him flee to France for his safety. This view that Baldwin's perception of Africa has a hazy dimension because of his dedication to fighting the overwhelming deficiencies of America is supported by Stanley Macebuh, who published a study of Baldwin in a bid to understand his "traumas of blackness."

In Macebuh's view, Baldwin has never been unduly impressed by theories of cultural survival, and only towards the end of his life did he seem to concede the possibility of a world view of blackness. Macebuh states that:

Baldwin appears quite early in his career to have made up his mind that a clear, definitive and irreversible rupture was established by the fact of slavery and the slave trade, and, consequently, the problem has been for him not one of re-establishing the black American's African ties . . . but of coming to terms with a condition that is at once immediate and permanent. ("Baldwin: The Traumas of Blackness," 9)

The consequence of this inability to lay claim to an African patrimony colored the portrayal of Africa in his writings. Although it may not be possible to assert as authoritatively as Stanley Macebuh that Baldwin conceives the historical reality of the African American as a rupture with Africa, it could be deciphered from his works that Africa was hazy in his scheme of things at the beginning.

However, the later statements Baldwin made concerning Africa, especially in terms of the general exploitation of the continent, enabled him to portray the links of suppressive attitudes that oppress both the African American and the African. It is this perception that ultimately makes Baldwin a writer who was not only important to the African-American reality but also to the African reality. His evolutionary development from an indifferent, somewhat negative attitude to a positive, sympathetic appraisal of the African reality, which may not have been acutely articulated, establishes him as an African-American writer relevant to the African reality. The oppression that he condemned in America could thus be seen as the same oppression manifested in Africa, but it is clear that "Baldwin preached that it was not only the oppressed who became delivered by the end of oppression; it was also perhaps especially—the oppressor himself" (Ndibe, 54).

In conclusion, Africa was real to Baldwin, but he did not conceive it as sensitively as he conceived his American heritage. This attitude clearly accounts for his lack of passionate fury in articulating the reality of that continent and also for his lack of sustained attention to the continent's predicament. However, his realization of that inadequacy towards the end of his career enabled him to make fairly distinct the evidence of the things he had seen concerning Africa.

BIBLIOGRAPHY

Baldwin, James. *Another Country*. London: Corgi Books, 1965.
———. *The Devil Finds Work*. London: Michael Joseph, 1976.
———. *Going to Meet the Man*. London: Corgi Books, 1976.
———. *Nobody Knows My Name*. London: Corgi Books, 1965.
———. *No Name in the Street*. New York: Dell Publishing Co., 1972.
———. *The Price of the Ticket: Collected Non-Fiction 1948–1985*. New York: St. Martins, 1985.
Dennis, Ferdi. "Baldwin's Unique Vision." *West Africa*, no. 3670 (December 14, 1987): 2445.
Fuller, W. Hoyt. "The New Black Literature: Protest or Affirmation." In *The Black Aesthetic*, edited by Addison Gaylie, Jr. New York: Anchor Books, 1972.
Furay, Michael. "Africa in Negro American Poetry to 1929." *African Literature Today*, nos. 1–4, combined volume 1972: 32–41.

Hill, Herbert, ed. *Soon One Morning: New Writings by American Negroes, 1940–1962.* New York: Knopf, 1963.

Hill-Lubin, Mildred. "Chinua Achebe and James Baldwin at the African Literature Association Conference in Gavinesville." *Okike,* no. 17 (1980): 1–5.

Iloeje, Azubuike. "The Dimensions of Captivity in James Baldwin's *If Beale Street Could Talk.*" In *Black Culture and Black Consciousness in Literature,* edited by E. N. Emenyonu. Ibadan, Nigeria: Heinemann, 1987.

Macebuh, Stanley. *James Baldwin: A Critical Study.* New York: Third Press, 1973.

———. "Baldwin: The Traumas of Blackness." *The Guardian* (Nigeria), December 12, 1987: 9.

Mphahlele, Ezekiel. "Notes from the Black American World, Part 4: +Images of Africa in Afro-American Literature." *Okike,* no. 10 (May 1976): 96–115.

———. "Notes from the Black American World, Part 5: Images of Africa in Afro-American Literature—Conclusion." *Okike,* no. 11 (November-December 1989): 54–155.

Ndibe, Okey. "Review of James Baldwin: The Legacy." *African Commentary* 1, no. 1 (October 1989): 54–55.

Ojo-Ade, Femi. "Black Burden, White Ways." *A.L.A. Bulletin* 14, no. 3 (Summer 1988): 17–23.

Troupe, Quincy, ed. *James Baldwin: The Legacy.* New York: Simon and Schuster, 1989.

9

Reviewing Gloria Naylor: Toward a Neo-African Critique

VINCENT O. ODAMTTEN

The biggest weapon wielded and actually daily unleashed by imperialism against [the] collective defiance [of the oppressed] is the cultural bomb. The effect of a cultural bomb . . . even plants serious doubts about the moral rightness of struggle. Possibilities of triumph or victory are seen as remote, ridiculous dreams.

—Ngugi wa Thiong'o
Decolonizing the Mind

The works of Gloria Naylor offer a peculiarly interesting challenge; because, rooted as they are in a decidedly African-American tradition, the distance between them and their African literary cousins may seem wider than the temporal and geographical separation of the Atlantic and the postpartum trauma of the Middle Passage. Yet, it is precisely this historical and cultural gap that must be reviewed if Naylor's "Authorial Dreams of Wholeness"[1] are to be appreciated in terms of a "parentage" that presupposes an extended family, rather than a nuclear one. This examination does not contest Michael Awkward's reading of Naylor's first work; rather, it seeks to explore a different path of literary inheritance that is carried, as it were, in the complex genetic code of Naylor's artistic creations. By looking at Naylor's first three novels—*The Women Of Brewster Place*, *Linden Hills*, and *Mama Day*—from this vantage point, I hope to contribute to the uncompleted critical project of, on the one hand, charting a Black reading that inhabits the text, even as it prevents a Eurocentric bias; and, on the other hand, placing these works with those of other writers from "writing communities that run parallel to it."[2]

One of those parallel writing communities is represented by African writers in general and African women writers in particular. Nevertheless, African criticism of Gloria Naylor's work is virtually nonexistent; it is primarily represented by Ebele Eko's article "Beyond the Myth of Confrontation: A Comparative

Study of African and African-American Female Protagonists."[3] Eko examines
the treatment of mother-daughter relationships as represented by four fictional
daughters. Of specific interest to this study are Anowa in Ama Ata Aidoo's play
Anowa and Kiswana Browne in Gloria Naylor's novel *The Women of Brewster
Place* (Eko, 139–40). Eko's essay reveals the similarities between Kiswana
Browne's "determination and commitment" and Anowa's "concern with the
'common pain and general good' " (147). Despite its brevity, the review does
point to the need for further investigations of works that overcome the effects
of imperialism and racism.

Michael Awkward's intertextual analysis of Naylor's first novel in relation to
Toni Morrison's *The Bluest Eye* (1970), Zora Neale Hurston's *Their Eyes Were
Watching God* (1937), Ntozake Shange's *for colored girls* (1976), and Jean
Toomer's *Cane* (1923), is excellent, because he grounds his examination on the
recognition of the historical and material contexts of each work. Thus, we understand Morrison's first novel to have arisen as a creative response to the
climate of the Civil Rights struggles of the sixties when the slogan "Black Is
Beautiful" was heard (Awkward, 108–9). What Awkward points to in his argument is analogous to the realization, on the African continent, that the formal
end of colonialism did not result in an egalitarian transformation of society. Just
as the post-independence writers in Africa recognized that their historical moment made it rather problematic to continue writing literature about the colonial
legacy and the clash of cultures in the pre-independence mode; so too, African-
American writers, like Naylor, began to focus their attention on the more immediate problems faced by African Americans in the post-Civil Rights and
Women's Rights era. Both on the continent and in the diaspora, this period has
been one of reassessment, of a long, hard look at the cold reality of African
and African-American life prefaced by the title question of Langston Hughes'
poem, "What happens to a dream deferred?," which Naylor uses as the epigraph
to *The Women of Brewster Place*.[4]

Naylor's first novel focuses on the lives of those African Americans who fell
through the cracks of the promised "Great Society." Ironically, the "Dawn,"
which is the title of the novel's prologue, describes the corruption that has
marked the birth of Brewster Place and briefly chronicles the various waves of
immigrants and wanderers who have tried to make this "bastard child of several
clandestine meetings" (1) a home. The prologue ends with a description of the
present inhabitants of the now walled-in street, "these multi-colored 'Afric'
children of its old age" who have little hope of escape, "because they had no
choice" (4). However, they, especially the women, worked as hard and were as
passionate as any of the former inhabitants of Brewster Place (4). Despite the
enormity of this knowledge, this seemingly premature termination of hope, the
women were not completely beaten into the gloom and anonymity of the gray
winter landscape, which signals the arrival of Mattie Michael to Brewster Place.

"Like an ebony phoenix, each in her own time and with her own season had
a story" (5) to tell us. Naylor's prologue, with its final declaration of the in-

evitability of each woman's need and ability to tell her own "story," recalls the opening prologues of Ama Ata Aidoo's *The Dilemma of A Ghost* and *Anowa*.[5] The story of Mattie Michael, framed by the images of a depressing winter evening, opens the body of the novel. This narrative strategy emphasizes the difference between what Mattie has left behind (4), while simultaneously indicating that, despite her memories of those seemingly benign times (8), Mattie's condition has not been radically altered. This recalls the situations described by Aidoo of the betrayal of the hopes for meaningful change, in her collection of short stories *No Sweetness Here*.[6] Similarly, both Naylor and Aidoo avoid direct mention of the White colonizers' role in creating the conditions in which their characters have their existence. That is to say, both writers are concerned with and depict why "the myth . . . lives on—even among black [people]"[7] and how, in the midst of such demoralizing conditions, many of their characters "maintain their defiance . . . against . . . the cultural bomb."[8]

In the same manner that Naylor's first novel explores the why and the how of the continued "defiance" in this cul-de-sac of the American Dream deferred, so the stories of the seven women of Brewster Place should not be seen as being bound, primarily, by the theme of misogyny.[9] The evidence of Naylor's care, insightful wit, and seriousness suggests that the canvas upon which these lives are drawn is larger, more complex than that implied by a narrow revisioning of patriarchal stereotypes of Black women. Some of Naylor's concerns, briefly outlined in "The Myth of the Matriarch,"[10] should give us reason to pause and reflect upon the interdependent and conflictual individual, familial, and social traumas depicted in *The Women of Brewster Place*. Similarly, Aidoo, in a 1985 article, resists the tendency to place in hierarchical categories the particular concerns of a (Black) woman writer:

Whatever gender, whatever nationality we belong to: we must also resist any attempts at being persuaded to think that the woman question has to be *superseded* by the struggle against any . . . exploitative system. . . . *For what is becoming clear is that in the long run, none of these fronts is either of greater relevance than the rest or even separate from them.*[11]

Naylor's novel is about how these women respond to their desperate lives, even as they are implicated by acts of omission and commission in a world system that seeks "to annihilate . . . belief in their names, in their languages, in their environment, in their heritage of struggle, in their unity, in their capacities and ultimately in themselves" (Ngugi, 3).

Mattie Michael is forced to begin "her long, winding journey to Brewster" (8) because, like her modern-day sisters in the poverty-stricken inner cities, she had not learned how to defend herself against the seductive talk of the world's Butch Fullers. Furthermore, the limited horizons of an impoverished South were not the best environment for creating lasting and supportive family units, especially for the Michaels. Samuel Michael, Mattie's father, was a man of very few words (19) and so did not know how to respond to the knowledge of his daughter's pregnancy, except in a blind rage. Naylor expertly sketches the contours of the assumptions that have molded this man. His possessiveness was not only restrictive of his daughter's maturation, but contributed in no small measure to her subsequent fall (21).

Samuel Michael's words echo throughout the novel with ironic intensity, insinuating themselves not only into Mattie's relationship with her son, Basil, but also other relationships, in which one partner's sense of what is "fit" for the other results in disaster. Samuel Michael's desire to see no fault in his daughter releases a similar desire in Mattie. She becomes overprotective of Basil, constantly making excuses for his immaturity, until his recklessness lands him in jail. Ultimately, Mattie loses her suburban home when Basil jumps bail, and she finds herself back on that "long, winding journey to Brewster." In the midst of all this, the wisdom of Miss Eva (Eve), "a yellow, blue-eyed spirit who had foreseen this day and had tried to warn her" (43), like that of Brewster Place itself, goes unheeded. Yet Brewster Place is not the same as Miss Eva's house in the suburbs, and Mattie's journey, like those of her sisters, is a flight from her individual and their collective pasts, which are seen as our long, wasted existence.

The novel's apparent end, "The Block Party," is, as Michael Awkward notes, a totalizing gesture (98). But the novel does not end with the suggestions of a mystical unity grounded on a shared dream, baptized in the rainstorm and riot of women breaking down a wall (187–88). Rather, the novel ends in the return of the omniscient narrator's ode to "Brewster Place [which] still waits to die" (192); because "the colored daughters of Brewster, spread over the canvas of time, still wake up with their dreams misted on the edge of a yawn" (192). Naylor's bracketing of the "Seven Stories" by the opening prologue, "Dawn," and the epilogue, "Dusk," mimics the closure of the socioeconomic and natural environment depicted in the stories themselves.

At the nexus of the converging narratives of the novel, and especially in the dream-consciousness of Mattie Michael, which seems to generate a recuperative magic that raises the possibility of these (anonymous) people achieving some tangible victories over their shrouded lives, a putative hope is born; but this, under terms of a Western imperialist paradigm, is "seen as [a] remote, ridiculous dream." Only under magical or dream conditions is the transcendence of the Brewster women's historical entrapment possible; however, a real resolution, Naylor seems to suggest, must be "out there," in the real world of her audience. It is in this respect that she seems to have traveled along one strand the double-helix of cultural memory, crossing that gap of geopsychic space and history to Africa, serendipitously reclaiming the use of the open-ended dilemma tale, which is much used in traditional African orature and by such contemporary writers as Sembene Ousmane and Ama Ata Aidoo.[12]

Naylor's closure of *The Women of Brewster Place*, although superficially unlike Aidoo's or Sembene's, effects a similar response. Whereas her narrator distances us throughout the stories, by using a third person omniscient voice, we are placed in an ideologically significant position in relation to the majority of the characters whose stories we are told—they belong to that class whose only legacy from the Civil Rights and (Black) Women's Rights struggles of the sixties and seventies is a dream deferred. Our ability to engage in an exercise such as this is precisely what drives Kiswana Browne from the middle-class comforts of Linden Hills to Brewster Place and prompts the protagonists of Aidoo's "Everything Counts" and *Our Sister Killjoy* (1966) to return to Africa with renewed commitment and passion. Many of us, who have left our respective Brewster Places "forever . . . [and have become] the exception rather than the rule" (4), may wish to think that Brewster Place is dead. But the "final" paragraph of Naylor's text denies that pusillanimous assertion (192). We realize that Naylor's authorial project asks that we do not forget those who have been scattered by the effects of a sociocultural bomb more immediately devastating, to its victims, than the strangely removed threat of nuclear destruction.

If we have been distanced by the narrative strategies of *The Women of Brewster Place* and its characters' socioeconomic status, then Naylor resolutely attacks any sense of consolation that we might have felt, because of that distance, by exposing the truth, as she sees it, beneath the middle-class hell of *Linden Hills*.[13] Naylor has stated, in an interview, that *Linden Hills* is "a microcosm of the Black middle class experience, the hyphenated American experience in its worst possible scenario."[14] This fiction is prefaced by an epigraph that records a conversation between Lester Tilson (although here unnamed) and Grandma Tilson, recalling the "multi-colored 'Afric' children" (4) and the ancestral wisdom of "Miss Eva" (43) in *The Women of Brewster Place*.

Much has been written about Naylor's use of Dante's *Inferno* as a structural and thematic model for *Linden Hills*, her second novel.[15] Indeed, she has encouraged this comparison in various interviews since the novel's first publication in 1985.[16] Since this critique's object is to explore the familial ties of those "significant others" who have been voiced-over, *(sm)othered* as it were, by the discursive preoccupation with the genealogical inheritance of the American/European forebears in the hyphenated experience Naylor's second novel recreates, discussion of Dante's influence will be circumscribed.[17] Margaret Homans's feminist reading of Naylor's second novel and Luce Irigaray's *Speculum of the Other Woman* (1985), while excavating the "real" Willa Nedeed from the basement in which her husband, Luther Nedeed (the Lucifer of Naylor's revisionary *Inferno*), had imprisoned her and their sick five-year-old child, does, however, create "a vexing set of issues concerning the politics of reading" (Gates, Jr., "Significant Others," 606; see note 15). In response to Homans's article, moreover, Henry Louis Gates, Jr., foregrounds many of the political and ideological concerns that are the pretext for this reading of Naylor's work in general and *Linden Hills* in particular. He notes that "master narratives of sexual oppression, crucial as they are, can so easily render the sociopolitical subtext opaque" (617). It is precisely that clouding of subtext(s), even in Naylor's explicit pronouncements about her precursors and models, her Bloomian "influences" if you will, which must be prevented. In his final comments about the novel's ending—Luther's house is burnt to the ground on Christmas eve and, as the central characters, Willie and Lester, walk away, their final words are echoed by the narrator: *"They let it burn"* (*Linden Hills*, 304)—Gates comments on the tension caused by the ambiguity of interpretation ("Significant Others," 620–21). Yet Gates inadvertently voices over the narrator's own repetition without comment, and so leaves *that "utterance"* out of earshot because he "hears" *only* two voices at the narrative's end.

Let us return to the epigraph that becomes the (pre)text for the narrative, an extended morality tale for a child, and for us—"the exception[s] rather than the rule", the "they" who, because they have gained a measure of formal education, exclude them-(our)selves from the Brewster Places of their (our) shared histories. Traditionally, within African and early African-American orature, it was through the spoken word that we received our *"culture, knowledge, [it was part of] the training of children"* (Interview, 1988; emphasis added).[18] Such knowledge was often articulated by our mothers and grandmothers, or by the professional story-teller (that is, the griot). Thus, it is appropriate that the opening frame of this tale should be a "heard" conversation between Grandma Tilson and her grandchild, before we read/hear it.

The epigraph poses the problem which troubles the child, Lester, and, one suspects, many who have grown up in the Judeo-Christian tradition: What is the nature of hell? Is it to be experienced after death, or in this life? And, who or what is the devil? Grandma Tilson's answer, "the highest bidder," leaves us in no doubt. Naylor's novel is concerned with the here and now; but, this interest is intertwined with a certain uneasiness for the souls of people who have relinquished their ties with family and community, with religious and spiritual values, and, finally, with "their own ethnocentric sense of self" (Interview, 1988), in order to realize the American Dream, or rather, Luther Nedeed's spiteful version of it.

Lester Tilson and his friend, Willie Mason, in order to get some Christmas money, move through Linden Hills doing odd jobs for the residents. Their journey, as Naylor intends, takes them down through the various Dantean/bourgeois Euro-American "Circles of Hell," now painted black. As they move from job to job, over a period of six days (December 19th to 24th), they realize that this collection of individuals is not the original Luther Nedeed's "ebony jewel that reflected the soul of Wayne County but reflected it black"; nor is it "a beautiful, black wad of spit right in the white eye of America" (9). The potential for this experience being interpreted as nihilistic by the two young men is prevented, in part, by the import of Grandma Tilson's observations about "hell on earth." Secondly, because these men are still in the process of acquiring a "street" education, as opposed to a formal one, they have not been seduced into buying into the dominant ideology's vision of success. Their education, like those of their forebears, was informal, was acquired by oral transmission, experience, and apprenticeship.

The present Luther Nedeed had also acquired an informal education from his father, but his education was not wholesome. It was predicated on a tradition of mimicry and envy. The original Luther Nedeed had a vision (9) that was sired by the knowledge that "the future of Wayne County—the future of America—was . . . going to be *white*" (8). Thus, his efforts were directed by motives similar to those of Milton's Satan, rather than a love of his own culture, a pride in his people and their often unacknowledged power. Even before he started to effect his vision for Linden Hills, Luther was doomed. The seemingly autogenetic Luther Nedeed wished to purge his paradise of those radicals and revolutionaries, like Nat Turner or Marcus Garvey, who saw their connection with their blackness, their Africanness in more than rhetorical terms (11). The society that becomes a mockery of the life-sustaining dreams of the women (and men) of the Brewster Places of our world, has indeed sold "that silver mirror . . . to the highest bidder." In doing so, the residents have exchanged the productiveness of harmony for insatiable appetites and the desire to possess material things for their own sake.

They have lost their "soul-name," their *kradin*; in other words, they have lost their humanity.[19] To be caught in the Western embrace or the internationalized American Dream is often reflected in the works of African and African-American writers as a death or madness. Sembene Ousmane's short story "The Promised Land" (in *Tribal Scars*, 1974) shows how a trip to France becomes the literal death of Diouana, the protagonist, who had been brought there as a somewhat naive domestic servant. In Ayi Kwei Armah's novel *Fragments*,[20] contamination with the West precipitated Baako's nervous breakdown. Against this poison are the traditions of the past and the harmony that is sought between the household and public gods. Significantly, Armah brackets *Fragments* with chapters dedicated to "Naana," the old woman who forms the link with the ancestors and those yet to be born (11–25, 278–86).

In *Linden Hills* there are many characters who are on the verge of nervous breakdowns, are insane and/or commit suicide because they find themselves in impossible situations. Unlike Armah's protagonist, whose residency in the asylum is temporary, Naylor's "ghosts" have bought themselves a more permanent "zip code" in the Linden Hills twilight area. One which "is also an area of knowledge, twisted knowledge perhaps, but knowledge resulting from real information" (Armah, 225). As Willie and Lester begin their journey, they encounter Norman Anderson and his wife, Ruth, who once lived in Linden Hills; Norman suggests that the two young men do odd jobs in the Hills (41). We learn that Norman suffers from his own personal affliction, "the pinks" (34–37). This malady seems to be an *epidermalization* of his soul's fear of insignificance, of a dissolution into the American nightmare (36). Norman's sickness is, in the words of Amiri Baraka, "[t]he flame of social dichotomy. Split down the center, which is the early legacy of the black man unfocused on blackness."[21] Although the Andersons live outside of Linden Hills, they are not immunized against the diseases of a world that has been able to manufacture a Linden Hills.

Similarly, the adolescent sexual chauvinism and nervous homophobia of Naylor's major characters begin to surface during this section. Such behavior should be seen in terms of the general ideology of a homophobic and patriarchal society. Against such ideological dominance, Willie and Lester have their poetry and memory as a means of resistance (44–45). Since Willie, unlike his fellow poet, Lester, refuses to write down his poetry, he has opted for the more customary role as oral poet; yet, traditionally, he cannot perform in public as a legitimate poet. He needs to find and establish a rapport with his *hadzivodu*, god of songs, as Kofi Awoonor notes in *The Breast of the Earth*.[22]

In this light, Willie and Lester's passage through Linden Hills gains a consequence that incorporates and transforms the notion that Naylor's authorial project only emulates a classical European tale and ignores the rich resources of African orature.[23] Even though Lester *writes* his poetry, both young men are on a voyage of discovery, working their way toward maturity and understanding as both poets and human beings. Each encounter with, and each task for, the residents of the Hills brings each young man closer to the recognition of his personal *hadzivodu*. The "diviners," or intermediaries in this case, are the "dead" and "half-dead" of Linden Hills—those who have sold "that silver mirror . . . to the highest bidder" (see frontispiece of *Linden Hills*) and for whom they work.

Their first day together in Linden Hills ends with dinner at Lester's home and an invitation for Willie to stay overnight. The evening ends with Lester and Willie smoking some marijuana as they listen to the incomprehensible "long, thin wail" they had heard before at the Anderson's home, and which still filled them with a spine-chilling fear. As poets, both failed to appreciate the meaning of that human cry; as human beings, they were too inexperienced (60). By this point, Naylor has established the thematic link between the education of our apprentices and "a woman who was crouching over the shrunken body of her son" (61), a woman who is also about to begin a journey toward self-articulation.

The next chapter, "December 20th," begins in the basement of Luther Nedeed's house where the nameless woman, now silent, clutches her dead son. She has not found her true medium, her personal god-image through which she might speak the poetry of her life. Upstairs, her husband prepares for a busy day, including being the guest of honor at the reception for the wedding of Winston Alcott, whom Lester rightly suspects of being a homosexual. Winston is only getting married so that he can remain in Linden Hills (73). Lester and Willie find their first menial job at this function (85–86). When the reception reaches its climax, the toasting of bridegroom and bride, Lester and Willie realize that David, the best man, is actually Winston's ex-lover (88–90). Willie, who has memorized all of Walt Whitman's poetry, recognizes the slightly altered poem David reads for Cassandra, Winston's new wife. This charade becomes the first lesson in their education—knowledge of the betrayal of friendship for the sake of greed.

Paralleling Willie and Lester's experience, Mrs. Nedeed, in the basement, finds the bible of Luwana Packerville, the wife of the first Luther Nedeed, and this leads to the beginning of *her* education: "Her mourning had begun" (94). On the next day, we meet Xavier Donnel, the "Super Nigger" of General Motors (who has actually fallen in love with Lester's sister), and Donnell's misogynistic, friend Maxwell Smyth. Countering Smyth's facile opinions about the cause of (Black) poverty in America, Lester becomes more eloquent in presenting his arguments. Comparably, Mrs. Nedeed's progress toward more completely articulating the meaning of her life, is advanced by the words of her *"grand-self"*, Luwana Packerville (118). The present Mrs. Nedeed learns that the recovery of one's voice, through whatever medium one's *hadzivodu* dictates, is the way to recuperate, to regain a harmonious balance with one's household and public gods. The former Mrs. Nedeed becomes both the ancestors' and the present Mrs. (Willa) Nedeed's *hadzivodu*; thus, they provide her, through their various epistles, with the knowledge and wisdom she lacked. Eventually, they give her the strength to confront her fate, no matter the consequences.

Each day brings the apprentice poets closer to Luther Nedeed's house and Willa closer to her confrontation with her husband. By the early morning hours of Christmas Eve, the paths seem to converge. We find Willie in his apartment in Putney Wayne, half-dreaming about the mysterious Willa Prescott Nedeed (273) and his last job in the Hills. He has come a long way in his education, and he begins the process of accepting himself for what he is, in all its complexities and contradictions. Just before he falls asleep, a poem comes to him in a terrifying possession by his *hadzivodu*. We never "hear" the whole of this poem; but we suspect that the events that take place on Christmas Eve at the bottom of Linden Hills will significantly alter its final expression. Both Willie and Mrs. Nedeed have dreamless sleeps. Willa Prescott Nedeed no longer calls herself "Mrs. Nedeed," because she realizes that she does have a will of her own. She can make choices still, just as she had done when she married Luther, just as she had done in being a "good wife" and when she walked down the steps to the basement (227–80). So the choice was hers, and no matter what that eventually meant, she resolved to be herself: "She awoke Willa Prescott Nedeed on Christmas Eve. And after she straightened the basement, she was going to start on the rooms upstairs" (289).

Since *Linden Hills* is an African-American version of the (Euro-)American bourgeois experience gone terribly wrong, we tend to focus our attention on the obviousness of the "American" component of that experience; because, as middle-class readers, we are interpellated by all the ideological baggage we have taken up as our burden (Aidoo, *Our Sister Killjoy*, 5). The reflections of our own subject-positions, as they are transformed in Naylor's phantasmagoria of late twentieth-century (Black) bourgeois society, prevent us from fully acknowledging the other familial heritage in that hyphenated experience. We do not remember, as Willie does, the poetry of our oral and slave beginnings. We look at the content, and if the beauty of form is ever hinted at in our discursive practices, it is in terms of a Western paradigm.

I would suggest that Naylor's first two novels are the beginning of a project of atonement, which comes to a ritual end in the third, *Mama Day*.[24] Naylor's second novel describes what happens in the affluent suburb of Linden Hills during the course of six days; it ends at the start of the seventh, Christmas Day. However, Naylor's narrator chooses to close the work with the following words: "Each with his own thoughts, they approached the chain fence. . . . Hand anchored to hand, one helped the other to scale the open links. *Then, they walked out of Tupelo Drive into the last days of the year*" (304; emphasis added). From this perspective, it is especially significant that Naylor's third novel, which is so unlike either of the previous works, should be concerned with the Day family and "the legend of Sapphira Wade. A true conjure woman" (*Mama Day*, 3).

The story of the twentieth-century descendants of this "true conjure woman" is told by three narrative voices. The first voice is that of the island of Willow Springs, an ancestral choral voice, which brackets and intermingles with the other two voices, of Ophelia (Cocoa) Day and her husband, George, an orphan. In many respects, these three voices perform a concert of remembrance and celebration to mark the occasion of a poet-cantor (Naylor), who has achieved a harmony with her "household and public gods." The voice of Willow Springs, an androgynous spirit, has two assistants (male and female), whose function is to teach their respective group the song (or knowledge) that is the history and heritage of Willow Springs.[25]

We are taken to an island between "two distinct worlds," ideologically and culturally speaking: one is on the "Mainside" (late twentieth-century America), and the other is the world of Sapphira Wade and "the Other Place" (a place of legend, magic, and the connection to a common African past). Mama Day's niece, Cocoa, is able to "go Mainside" and return each year in a ceremony of affirmation and renewal because her familial ties remain unbroken. The view that Willow Springs is a world completely apart from the modern world (Western bourgeois society) is only partially true (5). Although Willow Springs does not "belong" to Georgia or North Carolina, its geographical proximity to those two southern states evidences both a "historical" and a more mundane relationship. However, this connection only confirms the nature of Naylor's artistic choices, which give her fictional island a greater sense of *being there* in a sense that Shakespeare's island, in the *Tempest*, is not.

The first narrative voice we hear speaks with a power derived from a tradition in which life and death exist as a continuum. This is why Sapphira Wade's presence is felt throughout the novel. Ultimately, we hear the voices of Africa and its countless daughters and sons, who endured the Middle Passage, in the voice of the hurricane, which "will come, rest, and leave screaming . . . while prayers go up in Willow Springs to be spared from what could only be the workings of Woman. And She has no name" (249–51). The last sentence echoes the first line of Willie Mason's six hundred and sixty-sixth poem, which was forming in his mind in the early morning hours of Christmas Day in Linden Hills.

Willow Springs is not a piece of real estate, like Linden Hills, to be exploited by developers (6–7). It is a living community, with a vibrant complex of cultural traditions and practices, such as The Candle Walk (110–18). The island of Willow Springs is home, a spiritual focus, the geopsychic space that usually keeps the Dantean vision, refigured by Baraka and Naylor, safely across the bridge on Mainside. But, as Baraka reminds us, "Hell is actual. . . . One thinks of home, or the other "homes" we have had. . . . The struggles away or towards this peace is Hell's function" (*The System of Dante's Hell*, 154; see note 21). Similarly, the collective ancestral voice of Willow Springs echoes Grandma Tilson's warning in its positive form (48–49). But this fictional island is not without its problems and "dammed souls," like Junior Lee and his envious "wife," Miss Ruby, who puts a hex on Cocoa (246). Naylor, however, reminds us that there are other islands that have more than their share of problems.

Just over half of the first section of *Mama Day* takes place Mainside, on those other islands, Manhattan and Long Island, New York. We are introduced to Cocoa and George, whose meeting, courtship, and eventual marriage, Naylor describes through their individual voices, so that we get a layered, richly textured, polylectical view of the whole romance. As Rachel Hass observed, "George and Cocoa are two nations learning to speak one another's language."[26] George Andrews is an orphan who was brought up in an institution, the Wallace P. Andrews Shelter for Boys and believes that "Only the present has potential" (23). Although George is, in many ways, a product of his education in the orphanage, he lives without history. As an orphan, he has no familial ties. As an adult, he has no real friends, and he lives for his engineering job and football. He is able, however, to teach Cocoa to see people and "small towns" in his city of New York, rather than various "fruits" (61–63).

George is a man literally driven by a faulty heart, an inordinate desire for order, control, and a narrow empiricism. After a protracted and often humorous courtship and a few years of marriage "Mainside," George finally agrees to go to Willow Springs. This visit, which ends in his death, is necessary because it becomes the occasion for George's reeducation, his return to the source and immersion into his un-remembered history, as well as his confrontation with "the other place" and liberation. A crucial moment in his reeducation comes during the poker game with Dr. Buzzard. George, in his narrative segment, comments on the funeral dirge Dr. Buzzard and the other men sing: "I didn't understand the rhythm and I refused to spoil it by attempting to join in. *Perhaps if I had known that I only had to listen to the pulse of my blood . . .*" (214; emphasis added). The narrative, spoken in the past tense, shows that the speaker has learnt to trust what was inside of him as much as, if not more than, what he could empirically prove. Willow Springs, or more specifically, Mama Day, becomes the catalyst that leads him to recognize his god-image, to understand that life is shaped by history and experiences that go beyond simple demonstration. Ultimately, George's ability to learn, in spite of himself, allows him to accept "the Other place." As part of the choral narrative voice, he reveals that, as he lay on Cocoa's bed, after staggering from the chicken coop, bloodied and dying, he felt only "total peace" (302).

Cocoa's sickness to near death, like "the pinks" that afflict Norman Anderson in *Linden Hills*, is also necessary to purge her of certain habits of thought, which are injurious to her calling as the heir to the legacy of Sapphira Wade and Mama Day, the new medium between the two worlds that influence Willow Springs. She realizes that the world and its repetition in song is a complex polyrhythmic endeavor and that "there are just too many sides to the whole story" (311). To exist harmoniously with one's household and public gods cannot be achieved by a vision that insists on there being one, and only one truth. The admission of multiple "truths" should not be taken as the condoning of an extreme relativism, as that leads to an insulated monologue. Rather, we acknowledge these "other" truths, which have a coherence and validity in their specific context(s), because they enrich and help us to hear the multiple voices and counter-rhythms of "the whole story." George's peace is possible, because he is finally able to admit "the Other place" into his self. He can bring his self "home" to "the Other place" and the true Conjure Woman's Africa.

We may, therefore, see Naylor's three works as bearing a family resemblance that has been overlooked, for the most part. Chinua Achebe, in a short essay, "Named for Victoria," discloses that, "Although I did not set about it consciously in that solemn way I now know that my first book, *Things Fall Apart*, was an act of atonement with my past, the ritual return and homage of a prodigal son."[27] Like her literary cousin's declaration about his first work, this critic has attempted to show the evidence of a more extended atonement by another of Africa's unwilling prodigal daughters. Naylor's three works constitute a series of rituals that successfully establish her personal *hadzivodu*.

NOTES

1. This essay owes much to the illuminating work of Michael Awkward's *Inspiring Influences: Tradition, Revision, and Afro-American Women's Novels* (New York: Columbia University Press, 1989).

2. Hortense J. Spillers, "Afterword," in *Conjuring: Black Women, Fiction, and Literary Tradition*, edited by Marjorie Pryse and Hortense J. Spillers (Bloomington: Indiana University Press, 1985), 258.

3. Ebele Eko, "Beyond the Myth of Confrontation," *Ariel* 17, no. 4 (October 1986): 139–52.

4. Gloria Naylor, *The Women of Brewster Place* (New York: Viking/Penguin, 1988).

5. Ama Ata Aidoo, *The Dilemma of a Ghost and Anowa* (Harlow, U.K.: Longman African Classic, 1987), 7–8, 65–68.

6. Ama Ata Aidoo, *No Sweetness Here* (Harlow, U.K.: Longman African Classic,

1970, 1988). What is particularly interesting is the thematic similarities, the North-South reversal excepted, between the short stories "For Whom Things Did Not Change" and "Certain Winds from the South" and Naylor's focus on how her characters, despite themselves, contribute to their own oppression in an era of supposedly radical change.

   7. Gloria Naylor, "The Myth of the Matriarch," *Life* 11 (Spring 1988): 65.

   8. Ngugi wa Thiong'o, *Decolonizing the Mind* (London: James Currey Ltd., 1986), 3.

   9. Dorothy Wickenden, revision of *The Women of Brewster Place* by Gloria Naylor, *The New Republic* (September 6, 1982): 37–38.

   10. Naylor, "The Myth of the Matriarch," 65.

   11. Ama Ata Aidoo, "Sisterhood Is Global," *Essence* (March 1985): 137.

   12. Vincent O. Odamtten, *The Art of Ama Ata Aidoo: Polylectics and Reading against Neocolonialism* (Gainsville, Fla.: University Press of Florida, 1994), 18–21.

   13. Gloria Naylor, *Linden Hills* (New York: Penguin Books, 1986).

   14. *Gloria Naylor Interview with Kay Bonetti* (Colombia, Mo.: American Audio Prose Library, 1988), sound recording. All subsequent references to this recording will be marked "(Interview, 1988)" in the text.

   15. Among the many reviews and articles that focus on this male, European precursorial figure are Michiko Kakutani's "Dante in Suburbia," *New York Times*, February 9, 1985, 13; Catherine C. Ward's "Gloria Naylor's *Linden Hills*: A Modern Inferno," *Contemporary Literature* 28, no. 1 (Spring 1987): 67–81; Margaret Homans's "The Woman in the Cave: Recent Feminist Fictions and the Classical Underworld," *Contemporary Literature* 29, no. 3 (Fall 1988): 369–402; and Henry Louis Gates, Jr.'s "Significant Others," *Contemporary Literature* 29, no. 4 (Winter 1988): 606–23.

   16. "Gloria Naylor and Toni Morrison: A Conversation," *Southern Review* 21 (July 1985): 567–93.

   17. For instance, Cynthia Ward's article (see note 15 above) meticulously charts the similarities and differences in the two works and also notes Naylor's echoing of T. S. Eliot's "Gerontion" and her reversal of Roxanne's situation in Edmond Rostand's *Cyrano de Bergerac*.

   18. However, in the same interview, it becomes apparent that Naylor does not follow her own observations to their conclusion. Despite herself, she privileges the *written* *"WORD"* in such a way that the full impact of her awareness of the *"African"* *oral* heritage in her *"African-Americanness"* does not manifest itself in an overtly confrontational/liberating manner. The *oral* has not died. Though we sometimes do not consciously apprehend it as such, it continually speaks within us and insists (through ruptures in the scriptural texts we create) that we acknowledge its haunting presence.

   19. Kofi Owusu, "Interpreting Interpreting: African Roots, Black Fruits, and the Colored Tree (of 'Knowledge')," *Black American Literature Forum* 23, no. 4 (Winter 1989): 745.

   20. Ayi Kwei Armah, *Fragments* (originally published 1969; New York: Collier Books, 1971).

   21. Amiri Baraka (LeRoi Jones), *The System of Dante's Hell*, (New York: Grove Press/Evergreen Black Cat Edition, 1966), 153.

   22. Kofi Awonoor, *The Breast of the Earth* (New York: Anchor Press/Doubleday, 1976), 115–16.

   23. Jewelle Gomez, "Naylor's Interno," *The Women's Review of Books* 2, no. 11 (August 1985): 8.

24. Gloria Naylor, *Mama Day* (originally published 1988; New York: Vintage Books/Random House, 1989).

25. Awoonor's *The Breast of the Earth*; see his discussion of Ewe poets, 111–16.

26. Rachel Hass, review of *Gloria Naylor's Mama Day*, *Boston Review* 13 (June 1988): 29.

27. Chinua Achebe, *Morning Yet on Creation Day* (originally published 1975; New York: Anchor/Doubleday, 1976), 102.

BIBLIOGRAPHY

Naylor, Gloria. *Linden Hills*. New York: Penguin, 1986.

———. *Mama Day*. New York: Vintage Books/Random House, 1989.

———. *The Women of Brewster Place*. New York: Viking/Penguin, 1988.

10

Creative African Memory: Some Oral Sources of Toni Morrison's *Song of Solomon*

OUSSEYNOU TRAORE

Night is an African Juju man
weaving a wish and weariness together
to make two wings.

O fly away home fly away

Do you remember Africa?

Cleave the air fly away home

My gran, he flew back to Africa,
just spread his arms and
flew away home.
—Hayden

Some of the most crucial sources of the myth of flight in Toni Morrison's *Song of Solomon* are located in two areas of African-American expressive culture: the oral traditions (myth, spirituals, blues, genealogical recitation, family history) and the slave narrative. These two expressive matrices, which Morrison calls, respectively, "the oral origins" and "the print origins" of African-American literature ("Site of Memory" 103), are, in turn, largely rooted in African oral traditions of myth, folktale, oral history, and the epic. The African and African-American verbal art traditions constitute a significant part of the mnemonic and epistemological systems that inform Morrison's fiction.

In African-American oral traditions, for example, the myth of the flying Africans is a pervasive narrative of ethnic root-search, self-retrieval, and liberation. The trope of ancestral flight is centrally inscribed in the myth, where it is activated by a creative memory of Africa, the dream and desire to return to Africa, and, sometimes, the recovery and utterance of empowering African magical words. The story is replicated at the documentary level as personal, family and clan, or collective history. It is, as Morrison puts it, "a motivating thing for

Song of Solomon'' (Jones, 144). Morrison explains her creative use of the myth as follows:

Myths get forgotten. Or they may not have been looked at carefully. Let me give you an example: the flying myth in *Song of Solomon*. If it means Icarus to some readers, fine. But my meaning is specific: it is about black people who could fly. That was always part of the folklore of my life; flying was one of our gifts. I don't care how silly it may seem. It is everywhere—People used to talk about it, it's in the spirituals and gospels. Perhaps it was wishful thinking—escape, death and all that. But suppose it wasn't. What might it mean? I tried to find out in *Song of Solomon*. (LeClair, 255)

Song of Solomon is thus a fictional reinterpretation of the flying myth as a knowledge system, especially in terms of what it may mean historically and ideologically with regard to the claim of African ancestry, escape, death and the ethnic dream of magical self-empowerment.

The flying myth speaks symbolically of the ancestry of all African Americans, as confirmed by its multigeneric presence in the sacred and secular founding Black oral texts of folklore, the gospels and spirituals. The sacred reference points of the founding texts are ontological, and their expressive features are highly archetypal and metaphorical. The secular slave narrative mode, on the other hand, particularizes, through personal, family, and collective history; it is thus historically documentable. In her ideological and literary consciousness, Morrison creates formal connections between mythic and slave narrative modes as elements that inform her fictional explorations of the flying story:

[The story about flying Africans is] not so much . . . a legend but a given. . . . Later on I read a lot of slave narratives, and I remember the interviewers asking these people who were children of slaves and have been slaves themselves, "have you ever heard of anybody who could fly?" and I was struck by the fact [that] . . . they kept saying things like, "well, I never saw it, but so and so saw it. . . . " The flying thing was heavy and spiritual. . . . I began to think about it as a real thing—like literally flying. (Bonnetti; my transcription)

Morrison's interpretation of the flying myth from the sacred sphere to the secular one as "a real thing" enables her to re-present the ancestral model literally and symbolically. The slave narrative sources provide the technical means of the fictional refraction of the flight myth and bridge the gap between elements of Morrison's family history and the received slave accounts and mythic variants of the flight story.

In her re-presentation of the myth, Morrison interjects and mythicizes aspects of her own family history and elements from oral accounts by descendants of African-born slave ancestors. In this sense the sources of *Song of Solomon* are consciously "autobiographical" and communal, but blended into a highly creative fiction that transforms and conceals them almost beyond recognition. Thus, personal, family, and collective ethnic memory merge in the novel because Morrison negotiates creatively what she calls "the differences between self-recollection (memoir) and fiction, and also some of the similarities—the places where those two crafts embrace and where that embrace is symbiotic" ("Site of Memory," 103).

The thesis about Morrison's creative use of African or ethnic memory sources is supported through a detailed examination of her transformative method of fictionalizing and interweaving mythic and historical data in *Song of Solomon*. The present study focuses on identifying the multiple sources for the ancestral figure of Solomon in the children's "song of Solomon" (306–7), Morrison's own poetic and composite version of the flying myth, and in its prose narrative variant told by the fictional Susan Byrd (325–28), and in important data borrowed from other African-American family oral histories or accounts. The analysis is particularly interested in establishing crucial connections between *Song of Solomon* and the family history of John Solomon Willis, Morrison's grandfather, and those of Belali Mohomet and Uncle Calina, two African-born slave ancestors taken from published oral recollections by their slave-born descendants.

ANALYSIS OF SOURCES

Song of Solomon deals with the story of the Dead family. Milkman (Macon, Jr.) Dead is the son of Macon Dead, Sr., who is the son of Jake. Jake, one of the many children of Solomon, the African-born slave ancestor who flew back to Africa, is baptized Macon Dead by a drunken White officer during his registration with the Freedman's Bureau before his exodus from the South to the North. The Deads thus lose their ancestral family name and African past through this historic renaming that mythicizes their ethnic loss as a metaphorical death. When Milkman journeys from Michigan, where his father is now a prosperous landlord, to the South in search of a supposedly lost family treasure, he has no knowledge of his family history or the original names of his grandfather, Jake, or even the existence of Solomon or Shalimar, his great grandfather, whose African name was also borne by Jake (the first Macon Dead).

Armed with fragmentary information gathered from his father and family friends in Pennsylvania (on his way South), and a blues verse sung by his aunt Pilate, her daughter, and granddaughter back in Michigan, Milkman arrives in a small town named Shalimar, in Virginia. Here, the forty-odd families that make up the population bear the family name of Solomon with whom they claim kinship. Frustrated by his lack of success in his treasure hunt, Milkman's experience reaches a peak as he hears a song performed by boys and girls holding hands and dancing in a circle. At the center of the circle, a boy spins round and round, arms stretched like wings of a bird in flight or an airplane. In their reenactment of myth and history, the children sing Morrison's poetic version of the flying story, which contains a verse Milkman recognizes as Pilate's blues lyric:

Jake the only son of Solomon
Come booba yalle, come booba tambee
Whirled about and touched the sun
Come konka yalle, come konka tambee
. . .
Solomon and Ryna Belali Shalut
Yaruba Medina Muhammet too.
Nestor Kalina Saraka cake.
Twenty-one children, the last one Jake!
. . .
Solomon done fly, Solomon done gone
Solomon cut across the sky, Solomon gone home

(Song of Solomon, 306–7)

Green, the Only Son of Solomon

According to Susan L. Blake, the source for the fictional Solomon in the song is a reference to Solomon Davis, an individual mentioned in *Drums and Shadows*, a collection of slave memories (Blake, 81). The reference Blake bases her argument on reads as follows: "There had also been living in Tatemville 'Golla' Jones Davis, and African, who, as affirmed by his relative, Solomon Davis, has not been heard of since his departure for his native land, some five years ago" (*Drums and Shadows*, 67).

However, Blake's argument is incorrect since "Golla" Jones Davis is the African-born slave who returned to his native land. Solomon Davis, who does not fly away but merely reports "Golla" Jones Davis's escape, cannot be a model for Morrison's flying Solomon. There is no mention of a flying Solomon in any of the slave accounts of ancestral flight collected in *Drums and Shadows*.

The source for the fictional Solomon and the first line of the song is an oral fragment of Morrison's own family history. Morrison points to this personal oral source and the models for both Solomon and Jake when discussing her ties with her Alabama past in an interview with Jessie W. Jones:

Jones: Is that through your mother exclusively or do you go back yourself? Do you make that pilgrimage at anytime?

Morrison: No—I've been back more frequently than she has. She talks about it with affection, but she never goes. My father used to go back to Georgia every year, but although she remembers it with a great deal of pleasure, she never goes there. There is a huge wing of our family who lived in Greenville and then in Birmingham, and that portion of them that didn't come to Ohio went to California, and I only recently met some of them whom I have only heard stories about. The song in *Song of Solomon* is a song from that wing of the family in Alabama. The song that my mother and aunts know starts out, "Green, the only son of Solomon." And then there are some funny words that I don't understand. It is a long sort of a Children's song that I don't remember. But Green was the name of my grandfather's first son and it was a kind of genealogy that they were singing about. So I altered the words for *Song of Solomon*. These people were born in Greenville. (Jones and Vinson, 130)

The first line of the children's song in the novel, "Jake the Only Son of Solomon," is a revision of the first line of the genealogical song in Morrison's family: "Green, the only son of Solomon." In the context of the interview, one can safely deduce that Solomon is Morrison's grandfather. This deduction is confirmed by the fact that Morrison's "mother's family had migrated north from Greenville, Ala., around 1910" (Strouse, 53) and her grandparents were Ardelia and John Solomon Willis (Strouse, 54).

Morrison alters the name of the historical "Green" into "Jake" in her fiction but confers on Jake the identification of an "only son" attached to Green. In the fiction, Morrison also reverses the order in which her grandfather's son is recalled: Jake is thus identified as the fictional Solomon's "last one," contrary to Green, who is John Solomon Willis's "first son." The transformation from the historical Green to the fictional Jake enables Morrison to mythicize her grandfather, who now assumes the volitant powers of the mythical ancestor in the general myth of the flying Africans through his identification or association with the fictional Solomon. Morrison's family history is thus merged with the African-American myth of ancestral flight and the slave narrative as vehicles of collective memory. The 1910 migration north of Morrison's family is a part of a pattern of movement in African-American sociocultural history since slavery time in the form of escape and is parallel to the equally historic exodus after the Emancipation Proclamation, the time frame in which the Deads move north in the novel.

In the fictional process, Morrison transforms Greenville into Shalimar, an "ancestral" town named through the father (Solomon/Shalimar), unlike the historical model in which, through a mythical reinterpretation, Greenville is named for Green, the son of John Solomon Willis. The variant pronunciations of the fictional Solomon's name are particularly suggestive and explain Morrison's choice of Shalimar as a place name. Shalimar distances the historical Solomon from the fictional one through phonological shifts that mask Morrison's use of her family history. According to Susan Byrd, Milkman's Native American cousin, Jake, is "one of Solomon's children. Or Shalimar. Papa said Heddy always called him Shalimar" (*Song of Solomon*, 325). Mr. Solomon, a descendant of the fictional Solomon whose store is located at the center of Shalimar, pronounces the name of the town as "*Shalleemone*" (264), which is closer to Solomon than Shalimar. Milkman, who at first asks for "a town named Charlemagne" (262) when he arrives in Virginia, later on muses, "Even the name of the town sounded like Solomon: Shalimar, which Mr. Solomon and everybody else pronounced *Shalleemone*" (305).

The fact that the town of Shalimar, Virginia, a community settled by the fictional Shalimar/Solomon's descendants, is named after the African founding ancestor suggests another mythopoetic link between Morrison's family history and the myth of flight merged in the fiction of the novel. In her mythical imagination and memory, Morrison retroactively reinterprets Greenville, the birthplace of a segment of her family, as a town founded by and named for "Green, the only son of Solomon." Morrison also makes it clear that the song her mother and aunts know "is a long sort of children's song" and "a kind of genealogy" about some of her "people who were born in Greenville," Alabama. In the fiction, Milkman refers to the children's song as "a kind of ring-around-the-rosy or a Little Sally Walker game" (266); he identifies part of the children's lyrics as his aunt "Pilate's song" (306); and recognizes the genealogical content of the song as "names of people" (306) and Shalimar as a place of origin for his grandparents (286); the African-language words and names Morrison calls "funny words I don't understand" are, in the fiction, what Milkman calls "meaningless rhymes" (267) and "nonsense words" (305). We will return to these funny words in a later section.

The representatives of individual and family histories that Strouse and this study argue for is perhaps what Morrison expresses at a theoretical level and which underlines her practice when she writes: "There must have been a time when an artist could be genuinely representative *of* the tribe and *in* it; when the artist could have a tribal or racial sensibility and an individual expression of it" ("Rootedness," 339).

Morrison goes on to affirm that the autobiographical form provides African-American writers with the opportunity to be representative while at the same time being solitary (telling their individual stories). In Morrison's case, her family history is both distinct and representative, which makes it *of* the tribe and places it *in* the context of the tribe's experience. John Solomon Willis did not fly back to Africa leaving his wife and children behind like his fictional namesake. However, he did migrate from Greenville to Birmingham, leaving his wife and children behind in a manner reminiscent of Solomon's desertion of his wife, Ryna, and their twenty-one children. Morrison narrates the 1910 migration of her mother's family to Birmingham. She informs us that they were sharecroppers who had lost their land and therefore were always in debt. Her grandfather had left for Birmingham, playing the violin and sending money back home. In spite of that, her grandmother was very nervous, being alone with all the children, especially the girls reaching puberty and being at the mercy of White boys. Her grandmother decided to go north and sent an oral message to her husband: "We're heading north on the midnight train. If you ever want to see us again, you'll be on that train" (Strouse, 53).

Ryna's blues complaint in lines seventeen through twenty (*Song of Solomon*, 321) is a complex fictional and mythical reworking of this historical theme of male desertion and female nervousness about the sexual rapacity and economic oppressiveness of the White male presence. Morrison transforms the family history data by making the fictional Solomon's desertion a permanent one and the source of a personal sorrow accompanied by White male sexual threats only to Ryna who sings: "Solomon don't leave me here/ Cotton balls to choke me/

Solomon don't leave me here/ Buckra's arms to yoke me.'' Ryna's blues verse expresses the killing effect of the "cotton balls," which recalls the economics of slavery and White male rape structurally instituted by the peculiar institution and its legacy, sharecropping. Ryna's "yoke" metaphor evokes the mule in the cotton field, and, coupled with "Buckra's arms" and his cotton *balls*, is saturated with the violent racial and sexual assaults feared by Morrison's grandmother with regard to her girls reaching puberty and White boys circling. ("Buckra" means "master" and "white man" in the "negro patois of Surinam" as well as in Ryna's complaint. In the language of the Calabar Coast of Nigeria, "buckra" also means "demon, powerful and superior being" [Oxford English Dictionary].) These images capture the demonic economic chokehold the White man has on the African-American family.

There are of course vast differences between the specifics of the stories about the two Solomons; but the hard work in the fields, in the hills, where the fictional Solomon and his family tried to grow cotton (326), a fact comparable to sharecropping, is also a motivating factor in Solomon's desertion of Ryna and their numerous children. An examination of some of the sources of lines thirteen through sixteen of the children's song (326) reveals obscure references to John Solomon Willis's "girls reaching puberty." Shalut, Yaruba, and Medina in the children's song are, in fact, the names of some of the many daughters of Belali Mohomet, the African-born slave ancestor, who also serves as an additional model for the fictional Solomon. Katie Brown, a descendant of Belali, tells us: "Belali Mohomet? Yes'm, I knows about Belali. He wife Phoebe. *He had plenty daughtuhs*, Magret, Bentoo, Chaalut, Medina, Yaruba, Fatima, an Hestuh" (*Drums and Shadows*, 161; emphasis mine). The fictional Solomon and Morrison's grandfather had only one son each, Jake and Green, respectively. Belali Mohomet had seven daughters, according to Katie Brown, who refers to them as "plenty daughtuhs." As Morrison tells it, her grandmother did not know whether John Solomon got the oral message, but she went ahead and got her "six or seven children" on the train to Birmingham. The children were all crying at their father's absence. He showed up about an hour later from his hiding spot: he had, indeed, been there, but was afraid that if he were recognized, some creditor might have disallowed his family from leaving.

The number of the Solomon's daughters is magnified by another mythicizing process, whereby the fictional Solomon (and Willis by association) is made father of twenty-one children, of whom only Jake (and Green by association) is male. The accusatory crying of John Solomon Willis's children is a blues complaint about the absence or desertion of the father (albeit temporary), which in the novel is attributed to Ryna. This specific transformation of the source masks the autobiographical element or family history data. But the children's song itself is a complaint that contains Ryna's blues and glorifies at the same time that it accuses the runaway father. This intricate connection between the fiction and Morrison's family history source is strongly suggested by the author's own comment: "The fathers may soar, they may triumph, they may leave, but the children know who they are; they half remember, half in glory and half in accusation. That is one of the points of 'song': all the men left someone, and it is the children who remember it, *sing about it, mythologize it, make it a part of their family history''* (quoted in Demetrakopoulos and Holloway, 87; emphasis mine). The song Morrison's mother and aunts sing is clearly a part of their family history, poeticized and mythologized as an experience both particular and representative of the collective.

Belali Mohomet and Calina

Morrison's use of elements from Belali Mohomet's and Uncle Calina's family histories helps create further distance between her family history and her fiction at the same time that it reveals areas where they intersect. In the slave narrative sources, Belali Mohomet does not fly as Solomon does in Morrison's novel. But, Ben Sullivan, a grandson of Belali Mohomet, whose father's first name was also Belali, tells us: "Muh fathuh's fathuh came frum Africa too but wen muh fathuh Belali wuz a small young lad, muh granfathuh wehn tuh Dungeness on Cumberland Ilun tuh trade in slabes an nebuh wuz seen agen. It wuz muh fathuh Belali dat made rice cakes'' (*Drums and Shadows*, 182).

This pattern of patriarchal desertion in the case of Belali Mohomet is very close to the fictional Solomon's desertion: Belali Mohomet, the African-born slave, leaves his family and son, Belali Mohomet/Sullivan, and is never seen again; Solomon, the African-born slave, flies back home to Africa, leaving his family and son, renamed Jake, but whom Heddy calls Shalimar (Solomon). Even though Belali Mohomet does not fly in Ben Sullivan's narrative, his leaving never to return is identical to the flying Solomon's desertion. As part of the fictional recombination of mythic and historical data, Morrison changes the spelling of Belali Mohomet's last name and places some of Belali Mohomet's daughters' names between their father's first and family names: "Belali Shalut/ Yaruba Medina Muhammet too." The name catalog in this stanza suggests that Solomon and Ryna, who head the list and are known to be a prolific couple, begat or are related to those named in the genealogy.

Lines thirteen through eighteen are a combination of several real family trees woven into a symbolic genealogy that replaces the one in the original "song of Solomon" sung by Morrison's mother and aunts. The fictional Kalina in line fifteen is not a part of the Belali Mohomet story, but belongs to a different oral family history very closely related to that of Belali Mohomet. Julia Grovernor, a descendant of Uncle Calina and Hannah, tells us: "Muh gran, she Hannah. Uncle Calina muh gran too; dey bote Ibos. Yes'm, I membuh muh gran Hannah. She marry Calina an hab twenny-one chillun" (*Drums and Shadows*, 163).

As with the other African names, Morrison changes the spelling of the historical Calina's name and attributes Calina and Hannah's twenty-one children to Solomon in line sixteen of the children's song, leaving Hannah out of the history. Calina is a particularly significant additional source and model for the fictional Solomon because, through his ethnic designation as an Ibo, he is associated with the magical shoes and walk or flight across the Atlantic back to Africa that form the thematic core of the myth and the novel. Charles White reveals a different dimension of the myth relevant to Calina's ethnic designation and Morrison's use of oral sources when he says: "Heahd bout duh Ibo's Landing? Das duh place weah dey bring duh Ibos obuh in a slabe ship and when dey git yuh, dey ain lak it an so dey all staht singin an dey mahch right down in duh ribbuh to mahch back tuh Africa, but dey ain able tuh bit deah. Dey gits drown" (*Drums and Shadows*, 185).

Like Solomon's flight, the Ibos' march back to Africa is accompanied and enabled by a song. Even the fact that the Ibos drown in White's narrative is metaphorical of Solomon's flight, which is thus grounded in the historical model of symbolic and representative walk through the water. Morrison suggests her source and this reading when she allows Milkman to interpret Solomon's flight ambiguously, "meaning died or ran off" (*Song of Solomon*, 307). Morrison also refers to the rock Solomon uses to take off as "Solomon's Leap," which is described in the novel as "the higher of two outcroppings of rock. Both flat-headed, both looking over a deep valley" (339). "Solomon's Leap" is named in the same way that the Ibos' take-off point is named into a commemorative ethnic landmark: "Solomon's Leap" echoes very clearly the symbolic idea of "Ibo's Landing," as a point of arrival and departure, of entry and exit, which foregrounds the reversibility of the Middle Passage.

Kum Buba Yali Kum Buba Tambe

Lines one through fifteen of the children's song tell of Solomon's desertion of his wife and children as well as his failed attempt to take Jake with him in his flight back to Africa. The odd lines of these three stanzas are fairly clear, though elliptical in their poetic concentration and metaphorical language, all of which Susan Byrd explicates in full narrative terms later. The literal flight of the fictional Solomon is patterned on mythical and slave narrative models, which also provide the "funny" flight-related words that are repeated in the even lines of the first three stanzas. Here too, Morrison's creative ethnic memory is just as dazzling.

In the opening sentences of a variant of the myth of flight Caesar Grant says: "Once all Africans could fly like birds; but, owing to their many transgressions, their wings were taken away" ("All God's Chillum," 139). In interviews quoted earlier in this study, Morrison talked about her commitment to reviving and closely reexamining Black "myths [that] get forgotten"; she cited her use of "the flying myth in *Song of Solomon*" and claimed that "flying was one of our gifts" (Leclair, 255). Solomon's ability to fly is governed by the fact that he is an "untainted" African, straight from Africa. In the myth, this power is activated by memory and utterance of magical African words.

Solomon's flight is accompanied and enabled by the utterance of African-language magical spells and an African genealogical list that Milkman at first refers to respectively as "meaningless rhyme" and "nonsense words." These rhymes and words are symbolic replacements for what Morrison refers to as "funny words I don't understand [and] . . . a long sort of a children's song I don't remember" in her family's "Song of Solomon" (Jones, 130). The African-language words in the children's song are words Morrison takes from slave oral accounts and alters by appropriating them creatively as part of the collective African-American ethnic memory and history she has inherited.

The second and fourth lines of the first three stanzas, *"Come booba yalle, come booba tambe"* and *"Come konka yalle, come konka tambee,"* come from a narrative about flying Africans told by Prince Sneed, an old man of about sixty years (*Drums and Shadows*, 79). The "funny words" Morrison does not understand or remember in her family history but borrows from other representative oral accounts and incorporates into the children's song are clearly associated with magical preflight incantations. Morrison splits Sneed's phrases into two alternating lines, changes the spelling of the words, and uses them in a close repetitive pattern of incantation that gives Solomon the power to fly as he "whiled about and touched the sun." The incantatory African words may conceivably be uttered by the mythical Solomon who, like the newly arrived African "wut wuzn't climatize," *remembers his ancestral language*, as he stretches his arms out like an airplane or a bird and takes off.

The magical African words are also found, in some altered form, in an African song, performed by Tony William Delegal, a former slave "over a hundred years old." Delegal sings:

> Wa kum kum munin
> *Kum baba yano*
> *Lai lai tambe*
> Ashi boong a nomo
> Shi wali go
> Ashi quank.
> (*Drums*, 54–55; emphasis mine)

In the absence of Morrison's family song, the structure of Delegal's song serves as a formal model for the children's song in the novel.

The slaves in Grant's narrative—marked by ethnic memory and utterance of African words—are "native Africans just brought into the country" ("All God's Chillum," 139). The oldest man of them all, an ancestral figure like Solomon, speaks to the new and acclimatized slaves in "an unknown tongue." As he speaks to them in this forgotten African language, stretching out his arms, "they all *remembered what they had forgotten*, and *recalled the power which once was theirs*" and flew away (141; emphasis mine). The critical importance of memory and African language is essential and the words the old man utters are phonologically very close to the preflight words found in Morrison's fiction,

Sneed's narrative and Delegal's song: Grant concludes, "As [the old man] went over the last fence he made a sign in the master's face, and cried 'Kuli-ba! Kuli-ba!' I don't know what that means" (142).

Flying Africans: Theresa and Ryna

Ryna, wife of the mythical/fictional Solomon, is drawn from a narrative by Rosa Grant, whose grandparents were African-born slaves. Grant's narrative not only indicates the source of the name "Ryna" in Morrison's song, but also provides a personalized variant of Sneed's story of flight. Morrison turns Ryna, the deserted little girl, into a woman and the wife of Solomon. The original pattern of maternal desertion, which is identical to the pattern of paternal desertion in the fictional transformation, becomes the basis of Ryna's blues story as Morrison makes her the fictional "black lady" who sings, "Solomon don't leave me here." The fictional Solomon, in turn, takes on the mythic volitant power of Theresa and stands as the towering and soaring African ancestor who reverses the traumatic Middle Passage by recrossing the Atlantic. The gender alteration is a necessary operation that allows Morrison to reinvest the lost ethnic volitant powers in the mythicized figure of the Black father/grandfather who dies or deserts his family. *Song of Solomon* is not only dedicated to "Daddy," Morrison's father, but the text of the novel is also preceded by a significant inscription: *"The fathers may soar/And the children know their names."* Morrison mentions her father's yearly pilgrimage to Georgia in her interview with Jones (130) and connects in another context the writing of *Song of Solomon* with the death of her father in a way that suggests intersections of fiction, autobiography and family history ("Site of Memory," 123–24).

The inventive resources of Morrison's art are deeply grounded in the knowledge and memory systems of ancestral legacies. The search for original ethnic names, languages, and gifts is one huge cultural and ideological imperative in Morrison's work. The myth of the flight contains all of this. Milkman experiences the epiphany Morrison talks about at the end of the novel after he discovers his ancestral name, sings the song of Solomon to Pilate, borrowing both Ryna's complaint and Pilate's blues, of which he revises the gender address as "sugar girl don't leave me here," before he himself flies. The quest and knowledge Morrison talks about are experienced by Milkman, for, at the end of the novel, "he knew what Shalimar knew: If you surrendered to the air, you could ride it" (342). Coupled with Morrison's dedication, the pre-text inscription and the autobiographical impulse cited above, *Song of Solomon* is a memorializing and commemorative act close to ancestor worship.

CONCLUSION

The matter of Morrison's oral sources for *Song of Solomon* is a very complex one, requiring an investigation of the creative form from various oral sources.

The evidence analyzed in this study points out real and significant aspects of the mythopoesis at work in the novel. This study demonstrates, in terms of aesthetic traditions, the formal relationships between the novel and specific African-American oral and written sources. The continuum between African and African-American oral and literary traditions is an indispensable factor in any balanced study of African-American literature whose non-African connections are already well known in the Western canon and quite often overvalued to the point of diminishing and colonizing the masterpieces.

For example, Blake (82) reduces the significance of oral tradition in Morrison's art and thus fails to grasp the cultural theory and practice that produced the novel. The "difference" created by Blake between "the world of black folk consciousness" embodied by the paradigm of "the folk tale" and "Morrison's fictional world" suggests a disconnection between *Song of Solomon* and its actual tradition. Blake reduces the determining oral sources to endnotes.

Leslie Harris discusses the novel in terms of two central paradigms, "the Icarus motif of failure and death . . . balanced by the Daedalus success" (72). He concludes that "rather than picking up the Icarus motif of escape and doomed flight, Morrison creates her own myth of those who fumble in their efforts to fly and they soar higher—more Daedaluses than Icaruses" (76). While there may be validity in comparing the flight paradigms in Greek mythology and in Morrison's novel, suppressing the African and African-American sources and substituting them with the Greek ones is a canonical falsification. The failure of much of Western criticism lies not only in its ignorance of the linguistic, aesthetic, and ideological culture of *Song of Solomon* but, more significantly, in the critics' insistence on extraditing the work from its cultural and ideological context and placing it into their own Eurocentric canon, where it is burdened with dubious parentage, ancestry, and the authorized misreadings of alien critical tools. Morrison clearly objects to any imposed alien paradigm and critical discourse:

I do not like to find my books condemned as bad or praised as good, when that condemnation or praise is based on criteria from other paradigms. I would much prefer that they were dismissed or embraced based on the success of their accomplishment *within the culture out of which I write*. ("Rootedness," 342; emphasis mine)

NOTE

The analysis of oral sources can be extended to African oral epic materials, especially with regard to possible links between Belali Mohomet's story and the story of the seventh-century Bilali Ibn Ka Nama. Significant details imported into the novel from the slave narratives told by descendants of Belali Mohomet suggest strong connections between their African-born ancestor and the first muezzin appointed by the Prophet Mohammad to whom Allah revealed the religion of Islam. This matter is treated in a separate work.

BIBLIOGRAPHY

Blake, Susan L. "Folklore and Community in *Song of Solomon*." *MELUS* 7, no. 3 (Fall 1980): 77–82.

Bonnetti, Kay. *Interview with Toni Morrison*. American Audio Prose Library. New York, May 1983.

Demetrakopoulos, Stephenie A., and Karla Holloway. *New Dimensions of Spirituality*. Westport, Conn.: Greenwood Press, 1987.

Drums and Shadows: Survival Studies among the Georgia Coastal Negroes. Savannah Unit, Georgia Writers' Project, Work Projects Administration, 1940. Westport, Conn.: Greenwood Press, 1973.

Grant, Caesar. "All God's Chillum Had Wings." In *The Doctor to the Dead*, edited by John Bennett. New York, 1946.

Harris, Leslie. "Myth as Structure in Toni Morrison's *Song of Solomon*." *MELUS* 7, no. 3 (Fall 1980): 69–76.

Jones, Jessie W. "Interview with Toni Morrison." In *The World of Toni Morrison*, edited by Jessie W. Jones and Audrey L. Vinson. Dubuque, Iowa: Kendall/Hunt Publishing Company, 1985.

LeClair, Tom. "Interview with Toni Morrison." In *Anything Can Happen*, edited by Tom LeClair and Larry McCaffery. Urbana: University of Illinois Press, 1983.

Morrison, Toni. "Rootedness: The Ancestor as Foundation." In *Black Women Writers*, edited by Mari Evans. New York: Doubleday, 1983.

———. "The Site of Memory." In *Inventing the Truth: The Art and Craft of Memory*, edited by William Zinsser. Boston: Houghton Mifflin Co., 1987.

———. *Song of Solomon*. New York: NAL Penguin, Inc., 1978.

———. "Unspeakable Things Spoken: The Afro-American Presence in American Literature." *Michigan Quarterly Review* 28, no. 1 (Winter 1989): 1–34.

Strouse, Jean. "Toni Morrison's Black Magic." *Newsweek*, March 10, 1981, 52–57.

11

The Circle of Meaning: Paule Marshall, Modernism, and the Masks of History

SIMON GIKANDI

> To what extent can one speak of an African knowledge, and in what sense?
> —V. Y. Mudimbe,
> *The Invention of Africa*
>
> After struggling for some time, I was finally able . . . to bring together what I consider to be the two themes most central to my work: the importance of truly confronting the past, both in personal and historical terms, and the necessity of reversing the present order.
>
> —Paule Marshall,
> "Shaping the World of My Art"

The African reader of African-American literature shares a similar agenda with Paule Marshall: of all the writers of the African diaspora, she is the most attuned not only to the order of blackness and the tropes that represent it, but also the global dimensions of the colonizing structures that have stifled, but also provoked, a discourse of resistance in the African world. The question of representing and understanding this colonial structure, and of ultimately supplanting it with an African order of knowledge, is hence of utmost importance to Marshall; and if her Caribbean texts seem to keep on returning to the terms by which the colonized can articulate the past, it is because she believes that the present state of oppression and reification can only be reversed if its conditions of existence are fully comprehended. Marshall's novels are, in this sense, concerned with the articulation of an Africanist hermeneutics: they probe the rules by which the Black experience in the new world can be interpreted in the face of the historical conditions that have sought to repress the Black voice in the discourse of Western modernism.

Like many of her characters, the Marshall text often struggles with the linguistic and psychological blockage that hampers the hermeneutical act, the rules of over-determination that often make it impossible for the reader to gain access to those original meanings which have been suppressed in the Middle Passage of the Black experience. Marshall's major works often strive to provide a meta-commentary on the painful coexistence of European modernist institutions and fragments of the African tradition in the New World. Her works often return to the Caribbean islands of her ancestors to try and capture what she calls, in "Shaping the World of My Art," "thoughts and feelings about the Middle passage" (101) and to elaborate "the psychological damage brought on by history" (110). But this concern with pain and the nightmare of history is seen as an important prerequisite for reestablishing a new cultural base, for recreating the hermeneutical circle of new Black meanings. In other words, the utopian desire of Marshall's major novels (*Brown Girl, Brownstones*; *The Chosen Place, The Timeless People*; and *Praisesong for the Widow*) is the recuperation of an original voice, an echo of an African past that exists beneath the manifest discourse of colonialism.

Simple issues of meaning—in particular the process by which individual subjects develop a materialist understanding of their conditions of existence—constitute an important prelude to the larger historical questions that mark Marshall's novels. For example, the central motifs in *Brown Girl, Brownstones*—the mirror and the body—are intended to raise phenomenological questions about vision and representation. Confused and threatened by the harsh logic of material progress, Selina Boyce often struggles to define the meaning of her body, to even understand her own subjectivity. Her disjunctive relationship with the acquisitive world of her mother is often manifested in the self-division she feels between her self and her family. The ethic that drives her mother has no reality for her; indeed, it is this ethic—this need for material things as a signature of one's existence—that stifles Selina's growth.

A significant representation of this repression of selfhood comes early in the novel when Selina reflects on the family photograph "which did not include her": "She wanted suddenly to send up a loud cry to declare herself" (6). Because this family icon does not include Selina, it exists as a mark of her displacement; because the photograph has no reality for her, it is perceived as "[t]he picture of a neat, young family and she did not believe it" (7). It might as well have been a fanciful image in the picture books. Furthermore, Selina's world is one of illusionary and shifting figures which already point to a social situation marked by alienation and *dedoublement*. The family photograph signifies connections with an ancestral home in Barbados, but she does not belong there; nor does she belong to her mother's brave new world in New York. Indeed, the ancestral past has no meaning for anyone except her father: he is the only one who appears real in the picture, and because of this, he represents her tenuous connection to the ethics and impulses of the past: "For her, he was the one constant in the flux and unreality of life" (8).

But for the father, like all the other Barbadian immigrants who populate Marshall's novel, such important connections to the past rarely function as a source of certainty and true understanding; rather, they are a mark of fear and shame, foregrounding both the need by the subjects to be anchored in the past, and their concern that the past forecloses the future. Thus, Selina's father is proud of his Bajan past, but he fears that Suggie's codfish will "insinuate itself into his clothes and he would carry it with him all night as the undisputable sign that he was Barbadian and a foreigner" (22).

This uncertainty of self, as we will see later in this study, functions as a synecdochic representation of a larger crisis of consciousness in Marshall's works. Her characters are driven by a double, and often contradictory, movement: on the one hand, they want to write themselves into the scheme of things and to be recognized as subjects with a culture and history; but, on the other hand, they believe that their mastery of the codes of the dominant culture— especially wealth, property, and status—will win them recognition from the Other. The end result, however, is a process of repression and disguise, which is manifested in Du Bois's famous notion of double consciousness—the repressed Black subject has to function as itself and as the Other at the same time.[1]

In *Brown Girl, Brownstones*, this self-division is figurated by Selina as she tries to walk the tight rope between her mother's desire to be assimilated into the materialist ethic and her father's dream of returning to Barbados. When the mother forces Selina to wear "throw-offs"—which the little girl perceives as symbols of her own alienation—it is the father's "voice" that restores her to her own sense of self (11). However, the repressed or marginalized self can never find wholeness and deep meanings in the ideology of modernity; because this self cannot belong wholly to the Other's scheme of things, it must live as a fragment of both its culture and the value system of the dominant. For this reason, there is often a disjunction between the soul and the body in Marshall's text. In moments of despair, anger, and an acute sense of betrayal, Selina realizes that all attempts to secure the integrity of her inner self have come to naught because "She was not free but still trapped within a hard flat body" (62). The body belongs to the other—the dominant culture, her mother, the Barbadian community—and thus her attempts at transgression and self-engenderment are bound to fail.

The problem of self-identity in situations of displacement is further accentuated by the fact that one cannot develop a synthesis between the real (Black) self and an assimilated sense of self that masks and protects the former. Self-division does not restore authority to one part of the self; on the contrary, it nullifies both because there is always confusion about what is authentic and, hence, representable. The example of Jay Johnson in *Praisesong for the Widow* is very revealing in this aspect. Frustrated in his previous attempts at mastery— even after a painful process of self-education he will not get a job as an accountant because of his race—Jay will destroy his spontaneous and natural self and adopt the hard and cold logic of "progress." But what is the meaning of this new self? What are its values, and how is it to be interpreted? For his wife, Avery (who was responsible for nudging him toward this change in the first place), the new Jay is "like the vague, pale outline of another face superimposed on his, as in a double-exposure" (131).

A doubly-exposed image, of course, has no clear outline; it exists as a fragment of two things without the representative value of either. In the end, Jay is defined by distance and difference, rather than any mode of identity between the self and the signs that represent it. In striving to be the equal of the Other, Jay even speaks in a voice that his own wife finds "hard to recognize" (131). In the new Jay, there is marked tension between voice and tone, between demand and desire. Indeed, his voice has become a mask of the self, not its signifier.[2]

The persistent image of the veil or the mask in Marshall's works denotes the impossibility of developing an essentialist sense of self and of really knowing the Other. But this is not always a negative process: the mask, as scholars of African-American literature and culture have begun to realize, signifies deep meanings, contains within it what Henry Louis Gates, Jr., has called, in *Figures in Black*, "a coded, secret, hermetic world, a world discovered only by the initiate" (167).[3] In Marshall's *The Chosen Place, The Timeless People*, to cite just one example, the mask idiom reflects the subject's mastery of their most essential, and often hidden, meanings, so that for the outsider to try to read the masked figures of the African-American experience is to confront the limits of his or her own, Eurocentric, rules of understanding.

In *The Chosen Place*, which is one of the monumental texts on modernization and colonial historiography, the central question that all subjects have to confront sooner or later has to do with developing new modes of knowledge in a world in which the old relationships between master and slave, the colonizer and the colonized, have been refigured in the period of decolonization. More importantly, the Middle Passage of Black culture is shown to be a discursive space in which historical and other meanings cannot be taken for granted: the text postulates the problems, and possibilities, of recovering the most hidden meanings of a culture that has always used duplicity and self-masking as weapons of survival.[4] Nothing illustrates this problem as vividly as Saul's travail as he tries to understand the island of Bournehills. Nothing in his education and experience has trained the American anthropologist to read the subaltern's modes of representation.

This point becomes more resonant if we recall that Saul is a scholar who believes in the Weberian doctrine of modernization as a rational process that liberates the self from restrictive traditions.[5] As a matter of fact, Saul heads a research study that promotes rational knowledge as the key to historical change. In the first part of *The Chosen Place*, the proposed plan for Bournehills is presented in the methodical and dead language of modernization.

Once he encounters the island, Saul discovers that rational knowledge cannot measure up to the fleeting nature of reality in Bournehills; here, the traditional binary oppositions that sanction analysis are easily invalidated and the unconscious side of history plays a dominant part in the lives of the people. In his attempts to "read" the islands, the analyst is confronted by realities he cannot fix. We are told of his stumbling upon a real yet unreal world, combining both present and particularly the past.

It is clear that the signs that denote this "illogical" mode of representation—the motionless figures of the cane cutters and the "ancient windmills"—negate all the key assumptions in Saul's modernist discourse. Indeed, if we accept Lyotard's famous definition of the modernist imperative as the drive "to seize and systematize the world and so liberate human possibilities by mastering the conditions of life in a cognitive and manipulative system" (quoted in Kolb, 257; see note 5), then the admixture of the real and unreal that Saul encounters on the island undermines any notions of systematization. In other words, the binary oppositions—reality/illusions, past/present, and tradition/modernity—that the researchers hoped to establish conclusively to master the conditions of life on the island, are nullified by the "marvelous" reality of Bournehills, which does not allow for such divisions.

In contrast, Marshall's retextualization of the past is prompted by a cultural need: to reassemble the pieces of Black history and "to bring together all the various strands (the word is synthesis) and thus make of that diverse heritage a whole" ("Shaping the World," 106). But such wholeness does not come easily, if it ever comes at all; the authoritative tone of narration that characterizes all of Marshall's text conceals an inner anxiety about meanings; the authority of her speaking subjects is often compromised and questioned by their own crises of identity, or by the obvious contrast between their desire for settled and complete meanings and the historical discontinuity that surrounds them.

Thus, in *The Chosen Place*, Merle Kinbona has struggled for eight years to make sense of the history of the island, to resurrect the hidden and unofficial history of her people—built around the myth of Cuffee Ned and his slave revolt—but such discordant history is not easily written into the master text of colonial history: "Saul could see how the lonely eight-year search for coherence and vision had exhausted her" (229). The history of the Black experience in the Americas refuse to be pigeonholed into periods and movements; it flees from the logic of Western historiography which, as Michel de Certeau has argued so limpidly in *The Writing of History* "is legitimized by what it excludes" (5).

HISTORY AS NIGHTMARE

"Ah, well, ah, history. . . . It is a nightmare, as that Irishman said, and we haven't awakened from it yet" (*The Chosen Place*, 130). Merle Kinbona's invocation of James Joyce is not uncharacteristic of Marshall's other characters: her central subjects are often haunted by their sense or knowledge of history; an encounter with the past creates a sense of betrayal and often ends in bitterness, because this is a past of pain and loss. But if these characters see history as a nightmare, it is because they often start from a false premise—the belief that a knowledge of the past is an encounter with the heroic and monumental side of the Black experience and that knowledge of this positive polarity, the better side of an often rapacious and dehumanizing history, will become an antithesis to the reification that characterizes the present moment. And if the reader falls into the same trap as Kinbona—and thus assumes that history will yield the positive binary of Black history—it is because Marshall's text represents history as what Frederic Jameson calls a "ruse." Represented as "an absent cause" rather than a positive vision, history "is what hurts, it is what refuses desire and sets inexorable limits to individual as well as collective praxis" (102).

In Marshall's novels, history often begins as an architectural process—complete with monuments that supposedly figurate the "chosen place and the timeless people"—but these symbols of history are never complete. Take, for example, the brownstones in *Brown Girl, Brownstones*: for many of the Barbadian immigrants in New York, these buildings have become the very embodiment of the American Dream, the objects of desire at the end of an eschatological process in which hard work leads to wealth and hence happiness.[6] However, a closer look at these monuments of upliftment shows how Marshall has loaded the brownstones with meanings that reverse their overt intentions. If the ownership of a brownstone is the mark of engenderment, this notion of subjectivity is undermined by the buildings' uniformity: "they all shared the same brown monotony. All seemed doomed by the confusion of their design" (*Brown Girl*, 3).

The houses were supposed to be distinctive to emphasize the individuality of their owners, but this distinctiveness is suspect: "looking close, you saw under the thick ivy each house had something distinctively its own. Some touch of Gothic, Romanesque, baroque or Greek triumphed amid the Victorian clutter" (3). And this is precisely the problem of the modernity project: it draws fragments from different European styles, but it does not fuse them into a new, redesigned form—hence, the confusion that has doomed the brownstones even before their owners have paid for them. Furthermore, if the right to property has here been posited as signifying self-engenderment—and, hence, is conceived of as a source of pleasure and life—the ivy that covers the building (all were "draped in ivy as though in mourning") is a symbol of death and decay.

History also hurts in *The Chosen Place*, but this is not solely because the experience of the Middle Passage was so painful for Black people; it is also hurtful because what was brought over from Africa can not be fully recuperated, and therefore the subjects who desire wholeness from this history are condemned to live with the yawning gaps it has left behind. In the first part of the book (appropriately titled "Heirs and Descendants" because it is concerned with the genealogy of modernity in the Caribbean), the ruins of history appear in various guises: Merle's Bentley, the former state car of the colonial governor, has been much misused and is no more than a wreck; her body is also fast approaching the decline brought about by middle age. A succession of motifs reinforces this image of decay, decline, and incompleteness: Merle's dress and decorations are fragments from diverse cultures; their beauty is obvious, but their meaning and value are not coherent. Her outfit is bizarre, made of opposing items that she is trying to reconcile. She puts together all these pieces of clothing from her past with the hope of recovering something lost, perhaps her sense of being a woman.

The ruins or remnants of history in *The Chosen Place* are signs of a buried, but sinister, past. Take, for example, the room that houses the nightclub in Bournehills: it is described as a "long, high nave, whole areas of which were lost to the shadows dwelling beyond the reach of the touring lights" (81). But the room is just the visible part of something more important: the building used to be a sugar warehouse and if you dig beneath, you will possibly discover the slave barracoons. With this kind of antiquity, the island becomes a field of rubble where various things discarded from centuries are dumped. Bournehills is often compared to a dilapidated amphitheater or coliseum.

Furthermore, each character in the text has his or her own notions of history and definite views about its value and modes of representation. Merle is fired from her teaching job because she insists on teaching the history of the subaltern, of events that occurred centuries before the arrival of the English on the island. History is thus a contested terrain: on the one hand, there are those who believe in positive history—those who, like Allen Fuso, have an Aristotelian confidence in the rational doctrine that allows everything, including people, to be put in their categories; on the other hand, there are the poor people of Bournehills who believe in the performative power of history, and, hence, recover that history by reenacting it.

Merle, too, shares this faith in the performative function of history: when she retells the history of Cuffee Ned, her voice reveals a certain reverence, a certain mystique making one think that it is her first time of recounting it. The novel presents a wonderful contrast between performed history (retold by Merle), and Allen's decidedly objective rendering of the same history according to what is called historical records. Most importantly, as Hortense J. Spillers has observed in her brilliant reading of the novel, the history of Bournehills is not simply one of oppression and betrayal; rather it is fixed in a scene determined by "origins that must be appeased, at least recognized and named out loud" (Spillers, 158).

CARNIVAL AS A MARKER OF HISTORY

To quote Mikhail Bakhtin in *Rabelais and His World*, "Carnival is not a spectacle seen by the people; they live in it, and everyone participates because its very idea embraces all the people."

Spillers's apt characterization of carnival as Marshall's "master sign and controlling figure" (165) recognizes the centrality of the carnivalesque in the rewriting of Black history in the Americas.[7] There is another point that needs to be foregrounded: the displaced and poor people of Bournehills, like their slave ancestors, have found in the form of the carnivalesque and its discursive strategies, a space in which ancestral memories can be retained and the ideology of colonial modernism contested.

Indeed, the poor people of Bournehills, who appear so intransigent to outsiders because they resist change and movement, are compared, in the novel itself, to Anancy, the trickster in Afro-Caribbean folklore who "though small and weak, always managed to outwit the larger and stronger creatures in his world, including man, by his wit and cunning" (*The Chosen Place*, 224). Thus, as a subterranean and subversive force, the carnivalesque exists to challenge the dominance and ideology of Eurocentric modes of knowledge and representation. And, yet, because carnival in *The Chosen Place* figurates the paradoxes engendered by temporal shifts in the island, including a postcolonial situation that has consolidated the power of the Black elite and left the island as dependent as ever on the old political economy, it is susceptible to different interpretations. For the upper classes and the tourists, it is a meaningless spectacle that creates a temporal suspense which is useful because it represses class, racial, and caste differences; that is why Lyle Hurton describes it as "a marvelous sight, and a much needed one . . . in a world where all of us manage to be so ugly to each other, especially over this whole stupid question of race and color" (200).

But as a proponent of the neocolonial order, Hurton's interpretation of the carnival is over-determined by his deliberate detachment from the popular culture; he views the carnival from outside, as a spectacle that mirrors his own desire to master and control his people, but he will not negate it entirely because his authority as a member of parliament depends on his claim to represent the peasants of Bournehills. In contrast, the real meaning of the carnival and its true spirit, as Mikhail Bakhtin argues so eloquently in *Rabelais and His World*, derives from the fact that the people don't view it as a spectacle, but "live in it, and everyone participates because its very idea embraces all the people" (7).

At this junction, it is important to recall that the reason why the majority of islanders resist the participation of the people of Bournehills in the carnival is because the latter will not change their design, routine, or story. As Harriet puts it aptly in a letter to her friend Chessie, "for some reason people in Bournehills insist on enacting the same masque or story every carnival, which is against the rules. But they say it's cheaper, because then they don't have to buy new costumes" (*The Chosen Place*, 233). Why do the people of Bournehills insist on constituting a carnival within the carnival? The cost analysis that they offer as a reason for repetition and changelessness is already a ruse or mask; the real reasons have to do with a deliberately constituted oppositional stance vis-à-vis the dominant. They feel that the new carnival (the tourist spectacle) has become institutionalized in the capitalist system of exchange; by insisting on changelessness, these people have defied the logic of the neocolonial economy or representation. Indeed, when the peasants of Bournehills march against "the rules," they are in keeping with the true spirit of the carnivalesque as a subversive force, for as Bakhtin has noted, carnival celebrates "temporal liberation from the prevailing truth and from the established order" (10).

We must note that, in addition, the people of Bournehills insist on repeating the worn out history of the Cuffee slave rebellion; to the embarrassment of the modernists who prefer to look to the future rather than the past, the peasants come into town every year in their wretched clothes and recall events that so-called decent people have forgotten. This repetitiveness of history runs counter to Bakhtin's description of carnival as "the true feast of time, the feast of becoming, change and renewal" (10). What, then, is the value of a history that repeats itself?

In the end, Marshall and her characters are seeking to reclaim an essentialist African voice in the New World. The notion of continuity of ancient African traditions is paramount in Marshall's work, of "the oral mode by which the culture and history, the wisdom of the race had been transmitted" ("Shaping the World," 103). In the same manner as Edouard Glissant and Edward Brathwaite, Caribbean writers like herself, Marshall often posits the voice as a paradigm for the repressed African past in Caribbean and African-American cultures. In *Brown Girl*, Silla Boyce may strive to master the culture of capitalism and its celebration of property rights, but she cannot escape from the tradition of the voice that relives the past at every opportunity. For this reason, she has become "the collective voice of all the Bajan women, the vehicle through which their former suffering found utterance" (45).

In *The Chosen Place*, Merle's voice is at once what identifies her and the mask of a hidden and enigmatic self. The voice appears to have acquired a life of its own, grossing on the surface, out of control, refracting us from, rather than drawing attention to, the speaker. Very early in the novel, Merle's voice is shown caught up in "what seemed a desperate downhill race with itself" (11); her words flow unchecked and her desperate and anguished voice is described as rushing headlong toward destruction. As the novel progresses, however, we begin to realize that the voice masks an inner pain; her surface talk is a form of temporal suspense—by talking, Merle postpones confronting the past.

CONCLUSION: THE CIRCLE OF MEANING

In *Praisesong for the Widow*, Avery Johnson's crisis of identity is closely related to her uneasy relationship with a collective "black voice"; her cooption into the modern exchange system has ostensibly liberated her from echos of the past. But in the early scenes of the novel, the past seems to have returned to haunt her; she, who has always striven to erase the unpleasant from her memory, discovers that she cannot shake off her great-aunt Cuney from her mind. What needs to be stressed about this "eternal recurrence" of the past is the fact that Marshall poses it as a hermeneutical problem revolving around the central paradigm of Afro-American culture—the "Ring Shout" and its accompanying circle of meaning.

Now, in writing about this "circle of culture" in his monumental study, *Slave*

Culture (1987), Sterling Stuckey has stressed two points that are pertinent to any reading of *Praisesong for the Widow*: First of all, the circle functioned as an allegory of "African autonomy" in the new world; second, it marked the set of values and symbols that could condition the reading of the Black experience. Thus, early Afro-American storytellers "told tales in which the dominant spiritual configuration provided the means by which Africans, whatever their ethnic differences, found values proper to them when the slave trade and slavery divorced them from their homeland. Consequently, listeners in the slave community who had previously been unexposed to those tales immediately understood what was being related" (11). Similarly, the "Shout" signifies the beginning of a distinctive Afro-American discourse; at the beginning, says Glissant in his "Free and Forced Poetics," was the shout (96).

Avery Johnson is born into this circle of meaning; her first utterances are about the shout, her first discourse evolves around the story, told by her great-aunt Cuney, of the Ibos who had foreseen the tragedies of slavery and had decided to return home by walking across the sea. In a sense, Avery's mission was to carry into the future memories of the past: "in instilling the story of the Ibos in her child's mind, the old woman had entrusted her with a mission she couldn't even name yet had felt duty-bound to fulfill" (*Praisesong*, 42). Her crisis of consciousness has developed precisely because, in espousing the modernist notion of temporality as a form of progression from the past to the future, Avery has forgotten her ancestral duties; now her repressed past has returned to haunt her and "her memory seemed to be playing the same frightening tricks as her eyes" (57). But how can she recover the value of a past that now appears more remote from her than it ever was?

The idea of "return" is an important historical trope in *Praisesong* and is often proposed as a possible resolution of the crisis of temporality that grips characters like Avery Johnson. Let us recall that when the unconscious echoes from the past and forces Avery to abandon her cruiseship and return to her home, history ruses her into a Caribbean island in which the themes of return and historical continuity are inscribed into the collective memories of the people. Waking up in an island where the past still seems to be alive, Avery's mind has been cleared of the memories that repressed her Afrocentricity "so that she had awakened . . . like a slate that has been wiped clean, a *tabula rasa* upon which a whole new history could been written" (151). But how is this history written? Or rather, how is the subject inscribed into its old history?

Again, we must remember that the so-called Carriacou excursion is, like the carnival in Bournehills's, a performative act that has ensured the survival of the past in the present by annually repeating the African circle of meanings: in the great shout and dance, family and nation are recalled and reconnection with the past established. Every islander identifies with a nation or with a creole culture (175); in a sense, by recognizing her own place within this circle, it could appear that Avery has reconnected with her past and covered the "hole the size of a crater where her life of the past three decades had been" (196). However, a final question still remains: what is the value of this trope of return, of what Kubayanda has called the "phenomenon of recognition"? The answer is contained in a passage in which Avery tries to endow the dance of nations with meaning; she discovers value, not in the words of the songs, but in the emotions expressed:

It was the essence of something rather than the thing itself she was witnessing. . . . All that was left were a few names of what they called nations which they could no longer even pronounce properly, the fragments of a dozen or so songs, the shadowy forms of long-ago dances and rum kegs for drums. The bare bones. The burn-out ends. And they clung to them with a tenacity she suddenly loved in them and longed for in herself. Thoughts—new thoughts—vague and half-formed slowly beginning to fill the emptiness. (240)

The African ideal in the Americas is retained even in its shredded and fragmentary nature because it holds the hope of legitimating the Black self in a discursive formation that has often denied its very existence.

However, Paule Marshall will not succumb to the mystical belief that despite "separation and loss" an African "order of things" can be recuperated in a continuous and holistic way. What her narratives seem to propose is an archeological gesture that seeks to trace the conditions in which African-American culture emerged and the rules that governed the transformation of the African ideal in the Americas. At the end of *Praisesong*, Avery Johnson realizes that the power of the cultural circle in Carriacou does not lie in the object it proffers, but in "the unacknowledged longing it conveyed," which "summed up feelings that were beyond words, feelings and a host of subliminal memories that over the years had proven more durable and trustworthy than the history with its trauma and pain out of which they had come" (245). The African fragment has value precisely because it is the central focus of the unconscious rules that have governed Black discourse from the mercantile period, which sought to turn Blacks into voiceless objects, to our more contemporary period when late capitalism has evoked a new consumer culture that represses identities in the name of a global culture.

NOTES

1. In discussing the "veil" that divides the Black American in two, Du Bois is cognizant of the hermeneutical problems possible by the mediation of the Black self by the Other.

2. Lacan connects desire and marginality when he asserts that "Desire begins to take shape in the margin in which demand becomes separated from need" (311).

3. Houston Baker also recenters the mask, this time as a trope rather than a figure, in *Modernism and the Harlem Renaissance* (17).

4. My use of the notions of "middle passage" and "marginality" are indebted to V.

Y. Mudimbe. I read the "middle passage" as a numinous space between Africa and America.

5. In his excellent reading of Weber, David Kolb writes on how the famous proponent of modernization saw rationalization as the process by which the self became the creator of its own meanings; thus, modernity identity for Weber is "the unveiling" of what has been at the root of historical constructs [Kolb, *The Critique of Pure Modernity* (University of Chicago Press, 1986), 10].

6. There are two good discussions of architecture and architectural symbolism in Marshall's novels: Schneider's and Benston's. See also articles by Kapai and by Stoelting for discussions of time and historical archetypes in Marshall's fiction.

7. An excellent study of carnival in the Caribbean can be found in Warner (9–13).

BIBLIOGRAPHY

Baker, Houston A., Jr. *Modernism and the Harlem Renaissance*. Chicago: University of Chicago Press, 1987.

Bakhtin, Mikhail. *Rabelais and His World*. Cambridge, Mass.: M.I.T. Press, 1968.

Bentson, Kimberly. "Architectural Imagery and Unity in Paule Marshall's *Brown Girl, Brownstones*." *Negro American Literature Forum* 9 (1975): 67–70.

Brathwaite, Edward Kamau. "West Indian History and Society in the Art of Paule Marshall's Novel." *Journal of Black Studies* 1 (1970): 225–38.

Du Bois, W.E.B. *The Souls of Black Folk*. New York: New American Library, 1969.

Gates, Henry Louis, Jr. *Figures in Black: Words, Signs and the "Racial" Self*. New York: Oxford University Press, 1967.

Glissant, Edouard. "Free and Forced Poetics." In *Ethnopoetica*, edited by Michel Benamou and Jerome Rothenberg. Boston: Alcheringa, 1976.

Jameson, Fredric. *The Ideologies of Theory*. Minneapolis: University of Minnesota Press, 1988.

Kapai, Leela. "Dominant Themes and Techniques in Paule Marshall's Fiction." *CLA Journal* 16 (1972): 49–59.

Kubayanda, Josephat, B. "The Phenomenon of Recognition: The African Ideal in the Caribbean Text." Caribbean Literature and the African Diaspora Conference, Boston, May 19, 1988.

Lacan, Jacques. *Ecrits: A Selection*. Translated by Alan Sheridan. New York: Norton, 1977.

Marshall, Paule. *Brown Girl, Brownstones*. Originally published 1959. New York: Feminist Press, 1981.

———. *The Chosen Place, The Timeless People*. Originally published 1969. New York: Vantage, 1984.

———. "Shaping the World of My Art." *New Letters* 40 (1973): 97–112.

———. *Praisesong for the Widow*. Originally published 1983. New York: Dutton, 1984.

Mudimbe, V. Y. *The Invention of Africa: Gnosis, Philosophy, and the Order of Knowledge*. Bloomington: Indiana University Press, 1988.

Nazareth, Peter. "Paule Marshall's Timeless People." *New Letters* 40 (1973): 113–31.

Schneider, Deborah. "A Feminine Search for Selfhood: Paule Marshall's *Brown Girl, Brownstones*." In *The Afro-American Novel since 1960*, edited by Peter Bruck and Wolfgang Karrer. Amsterdam: Gruner, 1982.

Spillers, Hortense J. *"Chosen Place, Timeless People*: Some Figurations on the New World."* In *Conjuring: Black Women, Fiction and Literary Tradition*, edited by Marjorie Pryse and Hortense J. Spillers. Bloomington: Indiana University Press, 1985.

Stoelting, Winifred L. "Time Past and Time Present: The Search for Viable Links in *The Chosen People, The Timless Place* by Paule Marshall." *CLA Journal* 16 (1972): 60–71.

Warner, Keith Q. *Kaiso!: The Trinidad Calypso*. Washington, D.C.: Three Continents Press, 1985.

12

Homesick and Eurocentric?
Alice Walker's Africa

MWIKALI KIETI

Not knowing about Black American artists until completing college so infuriated Alice Walker that she set out to revisit her history in an attempt to relocate herself. As a result, she wrote *Langston Hughes: American Poet* (1974), a book intended especially to introduce Hughes to African-American children. Walker's determination to situate herself in history took her beyond her immediate environment to Africa, her distant ancestral homeland. While she acknowledges her love for Africa and Africans throughout *Warrior Marks*[1] and in various interviews, Walker's portrayal of Africa sometimes reveals latent Eurocentrism.[2] Despite Walker's sensitivity to various issues, her work is marred by the Eurocentrism that it uncritically reproduces. Moreover, Walker seems to reproduce the brand of feminist sisterhood she sets out to critique: that is, a feminism that generalizes women uncritically. In the process of distancing her work from the "Western liberal feminism" that has excluded African sisters, Walker relies on the Western liberal feminist practice of generalizing about African women. I will discuss Walker's Eurocentrism and feminism in this essay. However, my discussion of these two aspects in Walker's work proceeds from my recognition of Walker's tremendous contribution to literature and Black history as an essayist, activist, novelist, and poet.

Much of Western scholarship is Eurocentric. Major studies about Africa depict an Africa that is part of Said's orientalist discourse (see Said, *Orientalism*). This discourse defines an occidental (European) center through the textual creation of an oriental (non-European) other and relies upon scientific and social terms to describe societies in a manner that supports the ideology that the European view is universal. Thus, in a process closely related to the growth of the empire, literature is usually subsumed under the study of English. As such, "the study of English and the growth of Empire proceeded from a single ideological climate and the development of the one is intrinsically bound up with that of the other, both at the level of simple utility (as propaganda for instance) and at the unconscious level, where it leads to the naturalizing of constructed values (e.g., civilization, humanity, etc.) which, conversely, established 'savagery,' 'native,' 'primitive,' as their antitheses and as the object of a reforming zeal."[3] Accounts of Africa are replete with racist images of Africa, portraying Africa as wild, exotic, diseased, and dark.[4] Stories from Africa often assume the form of a reporter's adventure trip up the Congo or Nile, or a visit with mountain gorillas, lions, and/or elephants in East Africa. Familiar African countries are frequently synonymous with sprawling game parks and "real" natives, like the Masai in Kenya and Tanzania, who have become part of the tourist package.[5]

Obscured through this discourse is the history of colonialist rule where Africa, constructed as oriental and therefore distinct from occidental, became an image offering positive horror. The relationship between the "mother countries" and "children" of the empires was not negotiated but imposed by the mother countries on the colonies. The mother countries oversaw everything. Prevalent stereotypical images of Africa in Western popular culture occasionally find their way into Walker's Africa.

Sadly, the process of countering this Eurocentric and orientalist view of Africa has produced forms of Afro-essentialisms among some African Americans and Africans: for example, the different Afrocentricisms. Although they are reactions to imperialist efforts to homogenize Blacks, these essentialisms must be rebutted and challenged in terms of their totalizing tendencies. While originating in the domination and oppression within capitalism—more specifically racism—Afrocentrisms' totalizing discourse of Eurocentrism breeds an opposite one. A useful Afrocentrism needs to include an analysis of colonialism, racism, sexism, homophobia, and capitalism. European thought and domination systems must be removed through politics and a solid strategy that endeavors to do so, instead of the imaginary cultural clash that Asante and Collins (among others) create.[6] I will discuss how these problematic aspects of Afrocentric thought operate in Walker's work. Such an analysis will reveal Walker's own Eurocentric tendencies as well as some contradictions in her feminist analysis.

Introduced in *The Color Purple*, Tashi is the main character in *Possessing the Secrets of Joy*, after appearing briefly in *The Temple of My Familiar*.[7] While recreating and redefining African and African-American women's silenced voices, *Color* maintains an ambivalence to Africa that occasionally turns into stereotypical images of the continent, an ambivalence culminating in *Joy*. In *Color*, for instance, Nettie writes her sister many letters from the "dark" continent. "We celebrate [Christmas] here on the dark continent with prayer and song and a large picnic" (154). If Nettie says "dark" with tongue in cheek, this is not true of an earlier letter describing the journey into Olinka after landing in Africa (139). This description of Africa's jungle and its idle and lazy people is reminiscent of Joseph Conrad's *Heart of Darkness* (1902) or Henry Haggard's *She* (1885). Though Nettie compares the Olinka people's love for meat to that of her own people in America, her phrases evoke images of the cannibal Africans lurking around in the jungle, signaling earlier texts on Africa as well as the publicized stories of cannibalism.[8]

When Tashi resurfaces after her facial scarification and the rite of female initiation, Nettie reports that Tashi was "unfortunately ashamed of these scars." Soon after, Nettie is thankful that Tashi begins to appreciate the magnitude of her mistake. The villagers carve their identification as a people into their children's faces, and into this Nettie reads child molestation (*Color*, 214).

Walker looks at Africa without analyzing with whose eyes she sees the continent. Coinciding with increasing feminist studies today, theories about African women—for example, concepts of patriarchy and what constitutes women's oppression—have largely come from outside Africa. Without investigating the Olinka women's concepts of oppression, Nettie sees their friendships only as oppressive (153). Though Walker's women—in Africa and America—are silenced in many ways, the liberal feminist view of African "sisters," influenced by Eurocentrism, interferes with Walker's perception of this silencing in Africa. Sexual inequality is not a result of only the visible division of labor and the reproductive roles of women or men. Women's oppression in Africa (and other countries) is best understood if analyzed within specific people's histories and struggles against racism, sexism, colonialism, imperialism, and class divisions. This must be done much more rigorously than Walker suggests. The danger of a moral and religious analysis of any society is that religion positions the beginning of society outside society itself, in a supernatural world.

Walker also overlooks the divine purpose for missionaries in Africa, that is, "to civilize and educate" the *native*. Nettie and her family are doing God's work, presumably the God Celie rejects (*Color*, 175). Celie's attitude to God changes when she realizes that He has allowed Albert to keep Nettie's letters from her. God ceases to be the center of her universe as she redefines the concept of the supernatural as an "It" that resides in anyone: "It pisses God off if you walk by the color purple in a field somewhere and don't notice it" (178). But Nettie immerses herself more and more in this God, her Victorian puritanism apparent in her observations of Olinka culture (153).

That "men spend time away from the wives" bothers Nettie though she does not attempt to understand Olinka people's concepts of love, marriage, and sexuality. For example, spending more time with one's spouse(s) is neither demonstrative of love nor concern. Understanding how power relations work within different family members may indicate the meaning of love. Nettie finds Olinka women oppressed by work, an oppression not grounded in an international economic system exploiting both women and men in the world through unpaid and underpaid labor. Relocating this oppression to African men shifts the focus to the symptom, rather than the disease, and also essentializes African men's oppression of their women, thus implicitly absolving other men. "Man" or "woman" as a category of analysis is not useful since it assumes a superficial homogeneity, which presumes a unified consciousness and a universal subject. The Olinka women—like the Black women slaves—are not simply exploited and acted upon by the forces of imperialism, patriarchy, and capitalism; they resist these forces and struggle for social transformation. Black women slaves' industrial, agricultural, and reproductive labor was exploited simultaneously, in Africa, America, and the Caribbean—that is, as workers and "factories" for producing more slaves. They resisted slavery in many ways, as C.L.R. James documents in *The Black Jacobins* (1963).

Nettie's letter echoes the Western development aid rhetoric as she positions herself as a benefactor and teacher of the Olinka.[9] Like many colonial projects, development aid aims to help the poor in the Third World. Many aid projects, including those of nongovernmental organizations, although intended to "assist women and children at the grassroots" are often hijacked by bourgeois leaders (men and women) who use the funds for personal gain, like Nzingha Anne and her father, Dahvid in *Temple*.[10]

Development aid has now replaced the divine mission of early Christian missionaries and other imperialists in Africa and reversed the actors, though evangelism and religious fundamentalism are on the rise. Many African leaders have effectively appropriated the imperialist discourse of "knowing and understanding *their* natives." They embezzle public funds and mismanage their countries' economies using the administrative, judicial, and education systems instituted by the colonial governments; and they are often unaccountable to the country's people. The collusion between most African leaders and the former colonial masters has resulted in the neocolonialism that Walker critiques through Dahvid and his cronies in *Temple*.

Like Dahvid, most leaders in neocolonial Africa were "heroes" created by the colonial masters, specifically selected for their demonstrated propensity to collude with these masters after independence—either through a familial history of collaboration with the colonial governments, or their demonstrated greed for personal power and wealth. Rarely were they ever personally involved in the actual struggle for freedom.[11] Turning a new leaf, as Ola does, is only wishful thinking. The social, economic, and political climate that created Dahvid and his class of power-hungry neocolonial leaders has not changed, and neither does Walker call for such a change. Such a Dahvid can exist only as an idea. The Dahvids in Africa would not change so easily and start writing plays dedicated to their forgotten heroic wives. Though Walker clearly analyzes the behavior of these leaders, her desire to see a change in her African sisters is inconsistent with views of "feminists" like Dahvid.

Walker's feminism is equally problematic. When Walker recognizes Tashi "as my sister" in the reader's note to *Joy* (283), Tashi appears to represent a homogeneous African woman, with whom Walker easily bonds simply because she is an African woman. Walker's work implicitly assumes a Black sisterhood that ignores class, and sometimes race—a sisterhood that sees Black women as inherently less likely to oppress than men (Black or White). Rather than grounding men's actions in historical contexts, Walker tends to homogenize Black and White men as oppressors because they are men. She thus poses a men/women dichotomy that makes her feminist politics problematic. For instance, Celie's pants business will emphasize treating Black customers lovingly and with respect. Walker ignores the capitalist entrepreneurial aspect of the business as well as how the new Celie, as a property owner, might change her relations with her relatives and friends (both male and female). Similarly, situations and activities by women in Senegal and Gambia are presented as happening to the category "women" versus "men" in *Warrior*.[12]

Nettie and her family "teach" the Olinka people new ways to do what they have always done, such as working and caring for babies. Admittedly, hospitals introduced by colonialists curbed the number of birthing deaths among women. But the positive and negative consequences of colonialism must always be properly contextualized. Isolating and focusing on the benefits of colonialism to the colonized obscures the real evils of colonialism—and somehow justifies it.

The land issue in Olinka signifies more than the missionaries' role in helping the Olinka to pay rent for the barracks and land taxes and to buy water, wood and food. Land privatization has led to much social strife in neocolonial Africa, where land and water were previously regarded as everybody's. Until land demarcation and the individualization of land tenure began during colonization, land tenure was mostly corporate, and so were proprietary rights to land and water. Oppression of African women must be relocated within a wider exploitative world (dis)order.[13]

Doris Baines, a missionary in *Color*, speaks the Olinka language faultlessly, though she seems not to comprehend Olinka's diverse forms of marriages or concepts of gender. "In a burst of appreciation one day, I'm afraid the chief—not knowing what else to do, no doubt—presented me with a couple of wives. I don't think it was commonly believed I was a woman" (205). Despite speaking the Olinka language, interpreting terms in different settings and traditions can mislead, especially since syntactical possibilities and the meanings of words in two or more languages do not always correspond well. Language constitutes social reality in place of reflecting an already given social reality. Translations from African languages into English (or other colonial languages) happens where two unequal worlds meet, and power relations exist when one world is represented by another in the translation. Translating Olinka into English is a representation of a regional culture for a more powerful one that Baines seems unaware of. Social reality and the "natural" world don't have fixed innate meanings that language reflects or expresses. Different languages and discourses in the same language divide up the world and give it meaning in different ways that cannot be reduced to one another through translation or by appealing to universally shared notions indicating a fixed reality. Meanings for femininity and masculinity may vary among cultures and languages, or among discourses within a particular language, and are subject to historical changes.

Though certain African women marry other women, Baines's "marriage" to the two young women is unclear because little more is said on the subject. Marriages among African women have barely been researched.[14] Since different types of marriages exist, it is significant to understand why the Olinka people gave Baines the two girls.

Baines discusses the bloody traditions her adopted Olinka girls would change. Colonial education in Africa (usually carried within the Christian mission compound) aimed at transforming Africa, especially the "backward traditions" Africans practiced. Though her dialogue includes "positive" traditions too, Baines still considers these traditions uncivilized and plans to strive to ensure their end (*Color*, 206). At the same time, Baines castigates her country for its colonial policies in Africa (206).

Through Baines, Walker exposes the ambivalence of the benevolent British missionary: "saving" the African girls by sending them to school, while at the same time gloating about her property. The voice condemning England for colonizing Africa also takes pride in colonizing the Akwee village. Baines does not position herself within this imperial process. The "bit of bloody cutting" in *Color* becomes a full blown mutilation in *Joy*, which leaves women—Tashi in this case—with a "classic Olinka woman's walk, in which the feet appear to slide forward and are rarely raised above the ground" (*Joy*, 65).

Hall sees in *Color* "instances in which the human body is made to submit to and to register the forces of authority, where patriarchy maintains power by forcing the female body into a position of powerlessness" (Hall, 83). Celie learns to reshape those forces of oppression and to define herself through her letters, which act as a second body, mediating her relationship to the power structure in a way that gives her a voice. Hall also sees the rituals as an attempt to strip away the masculine in the female genitalia, advancing further Baines's concerns of the bloody actions—the major theme in *Possessing the Secrets of Joy*.

Hall's partly Freudian reading of *Color* does not reflect the Olinka understanding and interpretation of circumcision and facial scarification. Adam and Tashi both undergo face scarification. The concept of patriarchy for Hall is extracted from a "universal" theory of power, where (any) man rules over (any) woman. Thus, the male's desire to dominate is seen as inherent and natural, as socially displayed through "gender" relations. Social relations and contradictions illustrate this form of domination and are subsumed in the antagonism depicted in male-female gender relations. Seeing "woman" as a unified consciousness (and universal subject) obliterates real contradictions among women themselves. Concepts of "patriarchy," "masculinity," and "femininity" should be problematized rather than assumed when dealing with different cultures. For example, the social construction of and function of age-grades is important to understanding gender relations, rites of passage, and initiation to adulthood in some African societies.

Celie, Shug, and Albert quilt together at the end of *The Color Purple*, symbolizing what Awkward calls "the transmutation of tattered raiments of a familial and tribal history into a new and usable present form" (Awkward, 161).[15] Walker's reconstruction of history significantly draws a critical response regarding African women's understanding of feminism. Africa represents history and a desire for identity for many an African American; hence, the irony of Walker's Eurocentrism.

While examining questionable independence and exposing corrupt African leaders, Walker nevertheless vindicates Dahvid, Fanny's African father and the current minister of culture. Dahvid (the revolutionary) is the same man who imposes unwanted attentions on the unsuspecting Olivia (*Temple*, 150–51). Walker's Black men occasionally conform to racial stereotypes. The image of the "black male rapist" can be read in the characters of Mr.—(*Temple*), Harpo (*Color*), Dahvid (*Temple*), or the "hordes of intrusive men" who drove Walker and Deborah from swimming in the Gambian beach (*Warrior*, 53).

The Dahvid who writes political plays protesting his government's taxation is the same man who regrettably explains the "simplicity" of his house (*Temple*, 161), a set-up that contrasts sharply with his wife Nzingha Anne's "hut which she had made herself." Formerly "a brilliant fighter among the Mbeles"—the African underground that figures in *Joy*—she is abandoned by her husband and society after independence. She appears strangely isolated, even building her own hut, a task that other members of her community would help her in. This sequestered woman "saved many people's lives" (*Temple*, 255). Though reminiscent of many women freedom fighters whose participation is often marginalized by male-dominated African (or other) nations, the fact that her relatives abandon her is strange.

Nzingha Anne's inconsistent behavior with her mother is unexplained. At first, she loves her mother immensely (*Temple*, 256), but soon Nzingha is repulsed by her lonely and demented mother (258–59). Walker does not logically lead us to this emotional shift by daughter to mother. Her craziness seems to be part of her makeup, though we do not know the sequence of events that lead to her breakdown.[16] As does *Color*, *Temple* explores colonization and imperialism in America as well as in Africa. There is mention of Ola's forthcoming book, which would use Elvis Presley as a metaphor of White American's appropriation of Native American art. The man/god paradigm Shug and Celie reject in *Color* surfaces in *Temple*. This time, a man, Suwelo, preaches the reversed gospel. One wonders whether some of the women referred to above are in Olinka, the land where Fanny's father is the minister of culture (*Temple*, 244).

With tenderness and respect, *Joy* is dedicated to "the blameless vulva" and prefaced by a sinister statement by one Mirella Ricciardi in *African Saga*: "I had always got on well with the Africans and enjoyed their company. Black people are natural and possess the secret of joy, which is why they can survive the sufferin' and humiliation inflicted upon them" (vii). Since its publication, *Joy* has been widely acclaimed: "a powerful novel about brutal misogyny, both horrifying and readable"; "bold, intriguing and challenging, a novel that will trigger strong emotions." Walker has been praised for "conveying the passion, serenity and sense of freedom that comes from her ability to defy traditions that circumscribe women''; for "putting a beautiful spin on the tale of terror at the centre of *Joy*''; and for portraying "the struggles of an African woman to come to terms with the consequences of female circumcision. She teaches us about the tenderness with which we need to treat ourselves as we recover from our mistakes.''[17]

The domination of women and their enslavement in the world are connected with the mental and physical mutilation that Tashi goes through. Tashi, first introduced in *Color* as a minor character, is the protagonist in *Joy* who is grappling with a mutilation that traumatizes her. Tashi's "horrified self" represents "a truly universal self" for women's oppression. Besides universalizing women's oppression, Walker changes the "oppressed woman" into the "oppressed third world woman" category Mohanty critiques in *Third World Women and the Politics of Feminism* (72).

For Tashi, circumcision leads to a mental breakdown and a search into the "self" for redemption of the mistake through psychoanalysis. Tashi's psychiatric treatment—an individualizing process of healing—seems an ill-defined liberation. Though Walker uses circumcision as a metaphor for women's oppression, her privileging the genital mutilation itself over the notions of acceptable womanhood/manhood and how social power relations work within these notions eliminates the radical aspect of her project. Graphically, she describes the physical torture of the circumcision that is slightly alleviated by Tashi's going to America: "It now took a quarter of an hour to pee . . . .There was the odor, too, which no amount of scrubbing, until we got to America, ever washed off" (*Joy*, 64). Besides giving women the "classic Olinka walk," circumcision brings other complications. Evelyn-Tashi's first birthing becomes a spectacle in the North American hospital (57). Whereas circumcision traumatizes many women, separating it from the production and reproduction relations where it occurs is inadequate as a means to address the problem.[18] Similar researches to Saadawi's on circumcision in Sudan and Egypt are needed in other African countries.[19]

Walker's African women are more often than not shown as victims of male violence. She constructs them as a uniformly powerless group. Though it is useful to "increasingly draw the two discourses together (post-colonial and feminism)" (Ashcraft, 177), the danger in such a move lies in blurring the two issues and in failing to analyze exactly how women are discriminated against in First and Third worlds and how and where women meet as a "collective." Postcolonial theory faces the danger of merging these issues, and thus obfuscating different ways of analyzing phenomena.

In *Color*, Celie attempts to define herself through writing. Through her, Walker affirms the link between orality and the print culture. The spoken word becomes an active object that (re)members community and connects it to the voices from which it has been cut off, effectively forcing it out of its silence. But the spoken word also exists in a culture that privileges printing over orature. Giving Celie a pen is an attempt to reconcile the two.[20]

In *Joy*'s episodic structure, first-person accounts switch vertically and horizontally in time and place. Male/female Black/White characters give first-person accounts of events. From memory, the women's narrative voices form the women's representations and experiences in *Color*.[21] Similarly, oral narrators in Africa are often women. Tashi's fragmented self in *Joy* is illustrated in her different names at varying occasions, Tashi, Tashi-Evelyn, Evelyn, and Evelyn-Tashi. Her narrative voice also changes with her state of mind. As a colonial subject, though, Tashi's oppression as a colonial discourse is inadequately problematized.

In her discussion on AIDS in Africa, Walker does not refer to the Eurocentric problematic in the AIDS discourse—for example, the attempt to associate the origin of AIDS with Africans or other minorities: "I firmly believe that the reason AIDS spreads faster in Africa is because of these genital mutilations. And I think if it continues, it will depopulate the continent—maybe not in my lifetime, or even my child's lifetime, but it will happen."[22] While the spread of AIDS cannot be underestimated anywhere, confining it to "the genital mutilations" in Africa is erroneous. The politics surrounding AIDS, as well as the attempt to associate the origin of AIDS with the green monkey in Africa, is neither accidental nor isolated. The culture of imperialism has associated "backward societies" or "natives" with strange diseases. Columbus associated syphilis and gonorrhea with the Arawaks, for example. This influences the research and distribution of drugs for such stigmatized diseases. Whereas circumcision still occurs in Africa, it is difficult to determine how widespread it is, because its research, fraught with moral and state intervention, is only partly reliable.

Color, *Temple*, and *Joy* evoke a yearning for a "global" community of men and women and animals, probably Walker's metaphor for a peaceful, raceless, society. In her novels, most social structures collapse—marriage, heterosexuality, and racism. Pierre (*Joy*) is both bisexual and biracial, while Shug and Celie celebrate a lesbian relationship. Walker attempts to link imperialism to global women's oppression in France, China, Africa, and America, without tracing particular issues with different practices. Women's oppression is not homogeneous, and neither is feminism. Different experiences breed different "feminisms." Despite displaying elements of Eurocentrism, Walker's depiction of Africa is sometimes acutely perceptive; for example, her analysis of ruling African elites in *Temple*.

In *Temple*, the perception of racial differences is influenced by economic motives. Distinguishing between material and discursive practices allows us to understand more clearly the contradictions between the covert and overt aspects of colonialism. In all three texts, but especially *Joy*, the literary device of telling one's own stories effectively makes the book readable, likable and engaging. *Joy*, however, isolates the main character, Tashi, from herself and her world; and yet all her other problems—economic, racial, social, and political—are minimized and superseded by circumcision.

Walker's rewriting of a sharecropping Black family in her first novel,

Copeland, demonstrates her capacity to transcend stereotypes. Here, she takes on a senior man with a particular sensibility. Although female sensibility is not paramount in the novel, the grandfather's legacy that Ralph Ellison's narrator keeps wondering about in *Invisible Man* (1952) bypasses the son to the daughter, Ruth. Thus, *Copeland* becomes a rewriting of the Uncle Remus stories. In *Native Sun* (1940), Richard Wright could sympathize with the mother, but not empathize with the father, as Walker does in *Copeland* and her short stories.

In *Warrior*, Walker meets many "sisters," among them Bilaela, who heads the movement against female genital mutilation in the Gambia (41). Walker does not problematize Bilaela's preoccupation with getting more money. "Pratibha says I'm naive because I wanted to give Bilaela extra money—beyond what we'd paid for the interview and other help. But I had no idea until she told me that she'd already paid Bilaela seven thousand dollars" (52). While Walker easily overlooks this incident, it is indicative for me of the kind of people she interviewed for the film and, more importantly, of the problems projects like hers face. Which women does Bilaela represent in the Gambia?

My involvement with feminist organizations and nongovernmental organizations in Kenya has exposed me to the elitism and class inclination of participants—whether in or out of Kenya. While the rhetoric of these organizations may involve "grassroots," the women (and men) in the so-called grassroots often never know the existence of such organizations that claim to represent them. The activities of such organization revolve around conference rooms and aid offices in African cities and Western metropoles. While recognizing the importance of Walker's work on circumcision, I seek to problematize representational stances that may occur in aid projects through "sisters" or "brothers" whose class interests remain obscured and unexamined.

Walker considers economic independence crucial for women, a view probably prompted by her role model's life.[23] Not surprisingly, her characters often acquire material wealth—Celie, Suwelo, Carlotta, Arveyda and Evelyn-Tashi—usually without an attempt to situate and problematize this wealth within the oppressive structures she discusses. Overlooking class in the name of sisterhood/brotherhood is detrimental in political activities that seriously aim to make an impact. The crusade against circumcision appears to be such an activity.

Having seen Walker transcend stereotypes in her writings about African Americans, I believe she can equally transcend Eurocentrism and aspects of radical feminism in future works. Probably, a recrossing of the Atlantic in a way that helps merge the two sides of the African experience is necessary, a recrossing that recognizes that among sisters/brothers, blood is not "always thicker than water."

NOTES

1. Walker's texts will be abbreviated as follows: *The Third Life of Grange Copeland* (*Copeland*), *The Color Purple* (*Color*), *Possessing the Secret of Joy* (*Joy*), *Warrior*

Marks: Female Genital Mutilation and the Sexual Blinding of Women (*Warrior*), *The Temple of My Familiar* (*Temple*), and *In Search of My Mother's Gardens* (*In Search*).

2. Interviews in Gates and Appiah, eds., *Alice Walker: Critical Perspectives Past and Present* and in Walker and Parmar, *Warrior Marks*.

3. Bill Ashcroft et al., *The Empire Writes Back*, 3.

4. Among others, Karen Blixen's *Out of Africa*; Henry Haggard's *King Solomon's Mines* and *She: A History of Adventure*; Joyce Cary's *Aissa Saved*, *Mr. Johnson*, and *The African Witch*; and J. M. Coetzee's *Waiting for the Barbarians*.

5. A recent journalistic book by the African American Eddie L. Harris, *Native Stranger: A Black American's Journey into the Heart of Africa* (New York: Simon and Schuster, 1991) and George Ayittey's *Indigenous African Institutions* reinforce an occidentalist image of Africa, as do movies like *Jungle Fever* and *Out of Africa*.

6. In *The Afrocentric Idea*, Asante homogenizes "Europe or European" as monolithic categories and establishes an "African Perspective," while Patricia Hill Collins identifies Black women in the United States as "an oppressed group" in *Black Feminist Thought*. Despite appreciating experience as a category defining consciousness, her stance disregards the contradictory experiences of Black women in America.

7. The character Tashi only shares a name in the three texts, but is a different character altogether. (See Walker's note to the reader in *Joy*.)

8. Uganda's Amin Dada and Central African Republic's Jean-Baptiste Bokassa are two African dictators of the 1970s who supposedly routinely killed and ate their political enemies.

9. Her position also affirms the heterosexual family as the model (*Joy*, 214). Though Shug and Celie maintain a lesbian relationship, the end of the novel merges heterosexuality with homosexuality without any homophobic tensions arising from any character, including Mr.—.

10. Patricia Stamp examines the aid expert–aid relationship and the crisis in knowledge about Africa in her book *Technology, Gender, and Power in Africa*, 146.

11. Members of the Kenya Land and Freedom party (Mau Mau) who fought to liberate Kenya from British rule are officially forgotten in Kenya. The leaders who took over in December 1963 were mostly from the collaborator families, who continue to rewrite Kenya's history, showing the Mau Mau fighters as bandits and goons without an agenda or aim.

12. I have included the nonfiction text *Warrior* in this essay because it further expands Walker's Eurocentrism and brand of feminism that this essay discusses. The text (now a documentary film on genital mutilation) is a diary of events surrounding the making of the film.

13. Okey and Glazier, in separate works, examine land tenure among the Luo and Mbeere of Kenya.

14. Glazier discusses "fictive marriages" among the Mbeere of Kenya. What he calls "fictive" are *real* marriages in various Kenyan communities. Though this practice seems patriarchal today—being concerned with getting a male child for a barren woman or a woman without a son—little is known about its origin and different formations.

15. In the early 1980s, Chile's mothers of "the disappeared" got together and began quilting urgent messages to their government on *arpilleras* (quilts) demanding to know the fate of the disappeared and pressing for a stop to the practice. The *arpilleras* organized people so much that Pinochet's government banned the quilting, which, however,

continued underground. Smuggled out of Chile, the *arpilleras* publicized the plight of the "disappeared" and their families in other parts of the world.

16. The imperial process that produces "natives" like Nzingha and Dahvid is well illustrated in Tsitsi Dangarembga's *Nervous Conditions* (1988).

17. *Newsweek*, June 9, 1992, 56; *People Weekly*, July 13, 1992, 24; *Essence*, July 1992, 59; *The Globe and Mail*, July 18, 1992, c13; and *Santa Fe Reporter*, August 5–11, 1992, 27/29.

18. I use the term "circumcision" to refer to the practice called *nzaiko*—the events that accompanied (and still do) the cutting of the foreskin from the penis and parts of the clitoris and the labia from the vagina, while initiating boys and girls into adulthood. Among others in Africa, communities like the Luo in Kenya do not circumcize. (See Kieti and Coughlin for a discussion of circumcision among the Kamba in Kenya.)

19. Nawal el Saadawi's work among women in Egypt and Sudan is documented in *The Hidden Face of Eve* (1979). Her fiction also discusses women's problems in an Islamic culture; the problems may be generalized to non-Muslim cultures; for example, *Woman at Point Zero* (1975).

20. If Celie lived among the Olinka, she might have had somebody write her letters at her dictation. Also, learning to write alone is not sufficient empowerment.

21. This happens, too, in other female African-American authors: Gayl Jones's *Corregidora* (1975), Zora Neale Hurston's *Their Eyes Were Watching God* (1937), Toni Cade Bambara's *Gorilla My Love* (1972), and Toni Morrison's *Beloved* (1987) and *Song of Solomon* (1978).

22. Walker's interview in *Essence* (Giddings, 60).

23. Zora Neale Hurston is one of the earlier African-American women writers whose writings remained unknown for a long time. Walker was instrumental in publicizing her work. In Walker's opinion, Hurston's work reveals a "sense of black people as complete, complex, *undiminished* human beings, a sense lacking in much black writing and literature" (*In Search of Our Mother's Gardens*, 85). Hurston's remains lie in an unmarked grave in a segregated cemetery in Fort Pierce, Florida.

BIBLIOGRAPHY

Asante, Molefi K. *The Afrocentric Idea*. Philadelphia: Temple University Press, 1987.

Ashcroft, Bill, Gareth Griffiths, and Helen Tiffin. *The Empire Writes Back*. New York: Routledge, 1989.

Awkward, Michael. *Inspiriting Influences: Tradition, Revision, and Afro-American Women's Novels*. New York: Columbia University Press, 1989.

Collins, Patricia Hill. *Black Feminist Thought*. Boston: Unwin Hyman, 1990.

Fitzgerald, Judith. "A Harrowing Story, Beautifully Told." Book review in *The Globe and Mail*, July 18, 1992, c13.

Gates, Henry Louis, Jr., and K. A. Appiah, eds. *Alice Walker: Critical Perspectives Past and Present*. New York: Amistad, 1993.

Giddings, Paula. "Alice Walker's Appeal" (Interview with Walker). *Essence*, July 1992.

Glazier, Jack. *Land and the Uses of Tradition among the Mbeere of Kenya*. New York: University Press of America, 1985.

Hall, Wendy. "Lettered Bodies and Corporeal Texts in *The Color Purple*." *Studies in American Fiction* 16, no. 1 (Spring 1988): 83–89.

Harris, Trudier. "From Victimization to Free Enterprise: Alice Walker's *The Color Purple.*" *Studies in American Fiction* 14, no. 1 (Spring 1986).

Hite, Molly. *The Other Side of the Storm: Structures and Strategies of Contemporary Feminist Narrative.* Ithaca, N.Y.: Cornell University Press, 1989.

James, C.L.R. *The Black Jacobins.* New York: Random House, 1963.

Jones, Gayl. *Corregidora.* Boston: Beacon Press, 1975.

Kieti, Nwikali, and Peter Coughlin. *Barking, You'll Be Eaten! The Wisdom of Kamba Oral Literature.* Nairobi: Phoenix Publishers, 1990.

Mohanty, Talpade, Ann Russo, and Torres Lourdes. *Third World Women and the Politics of Feminism.* Bloomington: Indiana University Press, 1991.

Okeyo, A. P. "Daughters of the Lakes and Rivers: Colonization and the Land Rights of Luo Women." In *Women and Colonization: Anthropological Perspectives*, edited by Mona Etienne and Eleanor Leacock. New York: Praeger, 1980.

Peterson, V. R. Book review in *People Weekly*, July 13, 1992.

Said, Edward W. *Orientalism.* New York: Vintage, 1979.

Stamp, Patricia. *Technology, Gender, and Power in Africa.* Ottawa: IDRC, 1989.

Walker, Alice. *The Color Purple.* New York: Washington Square Press, 1982.

———. *In Search of Our Mothers' Gardens.* New York: Harvest and Harcourt Brace Jovanovich, 1983.

———. *Langston Hughes: American Poet.* New York: Crowell, 1974.

———. *Possessing the Secret of Joy.* New York: Harcourt Brace Jovanovich, 1992.

———. *The Temple of My Familiar.* New York: Pocket Books, 1989.

———. *The Third Life of Grange Copeland.* New York: Harcourt Brace Jovanovich, 1970; reprinted New York: Pocket Books, 1988.

———, and Pratibha Parmar. *Warrior Marks: Female Genital Mutilation and Sexual Blinding of Women.* New York: Harcourt Brace & Company, 1993.

13

"I is": Toni Morrison, the Past, and Africa

CHIMALUM NWANKWO

"I is" is an ontological declaration, especially if spoken consciously and deliberately as is the case when Spike Lee corrects one of his White interviewers who says "More Better Blues" instead of "Mo' Better Blues." The mission here is to unite a grammar of expression with a grammar of life. In juxtaposition with "I am," "I is" is wrong, but its wrongness is one predetermined by race, class, and all kinds of political and economic considerations. The most problematic program of any serious Black writing is the evolution of a form that mediates the paradox which makes "I is" adequate and inadequate simultaneously!

"I is" is adequate because it takes care of the base of the solution of all problems—the psychological base. "I is" instills confidence, affirms individuality and then communality. One is assured that he or she belongs in a world that exists in a reflexively definable sense, a sense that is autotelic. To understand that world, one has to be privy to all the rudiments of "I is" or remain an outsider. To be an outsider in all circumstances is somewhat unsafe, precarious, dangerous. To be an insider completely locked in is also unsafe because it creates its own sense and feeling of being locked out from the rest of the world, a world that is becoming increasingly complex. That is where the inadequacy comes in.

Can the paradox be mediated? Of course. Those who care to reflect about the shape of things in today's world, especially the relationship between literature and politics, with its ontological and epistemological implications, will ponder more about "I is." Political and ideological structures are collapsing before the economic forces in a subterranean global battle. Whether we like it or not, we live in a world of spaces. These spaces are generally culture-bound, and on that condition rests all the differences in value systems and judgments with their inescapable economic implications in a world of fortuitous and deliberate interdependencies. The African writer or critic who contemplates worthwhile participation must espy confluences and divergences between "I is" and "I am."

The most remarkable thing about Chinua Achebe's *Things Fall Apart* is the ability to adopt that ironic or paradoxical vantage point that keeps an eye on those who are caught between "I is" and "I am" with little cheer for either party. The world depicted by Achebe is not a self-conscious world. It lives, and it is a world that says "I is," a declaration that requires a special kind of sensitivity to appreciate, whether one belongs to that world or not. The relationship between the past and the present is clear, so are the confluences and divergencies. An African reader with the kind of sensitivity that produced *Things Fall Apart* and a reader with the kind of sensitivity that appreciates the nature of the conflict in the world of that novel will not miss the great similarity between Achebe's task and that of Toni Morrison.

The most crucial accomplishment of Morrison's art is the successful rejection of the current jargon of *otherness*, which very often unwittingly or deliberately subsumes Black, woman, and other culturally and economically disenfranchised people under one awkward umbrage. This strategy of emotional and intellectual convenience in nomenclature and classification reestablishes a unique monism that silences the radicalism of cultural independence. Morrison, who in African (Igbo) psychic parlance, is *seven-eyed*, is aware of all the traps. Graceful and elegant in her interviews as she is in her prose works, she declares: "I write what I have recently begun to call *village* literature, fiction that is really for the village, for the tribe. Peasant literature for my people which is necessary and legitimate but which also allows me to get in touch with all sorts of people" (LeClair, 26; emphasis mine).

Critics and readers of Morrison must recognize that, for her, there really is no other. Accepting the jargon of otherness means accepting the existence of a center, a first, which fixes that other as the periphery. This is why in the above statement as in other instances, words such as "village," "tribe," and "peasant" ostensibly sit in her text without apology or discomfiture, without any sense of the conventional baggage of disparagement. Morrison's private charity of cultural dignity makes her insist: "I cannot trust the literature and sociology of other people to help me know the truth of my own cultural sources" (Morrison, "Memory, Creation and Writing," 386). What other Black writers do is, of course, not her concern.

A cultural home is where everything begins, and that is where she directs her critics for answers. "Critics of my work have often left something to be desired," says Morrison, "because they don't always evolve out of the culture, the world, the given quality out of which I write" (McKay, 425). It is hard to read Morrison and not feel or witness many of those things only dreamed about and talked about in Black literature, not African-American, African, or Afro-Caribbean literature, but Black literature. This is what Morrison longingly expresses in the statement: "I also want my work to capture the vast imagination of black people. . . . Some young people don't want to look back to those embarrassing days when we were associated with 'haints' and superstitions. They want to get as far as possible into the scientific world" (McKay, 428).

Toni Morrison does not need to wonder about the accuracy of this sentiment. Euro-American culture, from German Romanticism through Poe to Steven King, remains enthralled by its own version of that kind of vision. If she were to be wrong, in theater practice, we would not have the tradition initiated by Antonin Artaud, that self-styled madman of the French avant-garde who insisted that modern European culture had sanitized the magic and mystery and wonder of living out the drama in the cause of realism. Neither would there be the anarchistic guerrillas of modern American theatre of the 1960s nor the feeble Afro-Orientalism of Richard Schechner's environmental theater movement, all efforts to fill the hiatus between a past teeming with humans and spirits and a present soporific in inertia because barren of spirits.

In Morrison, the issue of the past, as some African-American critics have tried to suggest, is not an issue of mythology—that is, mythology as a word suggesting a dead territory of named pseudospirits incapable of any kind of vitality because they existed in an extinct imaginative frame. That notion of mythology does not accommodate the "great supernatural" that Morrison writes about, where "birds talk" and "butterflies cry." It is true in her works that time, history, and space are collapsed, but that is part of a gesture that affirms the existence of the kind of traffic between humans and spirits prevalent in African culture. Rather than pursuing these points in the abstract, let us consider closely some of the instances in Morrison's works which an African reader or a Black reader who is not ashamed of haints and superstitions is most likely to identify with.

According to Achebe, "the African novel has to be about Africa. A pretty severe restriction, I am told. But Africa is not only a geographical expression, it is also a metaphysical landscape—it is in fact a view of the world and of the whole cosmos perceived from that particular position. . . . Ben-Gurion once said: 'If someone wants to be a Jew, that's enough for me.' We could say the same for being an African" (Achebe, *Hopes and Impediments*, 92–93). It is not a difficult thing to search for or to feel such resonances in Toni Morrison. In the interview with Thomas LeClair, she broadens this kind of perspective in trying to enforce an unapologetic distinction about the context of her work: "There is a level of appreciation that might be available only to people who understand the context of the language. . . . From my perspective there are only black people, when I say 'people' that's what I mean. Lots of books written by black people about black people have this 'universality' as a burden" (26).

The world of Morrison is different because it is a Black world, not, as LeClair says in the interview, a world of "Latin American enchantment" (26). It is a world of African enchantment: clear in Achebe's *Things Fall Apart* (1958) or *Arrow of God* (1964), where people do not call snakes by their names at night for fear that they might hear, or where children die and come again to torment their parents for one reason or the other, as is masterfully fleshed out in Ben Okri's *The Famished Road* (1993). It is clear in the world of Flora Nwapa's *Efuru* (1966) or Elechi Amadi's *The Concubine* (1966), where sea gods or goddesses incarnate or have spouses living in the world of humans. It is also most clear in Syl Cheney-Coker's *The Last Harmattan of Alusine Dunbar* (1990), where vibrant traffic and a humans-spirits cross communication is constantly on, and believe it or not, consequently human destiny is affected for ill or good.

In Morrison's *The Bluest Eye* (1970), Pecola prays for the blue eyes that will give her beauty and reverse the negative social fortunes and the stigma of an ugliness synonymous with being Black. Reading Pecola's prayer as only part of the insidious slippage into insanity, the result of White oppression, is only partial interpretation. For fuller understanding, one must situate the prayer in the realm of the different kind of individuation possible only in a Black universe. It is not possible in the other universe of White people except that it be done "scientifically." Jeanette Mahogany, the octoroon slave woman in *The Last Harmattan of Alusine Dunbar*, after deeply contemplating the human waste in slavery, somberly declares: "One day, the white men will know that the world has two faces, and they only have power over one" (Cheney-Coker, 6). "Morrison has always offered mythic possibilities in her emphasis on natural cycles, bizarre events and narrative echoes" (Davis, 334). Cynthia Davis's term "bizarre events" underscores the point under discussion. Pecola's wish is "bizarre," depending on who is reading or the perspective of the reader. But to Morrison and the kind of reader her works seek out, the bizarre is real.

In *Song of Solomon*, this reality is unmistakable. The story of the flight of Milkman is real in terms of what Africans think is possible. It is also symbolic as a number of readings try to suggest. Unfortunately, I think more people appear to be swayed by the symbolism than what the traditional Africans hold to be true. The "flight" of Milkman is as real as metempsychosis, or some kind of so-called paranormal phenomena such as possession and shamanism. That such things are real in Morrison's Black universe is clear in the behavior of people on the morning Mr. Smith attempts to fly. The people gathered thought Mr. Smith "was probably a nice man . . . they murmured to each other, you never really do know about people" (*Song of Solomon*, 8).

One might add here that you really do not know about the Black world because at that initial narrative point in *Song of Solomon*, mystery is piled upon mystery. Mr. Smith plunges to his death, a child is born; a child who at age four realizes "that only birds and airplanes could fly . . . to have to live without that single gift saddens him and left his imagination so bereft that he appeared dull even to the women who did not hate his mother . . . and called her son 'deep,' even mysterious" (8). Of course, in keeping with the atmosphere being established, a strategy for affirming how different Morrison's world is, the women venture confident diagnosis and prognosis for the brooding boy: "Did he come with a caul?" "You should have dried it and made him some tea from it to drink. If you don't he'll see ghosts" (9).

That is only the beginning of the double-vocality of *Song of Solomon*. Milkman's cold is a cultural cold that will dry after his exhilarating encounters with a variety of ghosts at the different atriums of his initiation and cognition. Flight will become a possibility and not a probability, but before then, we must learn how to love and endure, how to belong and how to share and give according to the book of the ancestors and the past, which is concealed in a lore sung by children, lived by the folk, and whispered by the wind. How else can we understand Ryna's gulch, or Circe and her multitude of dogs, or Solomon or Shalimar, and the marvelous environment of Pilate's death?

"Black lore, black music, black language and all the myths and rituals of black culture were the most prominent elements in the early life of Toni Morrison," writes Nellie McKay. "Her grandfather played the violin, her parents told her thrilling and terrifying ghost stories, and her mother sang and played the numbers by decoding dream symbols as they were manifest in the dream book that she kept" (McKay, 414). It is not difficult to see the impact of this background on Morrison's work. Whatever critics call myths in her work is not referential. If we consider them invented, it must only be because of their unfamiliarity in the context of what we know through the cultural lens of the West. A full appreciation of Morrison requires an African sensibility. By this, one is not speaking of a nebulous African past heaving its moribund throes under the weight of westernization. Morrison's peculiar artistic tendency marks out the lives of those described as inescapably bound to their own geography and culture in a manner deep enough to worry or baffle a cultural outsider. Three other Morrison novels, *Sula*, *Tar Baby*, and *Beloved*, affirm so in the manner in which the author delineates the world of these works.

"The whole book is junk. Morrison puts black people down. There is nothing positive about this book." Those were the irate declarations of one of my White students after reading *Sula* in an American literature class. It was not difficult to see where that student was coming from. Those who have not been objects of definition cannot recognize definition unless they are the definers. It is therefore understandable when some readers miss the potency of White absence in Morrison's works and attempt to knock back their visions violently into the Black world. Even then, they miss the implication in their acts; just as my student and Harold Beaver do, they miss the fact that definition is a question of power.

What Morrison accomplishes in the opening lines of *Sula* is the establishment of an unequal relationship between the powerful and the powerless. The rest of the novel then defines the character of the impaired world. Needless to say, the source of impairment is obvious without necessarily excusing the imperfections of the victim. Generally, what Morrison pleads is that the victim's world be left alone with its integrity measured against nothing but itself. It is significant that there is minimal visible presence of White characters in Medallion. Essentially, therefore, part of the thesis of this novel in that regard is that *blackness* would have existed within its imperfections, but, nonetheless, solving its own existential riddles successfully or unsuccessfully.

Once again, as in *Song of Solomon*, the crucial aspects of Black life and cosmology are summoned for that affirmation. Before Chicken Little's death,

Sula and Nel engage in a ritualistic earth-digging. The act seems meaningless, but not after one has affirmed its contextualization in the total world of the novel. Ominous and inexplicable actions of that nature can only assume appropriate significance in a world where omens are accepted as significant. That explains why various strange things happen before Hannah's death. Sula's return to Medallion is accompanied by a plague of robins. The phenomena of wind and rain and fire and dreams and, indeed, things such as Sula's birthmark possess meaning not only for the various people who witness them but for the entire community. Meaning is valid and unquestionable within its geographical territory, a territory spawning its own independent epistemological and ontological reality and status.

Thus, when I read *Tar Baby*, my African sensibility appreciates, above all things, how Morrison's muse naturalizes the supernatural. My interest is in the accomplishment of a credible and compelling cosmos of presences. I do not doubt that there is an Isle des Chevaliers, with its water-lady nurturing, controlling, or blighting Son at will, and that the island trees are peopled with mysterious spirit-women mocking or sympathizing or forsaking Jadine every now and then, or that the hills resound with the hoofs of horses galloping all over the place with naked, blind, male riders. I do not doubt that when Jadine visits Enloe, she has a portentous waking vision in which all kinds of women, dead and alive, assault her with their breasts, eggs, and so forth. Even though several readings tend to anchor the understanding of such phenomena in theory, I doubt that this accounts fully for Morrison's preoccupation with that mode of story-telling.

My inclination is to read these as essential aspects of a culturally based program that she is executing, a program of extensive redefinition. "In each of her narratives," observes Roberta Rubenstein, "a community functions as moral arbiter, the source of both individual and group norms. Her characters are defined in part through their acceptance of or challenge to certain collective presumptions" (149). As readers, we may reject these collective presumptions, but only from cultural sidelines. But whether we accept or reject them, it no doubt suffices that the writer successfully fulfills her role as witness, griot, custodian of all those things that deserve preservation.

One of the features that helps to define and affirm the peculiar world of *Beloved* is the relationship between the presumption of key individuals and the rest of the community. Once more, the central issue is associated with presences. It was communal knowledge that the principal setting of *Beloved*, in Cincinnati, was haunted, "spiteful. Full of a baby's venom" (*Beloved*, 3). For one of those key individuals, Sethe, whose problem comprised that baby and the past in a kind of chiasmus between the real and the ethereal, the abiding leitmotif of the novel, the solution is clear: "We could move," she suggested once to her mother-in-law. "What'd be the point" asked Baby Suggs. "Not a house in the country ain't packed to its rafters with some dead negro's grief" (*Beloved*, 5). The presences in *Beloved*, whether as ethereal grief or as haints, are so powerfully tangible that the strongest White character in the story, Amy, recognizes it during the crucial meeting with Sethe.

In *Beloved*, the writer deftly defines the traffic between the living and the dead with the relationship between the past and the present, and technically harmonizes all that with appreciable symbolic action. Beloved, a past agony, the lady who emerges from the deep, becomes what the Black people of Cincinnati want her to be. She is, in turn, synchronistic with the fortunes of the inmates of number 124—mysterious, passionate, loving, and diabolical. The fate of Beloved is also matched with the recommended attitude to the past: to be accepted, loved, and cherished when it is useful, functional and fulfilling; to be rejected and banished when it becomes a useless, consuming, and obsessive burden. Ultimately, Baby Suggs is actually stressing to the younger Sethe the need to deal squarely with the past. This is what the Black people of Cincinnati do with regard to 124. After acting fearfully by pretending and ignoring 124 and regarding the residence as one of the haints, after trying to wish it away ritually, after trying to vilify it with scorn and abuse, they finally come together and take a winning stand. The fruitful consequence is that Beloved evanesces, demonstrating that all communal presumptions can only be what the community wills such to be.

Beloved is a book "filled with marvels." If marvels constitute an essential aspect of the village literature that Morrison strives to accomplish, it is significant that Amy, a female White character, is one of those outsiders to the Black world who is capable of witnessing one of such marvels. The implication here is that the process of definition and re-cognition of the past is a multifaceted enterprise that is not exclusive, but expansive, in terms of input and participation. *Other* people are not necessarily excluded, otherwise Valerian and Margaret Street, who are Whites, would not be a crucial part of the drama of *Tar Baby*; and, indeed, Amy, who is pivotal in the survival of Sethe in *Beloved*, would not be there. In the aesthetics of Morrison, it would be reasonable to suggest that it is of capital importance that all that constitutes the Black polity and cosmology is not only what the inhabitants and makers of that territory want it to be. If outsiders call this world *Jazz* (the title of Morrison's latest novel) in derision, bafflement, or that peculiar awe that conceals the sophisticate's ignorance and qualified acceptance, that should not matter. Indeed, it seems that *Jazz* adds another whorl to this constantly evolving pattern of expression.

Consider how the narrator sets up the trigger of a psycholosomatic and historiographic investigation:

Hospitality is gold in this City, you have to be clever to figure out . . . when to love something and when to quit. If you don't know how, you can end up out of control or controlled by some outside thing like that hard case last winter . . . something evil ran the streets and nothing was safe—not even the dead. Proof of this being Violet's outright attack on the very subject of a funeral ceremony. (*Jazz*, 9)

This narratorial angle of the event sounds innocuous and almost noncommital and so does the mischievous sobriquet of "Violet," which displaces Violet's name. For the careful Morrison reader, there are other subtextual objectives:

1. The quibbling in name corresponds to the quibbling over the actual identity of Violet as an African-American woman.

2. The veiled sarcastic reference to the predilections of "a host of thoughtful people" draws attention to the habitual dismissal of certain aspects of Black life and world as superstitious and, therefore, of no serious consequence.

3. The superstitious aim of the event is finally subsumed in the kind of folkloric paradigm in certain Black works, such as Charles Chestnut's "The Gophered Grapevine" or "The Conjure Woman," where the marvel in the tale valorizes and validates multiple realities simultaneously. The world of the tale may be a world of superstition, but it is nonetheless a reality for the characters and their audience. For the reader, especially the cultural *outsider*, this may be a world of superstition, but it is nonetheless controlled by its own inner compelling logic, comprehensible or incomprehensible. And for Morrison, the complexity of this world becomes an opportunity to demonstrate that comprehensibility is available to those who are willing to unskein the convoluted fabric of this reality. At the end of all this, distant and effaced, Morrison makes her point: what is as simple and laughable as "I is," what is superstitious and what is facile become as serious and profound as "I am" and more. *Jazz* demonstrates that no present is comprehensible without the past, and that each past or present, in a cultural sense, validates itself and valorizes the norms of its polity on its own terms. Thus, we have this very peculiar story of Violet, whose act becomes meaningful only when we follow her and Joe carefully from the events in their very youthful days in rural Virginia into the new cosmopolitan world of Harlem.

Jazz, Morrison's novel, seeks to affirm itself like jazz itself, accessible, beautiful, and meaningful, but only to the willing initiate. It redefines culturally the kind of affinity that the African mind upholds between life and death, between the present and the past. And like jazz, it compels with the seductive subtlety of all powerful art, especially when complexity demands strict visceral access, from those who care.

In a recent collection of essays, Toni Morrison undertakes a critical responsibility that she defines in these eloquent words: "my project is an effort to avert the critical gaze from the racial object to the racial subject; from the described imagined to the describers and imaginers; from the serving to the served" (*Playing in the Dark*, 90). It is reasonable and pertinent to suggest that this critical responsibility also defines her responsibility as a writer. Morrison, no doubt, is fully aware of the dangers of ontological compromise and distortions were she to pursue other goals. She, therefore, presents the Black world as if there is no other world. The universe presented is independent and accorded legitimate tenancy. Missing are the diffident and self-deprecating blues characteristic of the writings of some well-known African-American women writers, who are afflicted with the syndrome of cultural homelessness and its concomitant peripatetic anguish. Even though Morrison's authorial stance is first and foremost a woman's, it is very important to stress that she is no mere celebrator of pain; nor can she be found, through her works, in the ranks of the dogmatic knights-at-arms for "this good woman" or "that bad man," or vice versa. Her commitment is a commitment to woman and man in a mystical strain traceable to the deep mysteries of many old African cultures. She functions like a medium, possessed by a truth that cuts both ways, undiscriminatingly.

When the numerous memorable characters in her works communicate in Black dialect, we know why they do so; and in the resonances from their words it is easy to see why there is no better way. "I is" is wrong in conventional grammar, but it suffices, at least to "some" extent, in this complex world. The perspicacious must decide the extent of territorial and functional relevance as we also know about pidgin usage in Africa. When many characters in Morrison's works look to the past, we also know why they have to do that. In that regard, caveat emptor is what resonates from *Beloved* as forcefully as the following declaration by Chinua Achebe, whose works appreciate the veritable peace redolent in the past. Achebe sees the necessity to recreate the past. He, however, insists on the writer's integrity and ability not simply to select features that flatter him: "It is not only his personal integrity as an artist which is involved, the credibility of the world he is attempting to create will be called to question and he will defeat his own purpose if he is suspected of glossing over inconvenient facts" ("The Role of Writers," 15).

The past is ubiquitous in Toni Morrison's novels. It is there either in direct references to Africa, such as we find in *Song of Solomon* and *Tar Baby*, or indirectly as the "superstitious" presences and vibrant mythological extants in *Tar Baby*. The past is there in the domesticated neoplatonic dualities expressed in the behavioral tendencies of characters such as Pecola and Violet in *The Bluest Eye* and *Jazz*, respectively. The past is present in the magical wisdom of characters like Eva in *Sula* or Pilate in *Song of Solomon*. It is there in the strangeness of the entire world of *Sula* and, indeed, in the total Black vision which must now be seen as synonymous with Toni Morrison.

In Morrison, either the novel is set in the past or the characters reach out to the past for questions and answers about physical survival or spiritual nourishment. The cultural lineaments that constitute that past may be intangible, invisible, or moribund in the reality of a Black world rapidly dying from the raging fire of Western technological culture; nonetheless, Morrison's efforts erect fireproof havens where the grammar of "I is" combines with haints, superstitions, and sundry "other-world" presences and actions to affirm an ontological and epistemological independence intrinsic and integral to the African universe before "things began to fall apart."

BIBLIOGRAPHY

Achebe, Chinua. *Hopes and Impediments: Selected Essays.* New York: Anchor/Doubleday, 1989.

———. "The Role of Writers in a New Nation." In *The Novels of Chinua Achebe*, edited by G. D. Killam. New York: Africana Publishing Corporation, 1969.

———. *Things Fall Apart*. London: Heinemann, 1958.

Cheney-Coker, Syl. *The Last Harmattan of Alusine Dunbar*. London: Heinemann, 1990.

Davis, Cynthia. "Self, Society & Myth in Toni Morrison's Fiction." *Contemporary Literature* 23, no. 2 (Summer 1982).

LeClair, Thomas. "The Language Must Not Sweat." Interview with Toni Morrison. *New Republic*, March 21, 1981.

McKay, Nellie. "Interview with Toni Morrison." *Contemporary Literature* 24, no. 4 (Winter 1987).

Morrison, Toni. *Beloved*. New York: Plume, 1987.

———. *The Bluest Eye*. New York: Washington Square Press/Simon and Schuster, 1970.

———. *Jazz*. New York: Alfred A. Knopf, 1992.

———. "Memory, Creation and Writing." *Thought* 59, no. 235 (December 1980).

———. *Playing in the Dark: Whiteness and the Literary Imagination*. Cambridge, Mass.: Harvard University Press, 1992, 381–88.

———. *Song of Solomon*. New York: Signet, 1977.

———. *Sula*. New York: Knopf, 1974.

———. *Tar Baby*. New York: Alfred A. Knopf, 1981.

Rubenstein, Roberta. *Boundaries of the Self: Gender, Culture, Fiction*. Urbana: University of Illinois Press, 1987.

Afterword: What's in a Name?

FEMI OJO-ADE

It is very easy to call yourself something, but to *be* that is something else.[1]

Do you feel a man's pain at not knowing his own name? What his name means? Alas! only our Mother Africa knows.[2]

It does not matter so much what the thing is called as what the thing is.[3]

I am a Negro. I am clean, black and I smile a lot. Whenever I want something—to get a job in motion pictures, for instance . . . I go to white folks. White folks have money. I do not.[4]

One problem with which I have had to grapple in editing this book—and I dare say it continues to nag me—is the matter of naming the Americans whose works have been analyzed by African critics. For me—Africans are never cognizant of how easy our life is!—the choice between "*Black* American" and "*African* American" is not in the least difficult, given the critical standpoint and thrust of the project. However, looking beyond my nose and attempting to know what exactly our American brothers and sisters want to name themselves, bothersome questions keep cropping up. A quick review of the history of naming further lays out the dilemma already seen in the essays.

In Africa, a name is not simply a matter of whims and caprices. A name has a meaning, with connotations of nature, ancestry, character, hopes, and desires, thus serving as one more symbol of the inextricable linkage between past, present, and future. It is a question of pride and joy, of survival, of continuity, a celebration of human life and of the newly born as one more proof that the family is the nucleus of the nation. Nowhere are these characteristics more visible than among the Yoruba, one of the major ethnic groups from whom those that were forcibly taken across the Atlantic descended; just as importantly, Yoruba culture has survived in the diaspora more than most other African ethos.

Besides the many meanings of names, besides their symbolism, a very significant factor of naming is the freedom of the people to choose, that is, to name
themselves and not suffer the shame of submitting themselves to names imposed
by the Other. That, indeed, is one major, forever traumatizing aspect of slavery.
Aimé Césaire's Henri Christophe, tragic hero of the drama of the same name,
talks of the opprobrium of the Haitians' losing their name, their identity, their
humanity, as a result of the slave trade. "Only our Mother Africa knows!" he
thunders. "Since we cannot snatch our names from the past, let it be from the
future!" (37). The challenge, therefore, is to create a new, authentic name, not
in isolation, not in a void, but upon a foundation prepared through a process of
linking the past to the present as a way of progressing towards the future. Christophe does not appear to have understood that. Symbol of Haiti's independence,
he shows how an ill-prepared re-naming is potentially ambiguous and problematic, making for a meaningless future in which new names could become a
rehashing of the rejected slave names. In other words, Christophe's call for
patriotism and the construction of the Citadel (symbol of the new name) soon
becomes, not a catalyst for nationalism but for neocolonialism.

In the American (United States) context, what strikes an African observer is
the controversy that always attends the matter of naming Black people. From
"African" (meaning, "savage," "closest to the jungles" of the slavery period)
through "nigger," "colored," "Negro," to "Black," "Afro-American" and,
now, "African American," there seems to have been a movement full-circle,
from depreciation to appreciation of Africa. While the evolution from notions
of color to those of culture is most welcome, one notes that the former nomenclature, in various forms, is still very much alive. For example, the National
Association for the Advancement of Colored Peoples (NAACP) is a most vibrant
organization, as is the United Negro College Fund (UNCF). And, in the 1990s,
the expression "men and women of color" has gained a great deal of support.

Carter G. Woodson and W.E.B. Du Bois, two great, progressive figures of
the 1920s and 1930s, made quite interesting statements on the question of
names. They felt "it does not matter what the thing is called" (Woodson) and
that "names are only conventional signs for identifying things" (Du Bois in
The Crisis 35 [March 1928]: 97), thus deemphasizing the importance of names,
which is undoubtedly a real shock to Africans. Du Bois, in that oft-quoted
comment in response to a high school student's (Roland Barton) letter to the
journal on the name "Negro," actually stated that, "Etymologically and pho-
netically ['Negro'] is much better and more logical than "African" or "colored" or any of the various hyphenated circumlocutions." In Du Bois's opinion,
"Negro" means "Us ... all those spiritual ideals, those inner bonds, those
group ideals and forward striving of this mighty army of 12 millions ... our
most precious heritage." His final exhortation to the perplexed young man who
would prefer the word "African": "It is not the name—it's the Thing that
counts. Come on, Kid, let's go get the Thing!"

Lerone Bennett, Jr., chronicler of Black history, makes a lucid analysis of Du

Bois's position in a 1967 article ("National Controversy rages over proper name for Americans of African descent," *Ebony* 23, no. 1 [November 1967]: 46–54). Bennett mentions the persuasiveness of Du Bois's argument. He also quotes other Blacks such as Keith Baird, who feels that Du Bois's premises are dubious and that "names and words determine, to a great extent, what we see and what we feel." One point excluded from Bennett's essay is that Du Bois, by referring to "the Thing," ambiguous and undefined, inadvertently and unfortunately has played into the hands of those who would rather objectify and dehumanize a whole people and would gleefully agree with him that names did not at all matter. (So, why not the name, "nigger"!) Moreover, Du Bois, famous for Pan-Africanism, showed in those comments a certain superiority complex vis-à-vis Africans. Since Negritude (the rehabilitation of "Negro" as a name and, essentially, the revaluation and rehumanization of the race) took a cue from the Harlem Renaissance (which, however, did not engage in the symbolism of words), one might say that the use of the word, "Negro," had a meaningful thrust in the 1920s and 1930s.

What remains disturbing is the great disparity among Blacks regarding the choice of name. Polls in *Jet* magazine (February 11, 1971, 8), *Ebony* (July 1989, 76–80), *The Washington Post* (October 16, 1990, A3), and *Time* (May 20, 1991, 15), among others, reveal that "African American" is far from being the choice of the majority; "Black" is. The promoters of the first name believe it is the essential step in cultural renaissance, while those who favor the latter see nothing wrong with its reference to their color. One statistic in the *Jet* data constitutes a kind of eye-opener: 71 percent of college-educated Blacks prefer the latter name to the former. Milton Morris of the Joint Center for Political and Economic Studies, who conducted the survey, suggests that part of the little popularity of the former term stems from "a failure on the part of African-American term advocates to solicit the opinions of mainstream Blacks in the terminology debate." "Mainstream Blacks" are, I believe, the middle class, with a lot of desire and, sometimes, desperation to realize the dream, to blend into the society, to be considered American—even with the color-epithet—without any African hyphenation.

To my mind, it is such people who would consider "African American" a segregated term, while preferring to be called "people of color." The class factor becomes glaring when one recalls that Negritude, that other color-conscious philosophy, was also a bourgeois search for self. Experiences have proven that, in the grassroots, the term "African" is very common. There, much less bickering goes on and one would be interested in finding out the results of polls taken specifically in the ghettos and housing projects: that is, among the lowest classes. In all probability, a choice between "African American" and "Black" would tilt the scale overwhelmingly in favor of the first term.

Witness the trend in the music, especially rap, that popular poetry steeped in the people's pride and imbued with a sense of cultural consciousness and the spirit of struggle. One of the groups involved in this Africanization is Arrested

Development, and the lyrics of their song "People Everyday" include references to the main character as an "African," proud, aware of who he is, peaceful. A sharp contrast is drawn between him and a group of Blacks harassing him and his woman, his "black queen." Other rap artists, such as Digable Planets, constantly use the name "African" to describe themselves and to express their humanity in situations of suffering and misery.

In combining the two words, "African" and "American," two forms are noticeable: "African-American" and "African American." In this book, the first is used as a qualifier while the second serves as a substantive. Yet, in other publications, I've observed both forms used as substantives. I see a possible difference in meanings between the two. Would the hyphenated word imply a double consciousness? And the latter, a split personality? Or could it be, in either case, that some ambivalence, deep, debilitating, remains? Whatever the case may be, it is incontrovertible that the promoters of the "African-American" nomenclature see the need to continue to affirm the viability of the culture and humanity of a people whose ancestors were enslaved and who, on the eve of the twenty-first century, have not succeeded in shaking age-old shackles. To some extent, that effort is simply using "Africa" as a means to attain rites of passage into "America." The question posed by that *Ebony* reader, Nathaniel Haynes, would be pertinent: "If our leaders are pushing for the term 'African-American,' what are they doing to educate our people toward Africa and her glorious history?" He affirms: "Many of our people have a negative image of Africa and lack knowledge of our past."

The essays in this collection underline the need to educate. One recalls the shocking statement made by the eminent African-American sociologist E. Franklin Frazier, as regards possible contributions to Africa:

Their [American Negro intellectuals and professionals] general outlook is dominated by the provincial and spurious values of the new Negro middle classes. They live in a world of make-believe and reject identification with the cultural traditions of American Negroes as well as with their African origin. They seek acceptance by white Americans at the price of losing all their racial and cultural identity and of being swallowed up in white America. (Présence Africaine: *Africa from the Point of View of American Negro Scholars* [1958], 278)

One has reason to hope that things have improved since Frazier's thought-provoking affirmation. But one knows full well that there is still quite some distance to go.

Just as important is the long overdue necessity to eradicate the sickness of racism. If racism continues to rear its ugly head, in whatever civilized formations, Blacks of African descent will continue to struggle in every which way to define themselves in order to lessen the burden of blackness. Which does not mean that the African and African-American connection is being condemned. In the best of times, there will be something useful in concretizing our convergences, in eschewing conflicts and contradictions. Yet, one must hope that there will come a time when African Americans will not have to think that they are "too Black" and therefore are desperate to make light-skinned babies, to save them from the trauma of racism (see *The Washington Post*, April 25, 1993, C1); when Whites will not "feel lucky about the color of [their] skin" (*The Washington Post*, January 28, 1993, A14); when naming oneself will not have today's political, socioeconomic, or other overtones, as eloquently enunciated by the playwright-actor Ossie Davis: "A black man means not to accept the system as Negroes do but to fight hell out of the system as Malcolm did. It can be dangerous. Malcolm was killed for it. Nevertheless, I like Malcolm much better than I like myself" (*Ebony*, November 1967, 54).

In short, it is difficult to be Black, to be human. The African American's struggle, ultimately, is to be accepted as a human being. Would that, however, be the same as being *American*, without qualifiers, without hyphens? Would America ever remove the hyphens? Would African Americans feel fulfilled without qualifiers that serve to affirm pride in their past, which continues to give meaning to their present and presence in a problematic condition? Some individuals do not seem to grasp the profundity of the problem being faced by the American descendants of Africans. They are depressed at being affiliated with the ancestral home and would rather be integrated into the American mainstream, as total beneficiaries of the dream. One such dreamer is Keith B. Richburg who, in his essay "Continental Divide" (*The Washington Post Magazine*, March 26, 1995, 19), writes:

Going from "colored" to "black" took some time to get used to. But now "African American"? Is that what we really are? Is there anything African left in the descendants of those original slaves who made that long journey over? Are white Americans whose ancestors came here as long ago as the slaves did "English Americans" or "Dutch Americans"? Haven't the centuries erased all those connections, so that we are all now simply "Americans"?

Richburg, in his naivete, would like to erase centuries of oppression and racism with a stroke of the pen or pencil. He would like to pretend that all cultures and colors can easily blend and mesh into the American rainbow. Unfortunately, his solution is nothing more than a mirage. The published responses to his "facile analysis" (see *The Washington Post Magazine*, May 21, 1995: 3–6) affirm that much. Thoughts of the continuing complexity of the relationship between Africans and African Americans remind us also of the controversial film *School Daze*, by Spike Lee. In his vehement reaction to a co–student-leader's call for African consciousness, the leader of the overtly retrograde fraternity controlling the cream of the female students—that is, the lightest-skinned—spits out defiantly: "We are Black Americans. . . . You can watusi your monkey ass back to Africa." It is noteworthy that Lee's movie was quite unpopular among certain African Americans.

One is still not sure where or when the current debate will end. The struggle of the Afrocentrists underscores the complexity of the issues discussed in these essays. While certain "buffer-Negroes" are helping to maintain the status quo of Eurocentricity, others, determinedly African, are committed to keeping alive the notion of "Africans in America" concretized in virile organizations that teach Africa's history and culture to younger generations. And, lest we forget, the struggle in America cannot be meaningful without the positive valuation of Africa, just as Africa cannot claim to be whole without striking an understanding with those whose ancestors were taken abroad centuries ago. And, when we talk of understanding, we are not referring to the colony of dollar-seeking exiles readily deconstructing their souls all in the name of progress.

NOTES

1. Nathaniel Haynes, letter to *Ebony* 45, no. 6 (April 1990); 132.

2. Aimé Césaire, *La Tragédie du Roi Christophe* (Paris: Présence Africaine, 1970), 37 (Translation mine).

3. Carter G. Woodson, *The Mis-Education of the Negro* (1st ed., 1933; Trenton, N.J.: Africa World Press, 1990), 200.

4. Ossie Davis in *Ebony* 23, no. 1 (November 1967); 54.

Index

About the Contributors

EDDIE OMOTAYO ASGILL, a Sierra Leonean, was educated at Fourah Bay College in Sierra Leone and has worked at his alma mater and at various institutions in the United States. He is presently employed at Bethune-Cookman College, Daytona Beach, Florida. He has published articles in major journals on the relationship between Africa and the African diaspora and is also interested in the preservation of the environment.

EZENWA-OHAETO teaches in the Department of Literature in English, Alvan Ikoku College of Education, Owerri, Nigeria. An award-winning poet, his collections include *I Wan Bi President* (1988) and *Bullets for Buntings* (1989). Ezenwa-Ohaeto is renowned for his mastery of the use of pidgin in creative writing and recognized as one of the truly committed writers in Nigeria.

SIMON GIKANDI hails from Kenya and is a professor in the Department of English at University of Michigan, Ann Arbor. He has written extensively on the African origins of African-American literature and culture. His theories on African literature are well expressed in his books, including *Reading the African Novel* (1987). A previous version of the Paule Marshall essay in this collection appeared as a chapter in his book *Writing in Limbo* (1993).

MWIKALI KIETI, a highly recognized Kenyan scholar, is currently finishing her doctorate at York University in Canada. She has done extensive work on the role of women in Africa and the world, as well as on the oppressed in neocolonial society. She is coauthor of *Barking, You'll Be Eaten! The Wisdom of Kamba Oral Literature* (1990). She has been both an editor and a drama producer in Kenya.

CHIMALUM NWANKWO has taught both in his home country, Nigeria, and in the United States, where he is presently a professor of English at North Carolina State University, Raleigh. His critical essays and poetry have appeared in many journals and anthologies. Winner of the Association of Nigeria Authors Poetry Prize in 1988 for *Toward the Aerial Zone*, he has also published a major critical text on Ngugi wa Thiong'o.

VINCENT O. ODAMTTEN, a Ghanaian who taught at the University of Cape Coast, won the 1976 Valco Fund Literary Award for Poetry. He holds a doctorate from the State University of New York at Stony Brook. His award-winning dissertation on the work of Ama Ata Aidoo has been published as an acclaimed book, *The Art of Ama Ata Aidoo* (1994). Odamtten is the director of the Africana Studies Program at Hamilton College, New York.

F. UGBOAJA OHAEGBULAM, a Nigerian, obtained his Ph.D. in International Studies from the University of Denver. He is professor of Government and International Affairs and former chair of the African/African-American Studies Program at the University of South Florida. He has published several books, including *The Nigeria UN Mission to the Congo* (1982) and *Towards Under-standing of the African Experience* (1990), and his articles have appeared in many journals.

TANURE OJAIDE is a renowned Commonwealth Poetry Prize winner from Nigeria. His collections include *The Fate of Vultures* (1990) and *The Blood of Peace* (1991). Currently a professor at the University of North Carolina, Charlotte, he has published a large number of articles on African literature.

FEMI OJO-ADE, former chair of the Foreign Languages Department at Obafemi Awolowo University in Nigeria, is presently professor of French and Francophone literature at St. Mary's College of Maryland. A critic and creative writer, he has written several books on the Black experience. His works have been translated into Portuguese in Brazil. He is preparing a critical text on African women writers and another on the Negritude poet, Aimé Césaire.

TESS ONWUEME, after obtaining her doctorate in her native Nigeria, became a university professor while honing her skills as a playwright. She is presently a Distinguished Professor at the University of Wisconsin, Eau-Claire. One of the most prominent creative artists of Africa, her titles include *The Broken Calabash* and *Go Tell It to Women*. She has won many awards, including the Martin Luther King Distinguished Authors Award in 1989.

OUSSEYNOU TRAORE is a Senegalese professor of Literature and Oral Traditions at William Paterson College of New Jersey, where he currently chairs the African-American Studies program. He has done a great deal of work on the literatures and cultures of Africa and the diaspora and is now engaged in a study of the works of Chinua Achebe and Toni Morrison. He is the founding editor of *The Literary Griot*.

ISBN 0-313-26475-9

EAN

9 780313 264757

90000>

HARDCOVER BAR CODE